Fodor's InFocus

ST. MAARTEN/
ST. MARTIN,
ST. BARTH &
ANGUILLA

W9-BVI-421

Excerpted from *Fodor's Caribbean*

15

TOP EXPERIENCES

St. Maarten/St. Martin, St. Barth &
Anguilla offer terrific experiences
that should be on every traveler's
list. Here are Fodor's top picks for
a memorable trip.

1 Shoal Bay, Anguilla

This 2-mile-long beach is covered with sand as fine and white as powdered
sugar, making it one of the best of many excellent beaches on this tiny
island. *(Ch. 4)*

2 Loterie Farm, St. Martin

On the slopes of Pic du Paradis, the highest mountain on the island, Loterie Farm is a wonderful family-friendly, family-run private nature reserve. *(Ch. 2)*

3 Shopping, St. Barth

Whatever you're shopping for, you will find no better place in all the Caribbean than St. Barth, especially the shops along Gustavia's Quai de la République. *(Ch. 3)*

4 Eden Rock, St. Barth

Since the Eden Rock's construction in the 1950s, extensive renovations and recent expansions have raised it into the top category of St. Barth properties, where it has remained. *(Ch. 3)*

5 Golf at CuisinArt, Anguilla

At this wonderful $50-million course designed by Greg Norman, 13 of the 18 holes are directly on the water. The island's only golf course is a winner. *(Ch. 4)*

6 Lunch at the "lolos," St. Martin

Some of the best dining bargains in St. Martin can be found at one of several roadside barbecue stands in Grand Case, the island's culinary capital. *(Ch. 2)*

7 Elvis' Beach Bar, Anguilla

You can have one of the best rum punches in the Caribbean at this bar (which is made from a beached boat) at Sandy Ground every day but Tuesday, when it's closed. *(Ch. 4)*

8 Anse de Grande Saline, St. Barth

Secluded, with a sandy ocean bottom, this is just about everyone's favorite St. Barth beach, and it's great for swimmers, too. Best of all, there's no major development here. *(Ch. 3)*

9 Marigot, St. Martin

St. Martin's lovely seaside French capital, with its bustling harbor, shopping stalls, open-air cafés, and boutiques, is a must-see destination. *(Ch. 2)*

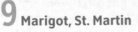

10 Butterfly Farm, St. Martin

This quiet, shady haven will mesmerize you with hundreds of beautiful tropical butterflies flitting about in a large, screened enclosure. *(Ch. 2)*

11 La Samanna Spa, St. Martin

One of the best places on the island to relax and rejuvenate is this spa in one of St. Martin's tonlest resorts. *(Ch. 2)*

12 Le Gaïac, St. Barth

Chef Stéphane Mazières' restaurant at Le Toiny showcases his gastronomic art on a dramatic, tasteful cliff-side dining porch. *(Ch. 3)*

13 KoalKeel, Anguilla

Dinner at KoalKeel is a unique culinary and historic treat not to be missed on Anguilla. A tour of the history-rich buildings is a must. *(Ch. 4)*

14 Baie Orientale, St. Martin

Many consider this 2-mile-long wonder the island's most beautiful beach, and it buzzes with lively water-sports outfitters, beach clubs, and hotels. *(Ch. 2)*

15 Yellow Submarine, St. Barth

A trip aboard this air-conditioned submarine shows you what's going on under the sea without requiring you to get your head or feet wet. *(Ch. 3)*

CONTENTS

MAPS

DID YOU KNOW?

Anguilla, an island only 16 miles long and 3 miles wide, has over 30 white-sand beaches.

ABOUT THIS GUIDE

Fodor's Ratings

Everything in this guide is worth doing—we don't cover what isn't—but exceptional sights, hotels, and restaurants are recognized with additional accolades. **Fodor'sChoice★** indicates our top recommendations; ★ highlights places we deem highly recommended. Care to nominate a new place? Visit Fodors.com/contact-us.

Trip Costs

We list prices wherever possible to help you budget well. Hotel and restaurant price categories from **$** to **$$$$** are noted alongside each recommendation. For hotels, we include the lowest cost of a standard double room in high season. For restaurants, we cite the average price of a main course at dinner or, if dinner isn't served, at lunch. For attractions, we always list adult admission fees; discounts are usually available for children, students, and senior citizens.

Hotels

Our local writers vet every hotel to recommend the best overnights in each price category, from budget to expensive. Unless otherwise specified, you can expect private bath, phone, and TV in your room. For expanded hotel reviews, facilities, and deals visit Fodors.com.

Restaurants

Unless we state otherwise, restaurants are open for lunch and dinner daily. We mention dress code only when there's a specific requirement and reservations only when they're essential or not accepted. To make restaurant reservations, visit Fodors.com.

Credit Cards

The hotels and restaurants in this guide typically accept credit cards. If not, we'll say so.

Ratings

- ★ Fodor's Choice
- ★ Highly recommended
- 👶 Family-friendly

Listings

- ✉ Address
- ✉ Branch address
- 📫 Mailing address
- ☎ Telephone
- 📠 Fax
- 🌐 Website
- 📧 E-mail
- 🎟 Admission fee
- ⏰ Open/closed times
- [M] Subway
- ✥ Directions or Map coordinates

Hotels & Restaurants

- 🏨 Hotel
- 🛏 Number of rooms
- 🍽 Meal plans
- 🍴 Restaurant
- ✍ Reservations
- 👔 Dress code
- 💳 No credit cards
- [$] Price

Other

- ⇨ See also
- ☞ Take note
- ⛳ Golf facilities

Experience
St. Maarten/
St. Martin, St. Barth
& Anguilla

WHAT'S WHERE

■ St. Maarten/St. Martin.
Two nations (Dutch and French), many nationalities, one small island, a lot of development. But there are also more white, sandy beaches than days in a month. Go for the awesome restaurants, extensive shopping, and wide range of activities. Don't go if you're not willing to get out and search for the really good stuff.

❷ St. Barthélemy. If you come to St. Barth for a taste of European village life, not for a conventional full-service resort experience, you will be richly rewarded. Go for excellent dining and wine, great boutiques with the latest hip fashions, and an active, on-the-go vacation. Don't go for big resorts, and make sure your credit card is platinum-plated.

❸ Anguilla. With miles of brilliant beaches and a range of luxurious resorts (even some that mere mortals can afford), Anguilla is where the rich, powerful, and famous go to chill out. Go for the fine cuisine in elegant surroundings, great snorkeling, and funky late-night music scene. Don't go for shopping and sightseeing. This island is all about relaxing and reviving.

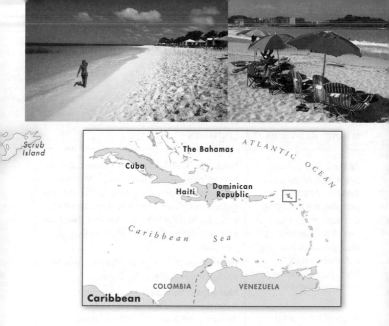

St. Barthélemy

Colombier Lorient Anse de Petit Cul do Sac

2

Lurin

PLANNER

Island Activities	Logistics
All three islands have beautiful **beaches**, but those on Anguilla are probably the best. Baie Orientale on St. Martin is one of the Caribbean's most beautiful beaches, but it's very busy. St. Barth has a wide range of lovely, relatively small beaches.	**Getting to the Islands:** Only Queen Julianna International Airport (SXM) in St. Maarten has nonstop flights from the U.S. But you can get a small plane or ferry to Anguilla (AXA) or St. Barth (SBJ) from St. Maarten; there are also connecting flights to Anguilla through San Juan.
Anguilla has a good **golf course**, but these islands are not a major golfing destination.	**Hassle Factor:** Low for St. Maarten, medium to high for Anguilla or St. Barth.
Water sports, including windsurfing, are popular, especially on St. Barth and St. Maarten/St. Martin. **Diving** is good but not great in the area. St. Maarten in particular also has many **land activities** and attractions.	**Nonstops:** There are nonstop flights to St. Maarten from Atlanta (Delta), Charlotte (US Airways), Chicago (United—seasonal), Fort Lauderdale (Spirit), Miami (American), New York–JFK (American, JetBlue), New York–Newark (Continental), Philadelphia (US Airways), and Boston (JetBlue). There are also some nonstop charter flights (including GWV/Apple Vacations from Boston).
Shopping is great on both St. Barth and St. Maarten/St. Martin.	**On the Ground:** Taxis are available on all three islands, but many hotels in St. Barth offer free airport transfers since they own and rent out cars themselves.
Fine dining is a popular activity on all three islands. Grand Case in St. Martin is renowned across the Caribbean for its great restaurants. But dining on any of these islands can be quite expensive.	**Renting a Car:** Most visitors to St. Maarten/St. Martin and St. Barth rent cars (taxis are particularly expensive on St. Barth). Driving is on the right on both islands. Visitors to Anguilla often rent cars, but it's possible to do without if you choose your accommodation carefully; taxis, however, are expensive. Driving is on the left in Anguilla. Gas is generally more expensive than in the U.S.

Where to Stay

Time-Shares: Only Dutch St. Maarten has a large number of time-share resorts; when the units are not being used by participants in the various points systems, they are often available to rent to anyone, but not during the busiest parts of the high season.

Large Resorts: Both St. Maarten/St. Martin and Anguilla have several fairly large resorts, and especially on Anguilla, many of the resorts can be quite luxurious and expensive. Some resorts in St. Maarten offer all-inclusive (AI) plans as add-ons, but there are no AI resorts on the island. There are no large resorts of any kind on St. Barth.

Small Hotels: All three islands have their share of small hotels (all the hotels and resorts on St. Barth are quite small, and most are rather expensive); in French St. Martin in particular, small hotels predominate, but there are a few larger resorts.

Villas: Most accommodations in St. Barth are in villas. Anguilla and St. Maarten/St. Martin also have many private villas for rent, though many of these are fairly large.

Hotel and Restaurant Costs

Restaurant prices are for a main course at dinner, and include any taxes or service charges. Hotel prices are per night for a double room in high season, excluding taxes, service charges, and meal plans.

Tips for Travelers

1

English is widely understood by most people involved in the tourism industry on all three islands; French is spoken in St. Barth and French St. Martin.

The minimum legal drinking ages: 18 in St. Maarten/St. Martin and St. Barth, 16 in Anguilla.

Electricity is 110 volts, just as in the U.S., on both St. Maarten and Anguilla; the standard in French St. Martin and St. Barth is the European, at 220 volts AC (60-cycle), requiring a plug adaptor and, for some appliances, a voltage converter.

U.S. currency is accepted almost everywhere in the islands, though the standard currency in French St. Martin and St. Barth is the euro.

Regardless of which island you choose, you'll need a valid passport and a round-trip ticket.

There's a $20 departure tax in Anguilla when you are departing by ferry; it must be paid in cash.

IF YOU LIKE

A Romantic Rendezvous

Anguilla, St. Barth, and St. Maarten/St. Martin are all popular destinations for weddings, honeymoons, second honeymoons, and other intimate getaways. Here are some of our favorites:

Hotel St. Barth Isle de France, St. Barth. Hide away with the rich and famous in this elegant classic with a white-sand beach and a magnificent spa with Natura Bissé products.

Karibuni Lodge, St. Martin. Eco-sensitive private suites with pools are new and surprisingly reasonable. Simple decor in a tropical garden setting offers amazing views over Pinel Island. Suites have kitchenettes, but breakfast is delivered.

La Samanna, St. Martin. Recent renovations and redecoration are on the mark, and the huge beachfront suites feel like private villas. The resort also has the best breakfast buffet on the island.

Le Sereno St. Barth. The name says it all. Serene, comfortable, tasteful, with delicious food, and right on the beach. Don't miss a massage in the private spa cabins on the beach.

The Viceroy, Anguilla. Design freaks swoon for the luxury; service is equally detailed.

Great Eating

You can find absolutely any cuisine you fancy, but you can't go wrong with these choices:

Absolutely Wine Le Bistroy, St. Barth. A gastro-pub/wine bar has sharable platters of salads, cheeses, and charcuterie; it's an open-air setting in a terrific shopping area.

Bacchus, St. Martin. The best local chefs cook lunch (only) in this unique wine shop/restaurant in the warehouse area (think SoHo) of Grand Case. You can also buy gourmet provisions.

Le Pressoir, St. Martin. French cuisine is beautifully and creatively presented in a carefully restored traditional house.

Le Ti St. Barth Caribbean Tavern, St. Barth. It's how you imagine St. Barth: with sexy cool, chic beauties dancing on the tables.

Straw Hat, Anguilla. Come for breakfast, lunch, or dinner on an airy terrace with a friendly crowd over gorgeous views of Mead's Bay.

Veya, Anguilla. A tree house–like verandah with a lively jazz lounge and sophisticated food to match the surroundings.

The Water

All three islands offer a number of ways to enjoy the beautiful Caribbean Sea with very little or a whole lot of exertion, but always plenty of fun. Here are some suggestions:

Wind Adventures St. Martin. Learn kitesurfing or windsurfing from the experts. They even have a five-day intensive package of instruction and practice.

Aqua Mania Adventures, St. Maarten. Great snorkeling trips or a "Rock n Roll Safari" are conducted on a motorized raft.

Tri Sports, St. Maarten. Try sea-kayaking, or join one of their bike trips.

St. Maarten 12 Metre Challenge. Compete on Actual America's Cup racing yachts or just enjoy the day on the water. (This is also one of the most popular cruise-ship excursions in the Caribbean, so book ahead.)

Scuba Diving, Anguilla. There is a great wreck dive off the north coast, or hunt stingrays in the coral of Ram's Head.

Jet Ski Tour of St. Barth. Guided tours around the island are tons of fun for the young.

Shopping

It's fun to bring home a memento for yourself and souvenirs for your friends and family. Here are some things you might like to enjoy on the island or take home:

Cuban Cigars. St. Barth's tobacconists stock the best Cubans to enjoy before you return stateside.

Natural Body and Beauty Products. Products from Ligne de St. Barth are crafted from tropical plants.

Island Arts and Crafts. Anguilla's Arts and Crafts Center in The Valley has charming local crafts, and there are several galleries showing work by a range of artists. Hibernia sells amazing pieces collected by the owners on their annual explorations in exotic parts of the world, in a gallery beside the excellent restaurant.

The Perfect Bikini. The hunt can be disheartening, but the prize makes it worthwhile. Look for labels like Pain de Sucre, Banana Moon, and ,HipUp where the tops and bottoms are bought separately, and for men, colorful Vilebrequin—all available both in St. Martin and St. Barth.

WHEN TO GO

The Caribbean high season runs from about December 15 through April 15—great for escaping winter. The Christmas holiday season is an especially expensive time to visit Anguilla and St. Barth, and you may very well pay double during this period, with minimum rental requirements for some villas and hotels. After April prices may be 20% to 50% less, and you can often book on short notice. Some hotels and restaurants close for all or part of September and October.

Climate

The Caribbean climate is fairly consistent, with slightly higher temperatures and more humidity when summer trade winds blow. But the warm ocean temperatures are a delight for swimmers. Hurricanes are most likely from August through October, although heavy rain can occur in any season. Major hurricanes are a relatively rare occurrence, and in recent years building standards have been raised to a much higher level to avoid some of the devastating damage of past storms.

Festivals and Events

Anguilla: Bankie Banx hosts **Moonsplash,** an annual full-moon Music Festival that brings Reggae acts and fans from all over. It's February 21–24 in 2013. The **Boat Races** start the first Monday in August, with 10 days of beauty pageants, nonstop partying, and Sailing Races of old-fashioned wooden boats. The "landracers" following onshore have as much fun as the boats. May 30 is **Anguilla Day,** and there is a round-the-island race.

St. Barth: Carnival celebrations begin in late January, leading up to **Mardi Gras,** which falls on Tuesday, February 12, 2013, but the festivities begin as of February 8, with a parade for school children to get the party started. **The St. Barth Music Festival** brings jazz and chamber music for the first three weeks of January. April brings the **Cinéma Caraïbe Film Festival,** and an International Regatta, **Les Voiles de Saint Barth.** Everyone loves shopping during the first two weeks of August during the **Shopping Festival.** On **New Year's Eve** locals join visiting boats for a round-the-island regatta, and a fantastic fireworks display over Gustavia Harbour.

St. Maarten: The **Heineken Regatta** in early March brings sailors and partygoers from all over the world. **Carnival** follows Easter with parades, great food, and music for all. November is foodie paradise during the **Culinary Month** events.

GREAT ITINERARIES

Here are some suggestions for how to make the most of your trip to the islands, whichever one you choose.

A Perfect Day in St. Maarten/St. Martin

In the morning head out to Loterie Farm on the slopes of Pic du Paradis and take advantage of some of the hiking trails or try the zip line. You can stay and have lunch in the Hidden Forest Café, but if you are hot, head right to Baie Orientale, where you can rent some chairs and umbrellas from one of the beach clubs and take advantage of the lovely surf. If you get hungry, you can have lunch there, too. The afternoon is a good time to stroll along Front Street in Philipsburg, because you can duck into one of the many air-conditioned stores to escape the heat. In the late afternoon, a nap is in order, but you have to be awake before sunset. For a splurge, have your sunset cocktail at the bar of La Samanna before heading to one of the restaurants in Grand Case for a perfect dinner. Dance the whole night away in Maho. The party starts at Sky Beach then moves on to Tantra.

A Perfect Day in Anguilla

The perfect day in Anguilla often involves the least activity. After breakfast, head to powdery Shoal Bay. If you get tired of sunning and dozing, take a ride on Junior's Glass Bottom Boat, or arrange a wreck dive at Shoal Bay Scuba. Have lunch at one of the beachside restaurants and relax a little more. In the late afternoon, head back to your hotel room to shower and change before going to Elvis' Beach Bar to watch the sunset with a cold rum punch. Have dinner at one of the island's great restaurants.

A Perfect Day in St. Barth

Have your café au lait and croissant in a harbor-side café in Gustavia, and then explore some of the many boutiques on Quai de la République. If you tire of the relative hubbub, have lunch in quieter St-Jean and then shop and stroll some more. If you're not a shopper, take a snorkeling excursion or go deep-sea fishing. Be sure to get a late-afternoon nap, because the nightlife in St. Barth doesn't get going until late. After a sunset cocktail in Gustavia, have dinner at one of the island's many great restaurants. Perhaps you'll choose Le Ti St. Barth Caribbean Tavern, which is as much a gathering spot as a restaurant. By the time dessert comes, someone is sure to be dancing on the tables; perhaps it will be you. Late night partying starts after midnight.

WEDDINGS AND HONEYMOONS

There's no question that St. Maarten/St. Martin, St. Barth, and Anguilla are three of the Caribbean's foremost honeymoon destinations. Romance is in the air here, and the white, sandy beaches and turquoise water, swaying palm trees, balmy tropical breezes, and perpetual summer sunshine put people in the mood for love. Destination weddings—no longer exclusive to celebrities and the super rich—are also popular on Anguilla and St. Maarten, but French laws make getting married in French St. Martin or St. Barth too difficult. All the larger resorts in Anguilla and St. Maarten have wedding planners to help you with the paperwork and details.

The Big Day

Choosing the Perfect Place. When choosing a location, remember that you really have two choices to make: the ceremony location and where to have the reception, if you're having one. For the former, there are beaches, bluffs overlooking beaches, gardens, private residences, resort lawns, and, of course, places of worship. As for the reception, there are these same choices, as well as restaurants. If you decide to go outdoors, remember the seasons—yes, the Caribbean has seasons. If you're planning a wedding outdoors, be sure you have a backup plan in case it rains. Also, if you're planning

an outdoor wedding at sunset—which is very popular—be sure you match the time of your ceremony to the time the sun sets at that time of year.

Finding a Wedding Planner. If you're planning to invite more than a minister and your loved one to your wedding ceremony, seriously consider an on-island wedding planner who can help select a location, help design the floral scheme and recommend a florist as well as a photographer, help plan the menu, and suggest any local traditions to incorporate into your ceremony.

Of course, all the larger resorts have their own wedding planners on-site. If you're planning a resort wedding, work with the on-site wedding coordinator to prepare a detailed list of the exact services they'll provide. If your idea of your wedding doesn't match their services, try a different resort. Or look for an independent wedding planner. Both Anguilla and St. Maarten have independent wedding planners who do not work directly for resorts.

Legal Requirements. There are minimal residency requirements on both Anguilla and St. Maarten, and no blood tests or shots are required on either island. On Anguilla, you can get a wedding license in two working days; paperwork in St. Maarten has to be submitted 14

days in advance, but there is no residency requirement there. You need to supply proof of identity (a passport or certified copy of your birth certificate signed by a notary public, though in Anguilla even a driver's license with a photo will do). If you've been married before, then you must provide proof of divorce with the original or certified copy of the divorce decree if divorced, or copy of the death certificate if you are a widow or widower.

Wedding Attire. In the Caribbean, basically anything goes, from long, formal dresses with trains to white bikinis. Floral sundresses are fine, too. Men can wear tuxedos or a simple pair of solid-color slacks with a nice white linen shirt. If you want formal dress and a tuxedo, it's usually better to bring your formal attire with you.

Photographs. Deciding whether to use the photographer supplied by your resort or an independent photographer is an important choice. Resorts that host a lot of weddings usually have their own photographers, but you can also find independent, professional island-based photographers, and an independent wedding planner will know the best in the area. Look at the portfolio (many photographers now have websites), and decide whether this person can give you the kind of memories you are look-

ing for. If you're satisfied with the photographer that your resort uses, then make sure you see proofs and order prints before you leave the island. In any case, arrange to take a CD home with you of HD photos, because uploading them via the Internet is a time-consuming frustration what with typically slow Caribbean connections.

The Honeymoon

Do you want champagne and strawberries delivered to your room each morning? An infinity-edged swimming pool in which to float? A five-star restaurant in which to dine? Then a resort is the way to go, and both Anguilla and St. Maarten have options in different price ranges (though Anguilla resorts are more luxurious and expensive as a rule). Whether you want a luxurious experience or a more modest one, you'll certainly find someplace romantic to which you can escape. You can usually stay on at the resort where your wedding was held. On the other hand, maybe you want your own private home in which to romp naked—or your own kitchen in which to whip up a gourmet meal for your loved one. In that case, a private vacation-rental home or condo is the answer.

KIDS AND FAMILIES

The three islands have plenty of activities and attractions that will keep children of all ages (and their parents) busy and interested. Children are generally welcomed at restaurants, especially earlier in the evenings.

Anguilla

CuisinArt Golf Resort and Spa offers children's programs, babysitting, and a great beach. Many activities are included at **Cap Juluca,** and **Viceroy** has programs both for little kids and a media room and club for teens. **Anacaona Beach Resort** has some great family-sized villas at a budget-friendly price.

Family dining options include **Smokey's at the Cove, Blanchard's Beach Shack,** and **Picante.** Don't miss a family excursion to gorgeous **Scilly Cay;** wave from the dock and a boat will take you out to the island for a day of snorkeling. Thursday night head to **Fire Fly** at Anacaona for the Anguillian buffet and folkloric dance performance. Even non-swimmers can enjoy an excursion on **Jonno's Glass Bottom Boat.**

St. Barth

Children are welcome at most resorts. **Hotel Guanahani & Spa** offers children's programs for ages 2–12, a good list of local babysitters, and activities galore. **Hotel Le Village St. Jean** makes is an easy to walk to beaches or shopping.

Only in St. Barth would you find a **Yellow Submarine** from which to observe undersea life in air-conditioned comfort. Don't leave without a visit to the **Inter Oceans (Shell) Museum.** Casual dining options include Gustavia's **La Crêperie,** Gloriette's beachy **picnic tables and hammocks,** and myriad takeout grills and pizzas.

St. Maarten/St. Martin

The **Radisson Blu Marina & Spa** is great for families, with a huge pool and activities for all with full- or half-day Kids' Club for supervised fun. **The Sonesta Maho Beach Resort & Casino** has a playground, an all-inclusive option, and gentler prices. Try to book rooms on the higher floors, though. **Le Petit Hotel,** a boutique property in Grand Case, has full apartment units and a caring management team. Don't miss the zip line at **Loterie Farm** or a visit to the **Butterfly Farm;** ride the **Carousel,** try kitesurfing on **Orient Beach,** wade in surf gentle enough for babies at **Le Galion Beach,** and enjoy incredible water sports all over the island. **Pineapple Pete's** suits for easy meals all day long, or try the creole specials in Marigot's **Enoch's Place,** and the jerk chicken and salads at **Taloula Mango's** in Phillipsburg. Vegetarians flock to **Top Carrot.**

St. Maarten/
St. Martin

WORD OF MOUTH

"[A] don't-miss activity would be an afternoon on Maho Beach watching the planes come in. [It's the o]nly place in the world where planes land and take off so close over your head."

—riverbirch

By Elise
Meyer

ST. MAARTEN/ST. MARTIN IS VIRTUALLY UNIQUE among
Caribbean destinations. The 37-square-mile (96-square-km)
island is a seamless place (there are no border gates), but it
is governed by two nations—the Netherlands and France—
and has residents from 70-some different countries. A call
from the Dutch side to the French is an international call,
currencies are different, and the vibe is even different. Only
the island of Hispaniola, which encompasses two distinct
countries, Haiti and the Dominican Republic, is in even a
similar position in the Caribbean.

Happily for Americans, who make up the majority of
visitors to St. Maarten/St. Martin, English works in both
nations. Dutch St. Maarten might feel particularly comfortable for Americans: the prices are lower (not to mention in
U.S. dollars), the big hotels have casinos, and there is more
nightlife. Huge cruise ships disgorge masses of shoppers
into the Philipsburg shopping area at midmorning, when
roads can quickly become overly congested. But once you
pass the meandering, unmarked border into the French
side, you will find a bit of the ambience of the south of
France: quiet countryside, fine cuisine, and in Marigot, a
walkable harbor area with outdoor cafés, outdoor markets,
and plenty of shopping and cultural activities.

Almost 4,000 years ago it was salt and not tourism that
drove the little island's economy. Arawak Indians, the
island's first known inhabitants, prospered until the war-
ring Caribs invaded, adding the peaceful Arawaks to their
list of conquests. Columbus spotted the isle on November
11, 1493, and named it after St. Martin (whose feast day is
November 11), but it wasn't populated by Europeans until
the 17th century, when it was claimed by the Dutch, French,
and Spanish. The Dutch and French finally joined forces
to claim the island in 1644, and the Treaty of Concordia
partitioned the territory in 1648. According to legend the
border was drawn along the line where a French man and
a Dutch man, running from opposite coasts, met.

Both sides of the island offer a touch of European culture
along with a lot of laid-back Caribbean ambience. Water
sports abound—diving, snorkeling, sailing, windsurfing,
and in early March, the Heineken Regatta. With soft trade
winds cooling the subtropical climate, it's easy to while
away the day relaxing on one of the 37 beaches, strolling Philipsburg's boardwalk, and perusing the shops on
Philipsburg's Front Street or the *rues* (streets) of the very

Oyster Pond, St. Maarten

French town of Marigot. Although luck is an important commodity at St. Maarten's 13 casinos, chance plays no part in finding a good meal at the excellent eateries or after-dark fun in the subtle to sizzling nightlife. Heavy development—especially on the Dutch side— has stressed the island's infrastructure, but slowly some of the more dilapidated roads are showing some signs of improvement. A series of large roundabouts, with the beginnings of some decent signage, and attractive monumental sculptures has improved traffic flow (remember, the cars already in the roundabout have right-of-way). At long last, the eyesore of hurricane-wrecked buildings that lined the golf course at Mullet Bay have been demolished, and a particularly rainy 2011 has painted the island a particularly vibrant shade of green.

When cruise ships are in port (and there can be as many as seven at once), shopping areas are crowded and traffic moves at a snail's pace. We suggest spending the days on the beach or the water, and planning shopping excursions for the early morning or at cocktail hour, after "rush hour" traffic calms down. Still, these are minor inconveniences compared with the feel of the sand between your toes or the breeze through your hair, gourmet food sating your appetite, or having the ability to crisscross between two nations on one island.

LOGISTICS

Getting to St. Maarten/St. Martin: There are nonstop flights to St. Maarten from the United States, as well as connecting service through San Juan. Further, St. Maarten is a hub for smaller, regional airlines. The island's main airport is Princess Juliana International Airport (SXM), on the Dutch side. Aeroport de L'Espérance (SFG), on the French side, is small and handles only small planes.

Hassle Factor: Low to medium.

On the Ground: Most visitors rent a car upon arrival, but taxi service is available at the airport with fixed fares to all hotels on the island, and you'll be able to pay the fare in U.S. dollars. Although the island is small, it's still a long drive to many hotels on the French side, and the fares will add up.

Getting Around the Island: Most visitors rent a car because rates are fairly cheap and the island is easy to navigate. It's possible to get by with taxis if you are staying in a major hub such as Philipsburg or Baie Orientale, but you may spend more money than if you rented a car.

PLANNING

WHEN TO GO

The high season begins in December and runs through the middle of April. During the off-season, hotel rooms can be had for as little as half the high-season rates.

The French side's **Carnival** is a pre-Lenten bash of costume parades, music competitions, and feasts. Carnival takes place after Easter on the Dutch side—the last two weeks of April—with a parade and music competition.

On the French side, parades, ceremonies, and celebrations commemorate **Bastille Day** on July 14, and there's more revelry later in the month on **Grand Case Day.**

The Dutch side hosts the **Heineken Regatta** in early March, with as many as 300 sailboats competing from around the world. (For the experience of a lifetime, you can sometimes purchase a working berth aboard a regatta vessel.) Other local holidays include November 11 (St. Martin Day), and April 30, the birthday of Queen Juliana.

ACCOMMODATIONS

The island, though small, is well developed—some say over-developed—and offers a wide range of lodging. The larger resorts and time-shares are mostly on the Dutch side; the French side has more intimate properties. Just keep in mind that the popular restaurants around Grand Case, on the French side, are a long drive from most Dutch-side hotels. French-side hotels often charge in euros. Be wary of some of the very lowest-price alternatives, as some of these can be very run-down time-shares, or properties that function as short-term housing for temporary workers or tourists with very low-end tour companies. Additionally, make note of locations of properties very close to the airport, to avoid unpleasant surprises related to noise. In general, the newer a property, the better off you will be.

Resorts and Time-Shares: In general, many of the older properties, especially the time-shares, are suffering from the wear-and-tear of multiple owners, and it is hard to recommend them because of great variances from unit to unit.

Small Inns: Small guesthouses and inns can be found on both sides of the island. It is worth exploring these, especially if you are not the big-resort type.

Villas and Condos: Both sides of the island have a wide variety of villas and condos for every conceivable budget. Some of the resorts offer villa alternatives, which make for a good compromise. In addition, some of the high-end condo developments are offering unsold units as rentals, and some are brand-new and terrific bargains.

HOTEL AND RESTAURANT PRICES

Prices in the restaurant reviews are the average cost of a main course at dinner or, if dinner is not served, at lunch; taxes and service charges are generally included. Prices in the hotel reviews are the lowest cost of a standard double room in high season, excluding taxes, service charges, and meal plans (except at all-inclusives). Prices for rentals are the lowest per-night cost for a one-bedroom unit in high season.

EXPLORING ST. MAARTEN/ ST. MARTIN

The best way to explore St. Maarten/St. Martin is by car. Though often congested, especially around Philipsburg and Marigot, the roads are fairly good, though narrow and winding, with some speed bumps, potholes, roundabouts, and an occasional wandering goat herd. Few roads are marked with their names, but destination signs are common. Besides, the island is so small that it's hard to get really lost—at least that is what locals tell you.

If you're spending a few days, get to know the area with a scenic "loop" around the island. Be sure to pack a towel and some water shoes, a hat, sunglasses, and sunblock. Head up the east shoreline from Philipsburg, and follow the signs to Dawn Beach and Oyster Pond. The road winds past soaring hills, turquoise waters, quaint West Indian houses, and wonderful views of St. Barth. As you cross over to the French side, turn into Le Galion for a stop at the calm sheltered beach, the stables, the butterflies, or the windsurfing school, then keep following the road toward Orient Bay, the St-Tropez of the Caribbean. Continue to Anse Marcel, Grand Case, Marigot, and Sandy Ground. From Marigot, the flat island of Anguilla is visible. Completing the loop brings you past Cupecoy Beach, through Maho and Simpson Bay, where Saba looms in the horizon, and back over the mountain road into Philipsburg.

DUTCH SIDE

WHAT TO SEE

PHILIPSBURG

The capital of Dutch St. Maarten stretches about a mile (1½ km) along an isthmus between Great Bay and the Salt Pond and has five parallel streets. Most of the village's dozens of shops and restaurants are on Front Street, narrow and cobblestone, closest to Great Bay. It's generally congested when cruise ships are in port, because of its many duty-free shops and several casinos. Little lanes called *steegjes* connect Front Street with Back Street, which has fewer shops and considerably less congestion. Along the beach is a ½-mile-long (1-km-long) boardwalk with restaurants and several Wi-Fi hot spots.

Wathey Square (pronounced *watty*) is in the heart of the village. Directly across from the square are the town hall

St. Maarten/St. Martin
Top Reasons to Go

A two-nation vacation is what you get with St. Maarten/St. Martin. But the island has much more going for it than that.

■ Philipsburg is one of the best shopping spots in the Caribbean; though it has fewer bargains (and fewer stores) these days with competetive Internet pricing, the growing strength of the euro, and worldwide economic woe. Marigot (the capital of French St. Martin) is fun to explore, especially on Wednesday or Saturday when the market is open, and if beachwear is on your shopping list, every body can find the perfect one before or after a terrific lunch in the boutiques around Marina Royale. Non-shoppers can watch the boats or sample some of the great fruit-infused rums proudly made by nearly every resturanteur.

■ Grand Case is the gastronomic capital of the French side, and Maho–Coupecoy of the Dutch, but there are great restaurants all over the Island. We suggest spending an evening in each of the Islands' different areas, checking out restaurants, nightlife, and the general vibe. Taking taxis Is a great way to get around in the evening, no worries about routing, parking, or designated drivers. At the end of the night any restaurant or club will call for a cab. (Rates are regulated—only use taxis with official stickers, and don't fall for any attempts for added charges.) You'll find plenty of great restaurants in Philipsburg and Simpson Bay as well.

■ Thirty-seven perfect beaches are spread out all over the island (and most of the island's hotels are not on the best beaches, one reason so many people choose to rent a car). Whether you are looking for the busy scene at Baie Orientale or the deserted stretches of sand at Simpson Bay, each is unique.

■ The wide range of water sports—from sailing to waterskiing, snorkeling to deep-sea fishing—will meet almost any need.

---

and the courthouse, In the striking white building with the cupola. The structure was built in 1793 and has served as the commander's home, a fire station, a jail, and a post office. The streets surrounding the square are lined with hotels, duty-free shops, fine restaurants, and cafés. The **Captain Hodge Pier,** just off the square, is a good spot to view Great Bay and the beach that stretches alongside.

Sint Maarten Museum. The Sint Maarten Museum hosts rotating cultural exhibits and a permanent historical display called Forts of St. Maarten–St. Martin. Artifacts range

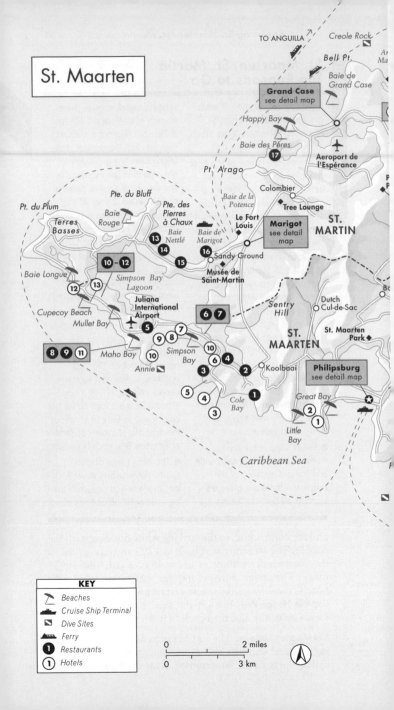

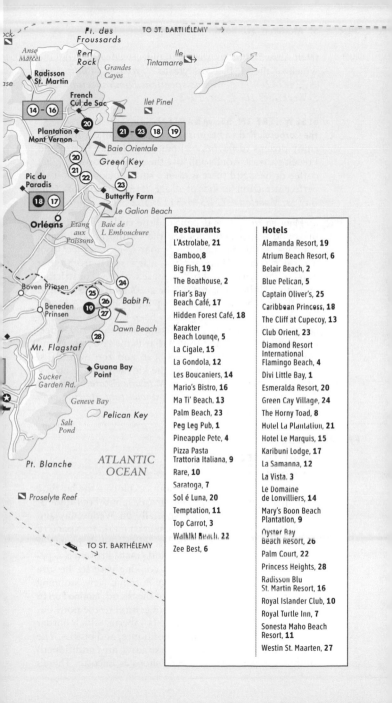

Restaurants

L'Astrolabe, **21**

Bamboo, **8**

Big Fish, **19**

The Boathouse, **2**

Friar's Bay
Beach Café, **17**

Hidden Forest Café, **18**

Karakter
Beach Lounge, **5**

La Cigale, **15**

La Gondola, **12**

Les Boucaniers, **14**

Mario's Bistro, **16**

Ma Ti' Beach, **13**

Palm Beach, **23**

Peg Leg Pub, **1**

Pineapple Pete, **4**

Pizza Pasta
Trattoria Italiana, **9**

Rare, **10**

Saratoga, **7**

Sol é Luna, **20**

Temptation, **11**

Top Carrot, **3**

Waikiki Beach, **22**

Zee Best, **6**

Hotels

Alamanda Resort, **19**

Atrium Beach Resort, **6**

Belair Beach, **2**

Blue Pelican, **5**

Captain Oliver's, **25**

Caribbean Princess, **18**

The Cliff at Cupecoy, **13**

Club Orient, **23**

Diamond Resort
International
Flamingo Beach, **4**

Divi Little Bay, **1**

Esmeralda Resort, **20**

Green Cay Village, **24**

The Horny Toad, **8**

Hotel La Plantation, **21**

Hotel Le Marquis, **15**

Karibuni Lodge, **17**

La Samanna, **12**

La Vista, **3**

Le Domaine
de Lonvilliers, **14**

Mary's Boon Beach
Plantation, **9**

Oyster Bay
Beach Resort, **26**

Palm Court, **22**

Princess Heights, **28**

Radisson Blu
St. Martin Resort, **16**

Royal Islander Club, **10**

Royal Turtle Inn, **7**

Sonesta Maho Beach
Resort, **11**

Westin St. Maarten, **27**

from Arawak pottery shards to objects salvaged from the wreck of the HMS *Proselyte*. ✉ *7 Front St., Philipsburg* ☎ *721/542–4917* ⊕ *www.speetjens.com/museum* 🎫 *$1* ⊙ *Weekdays 10–4, Sat. 10–2.*

ELSEWHERE IN ST. MAARTEN

Ⓒ **The Carousel.** Ride a beautiful restored Italian carousel and enjoy dozens of flavors of homemade Italian gelato and French pastries. Adults will love the espresso bar with great coffee drinks, and there is even a small cocktail bar. It's a perfect attraction for kids of all ages. ✉ *60 Welfare Rd., Cole Bay, St. Maarten* ☎ *721/544–3112* 🎫 *$2* ⊙ *Tues.–Sun. 2–10.*

Ⓒ **St. Maarten Park.** This delightful little enclave houses animals and plants indigenous to the Caribbean and South America, including many birds that were inherited from a former aviary. There are also a few strays from other parts of the world and a snake house with boa constrictors and other slithery creatures. The zoo's lone male collared peccary now has a female to keep him company. A family of cotton-topped tamarins also have taken residence at the zoo. All the animals live among more than 100 different plant species. The Monkey Bar is the zoo's charming souvenir shop, and sells Caribbean and zoo mementos. This is a perfect place to take the kids when they need a break from the sand and sea. ✉ *Madame Estate, Arch Rd., Philipsburg* ☎ *721/543–2030* ⊕ *www.stmaartenzoo.com* 🎫 *$10* ⊙ *Daily 9–5.*

FRENCH SIDE

WHAT TO SEE

MARIGOT

It is great fun to spend a few hours exploring the bustling harbor, shopping stalls, open-air cafés, and boutiques of St. Martin's biggest town, especially on Wednesday and Saturday, when the daily open-air craft markets expand to include fresh fruits and vegetables, spices, and all manner of seafood. The market might remind you of Provence, especially when aromas of delicious cooking waft by. Be sure to climb up to the fort for the panoramic view, stopping at the museum for an overview of the island. **Marina Port La Royale** is the shopping–lunch-spot central to the port, but rue de la République and rue de la Liberté, which border the bay, have duty-free shops, boutiques, and bistros. The West Indies Mall offers a deluxe (and air-conditioned) shopping experience, with such shops as Lacoste. There's

Concordia

The smallest island in the world to be shared between two different countries, St. Maarten/St. Martin has existed peacefully in its subdivided state for more than 360 years. The Treaty of Concordia, which subdivided the island, was signed in 1648 and was really inspired by the two resident colonies of French and Dutch settlers (not to mention their respective governments) joining forces to repel a common enemy, the Spanish, in 1644. Although the French were promised the side of the island facing Anguilla and the Dutch the south side of the island, the boundary itself wasn't firmly established until 1817, and then after several disputes (16 of them, to be exact).

Visitors to the island will likely not even notice that they have passed from the Dutch to the French side unless they notice that the roads on the French side feel a little smoother. In 2003 the population of St. Martin (and St. Barthélemy) voted to secede from Guadeloupe, the administrative capital of the French West Indies. That detachment became official in February 2007, and St. Martin is now officially known as the Collectivité de Saint-Martin.

---

less bustle here than in Philipsburg, but the open-air cafés are still tempting places to sit and people-watch. Marigot is fun into the night, so you might wish to linger through dinnertime. From the harborfront you can catch ferries for Anguilla and St. Barth. Parking can be a real challenge during the business day, and even at night during the high season.

Fort Louis. Though not much remains of the structure itself, Fort Louis, which was completed by the French in 1789, is great fun if you want to climb the 92 steps to the top for the wonderful views of the island and neighboring Anguilla. On Wednesday and Saturday there is a market in the square at the bottom. ⊠ *Marigot.*

Saint Martin Museum. At the southern end of Marigot, next to the Marina Port La Royale, is a museum dedicated to preserving St. Martin's history and culture. A new building houses a variety of pre-Columbian treasures unearthed by the Hope Estate Archaeological Society. ⊠ *Terre Basse Rd., Marigot* ☎ *0690/29–48–36* ⊕ *www.museesaintmartin.com* ☎ *$5* ☉ *Daily 9–1 and 3–5.*

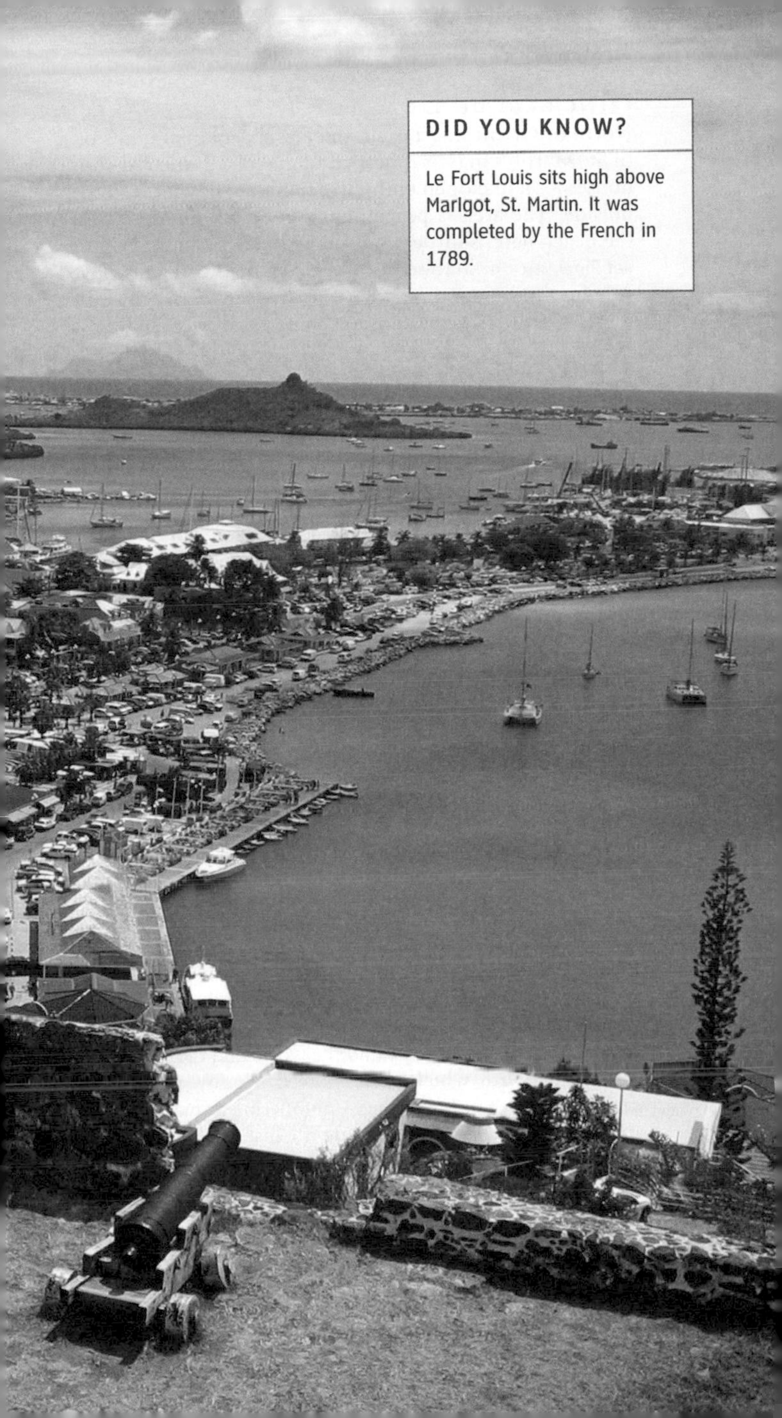

DID YOU KNOW?

Le Fort Louis sits high above Marigot, St. Martin. It was completed by the French in 1789.

FRENCH CUL DE SAC

North of Orient Bay Beach, the French colonial mansion of St. Martin's mayor is nestled in the hills. Little red-roof houses look like open umbrellas tumbling down the green hillside. The area is peaceful and good for hiking. From the beach here, shuttle boats make the five-minute trip to **Ilet Pinel,** an uninhabited island that's fine for picnicking, sunning, and swimming. There are full-service beach clubs there, so just pack the sunscreen and head over.

GRAND CASE

The Caribbean's own Restaurant Row is the heart of this French-side town, a 10-minute drive from either Orient Bay or Marigot, stretching along a narrow beach overlooking Anguilla. You'll find a first-rate restaurant for every palate, mood, and wallet. At lunchtime, or with kids, head to the casual lolos (open-air barbecue stands) and feet-in-the-sand beach bars. Twilight drinks and tapas are fun. At night, stroll the strip and preview the sophisticated offerings on the menus posted outside before you settle in for a long and sumptuous meal. If you still have the energy, there are lounges with music (usually a DJ) that get going after 11 pm.

ORLÉANS

North of Oyster Pond and the Étang aux Poissons (Fish Lake) is the island's oldest settlement, also known as the French Quarter. You can find classic, vibrantly painted West Indian–style homes with the original gingerbread fretwork, and large areas of the nature and marine preserve that is working to save the fragile ecosystem of the island.

ELSEWHERE IN ST. MARTIN

★ **Fodor's Choice Butterfly Farm.** If you arrive early in the morning
☼ when the butterflies first break out of their chrysalis, you'll be able to marvel at the absolute wonder of dozens of butterflies and moths from around the world and the particular host plants with which each evolved. At any given time, some 40 species of butterflies—numbering as many as 600 individual insects—flutter inside the lush screened garden and hatch on the plants housed there. Butterfly art and knickknacks are for sale in the gift shop. In case you want to come back, your ticket, which includes a guided tour, is good for your entire stay. ⊠ *Le Galion Beach Rd., Quartier d'Orléans* ☎ *590/87–31–21* ⊕ *www.thebutterflyfarm.com* ☞ *$12* ☼ *Daily 9–3:30.*

DID YOU KNOW?

Not counting Trinidad, the Caribbean has about 300 native species of butterflies, far fewer than in Central America, which has more than 2,000.

★ Fodor'sChoice **Pic du Paradis.** Between Marigot and Grand Case, "Paradise Peak," at 1,492 feet, is the island's highest point. There are two observation areas. From them, the tropical forest unfolds below, and the vistas are breathtaking. The road is quite isolated and steep, best suited to a four-wheel-drive vehicle, so don't head up here unless you are prepared for the climb. There have also been some problems with crime in this area, so it might be best to go with an experienced local guide.

Loterie Farm. Halfway up the road to Pic du Paradis is Loterie Farm, a peaceful 150-acre private nature preserve opened to the public in 1999 by American expat B. J. Welch. There are hiking trails and maps, so you can go on your own (€5) or arrange a guide for a group (€25 for six people). Along the marked trails you will see native forest with tamarind, gum, mango, and mahogany trees, and wildlife including greenback monkeys if you are lucky. In 2011 Loterie opened a lovely spring-fed pool and Jacuzzi area with lounge chairs, great music, and chic tented cabanas called L'Eau Lounge; if you're with a group, consider the VIP package there. Don't miss a treetop lunch or dinner at **Hidden Forest Café** (⇨ *Where to Eat, below*), Loterie Farm's restaurant, where Julie Perkis cooks delicious, healthy meals and snacks. If you are brave—and over 4 feet 5 inches tall—try soaring over trees on one of the longest zip lines in the Western Hemisphere. ✉ *Rte. de Pic du Paradis 103, Rambaud* ☎ *590/87–86–16, 590/57–28–55* ⊕ *www. loteriefarm.com* ⚎*€35–€55* ☉ *Tues.–Sun. 9–4* ✉ *Rte. de Pic du Paradis, Pic du Paradis.*

BEACHES

DUTCH SIDE

Several of the best Dutch-side beaches are developed and have large-scale resorts. But others, including Simpson Bay and Cupecoy, have little development. You'll sometimes find vendors or beach bars to rent chairs and umbrellas (but not always).

Cupecoy Beach. This picturesque area of sandstone cliffs, white sand, and shoreline caves is a necklace of small beaches that come and go according to the whims of the sea. Even though the western part is more developed, the surf can be rough. It's popular with gay locals and visitors. It's near the Dutch-French border. Break-ins have been reported in cars, so don't leave anything at all in your

Cupecoy Beach, St. Maarten

vehicle. **Amenities:** none. **Best for:** sunset. ✉ *Between Baie Longue and Mullet Bay, Cupecoy.*

★ **Dawn Beach.** True to its name, Dawn Beach is the place to be at sunrise. On the Atlantic side of Oyster Pond, just south of the French border, this is a first-class beach for sunning and snorkeling. It's not usually crowded, and there are several good restaurants nearby. To find it, follow the signs to Mr. Busby's restaurant. **Amenities:** none. **Best for:** snorkeling, sunrise. ✉ *South of Oyster Pond, Dawn Beach.*

Great Bay. This is probably the easiest beach to find because it curves around Philipsburg. A bustling, white-sand beach, Great Bay is just behind Front Street. Here you'll find boutiques, eateries, and a pleasant boardwalk. Busy with cruise-ship passengers, the beach is best west of Captain Hodge Pier or around Antoine Restaurant. **Amenities:** food and drink. **Best for:** swimming, walking ✉ *Philipsburg.*

Little Bay. Despite its popularity with snorkelers and divers as well as kayakers and boating enthusiasts, Little Bay isn't usually crowded. Maybe the gravelly sand is the reason. But it does boast panoramic views of St. Eustatius, Philipsburg, the cruise-ship terminal, Saba, and St. Kitts. The beach is west of Fort Amsterdam and accessible via the Divi Little Bay Beach Resort. **Amenities:** food and drink, parking, toilets. **Best for:** snorkeling, swimming, walking. ✉ *Little Bay Rd., Little Bay.*

Mullet Bay Beach. Many believe that this mile-long, powdery white-sand beach near the medical school is the island's best. Swimmers like it because the water is usually calm. When the swell is up, the surfers hit the beach. It's also the place to listen for the "whispering pebbles" as the waves wash up. **Amenities:** none. **Best for:** surfing, swimming. ⊠ *South of Cupecoy, Mullet Bay.*

Simpson Bay Beach. This secluded, half-moon stretch of white-sand beach on the island's Caribbean side is a hidden gem. It's mostly surrounded by private residences. There are no big resorts, no Jet Skiers, no food concessions, and no crowds. It's just you, the sand, and the water. Southeast of the airport, follow the signs to Mary's Boon and the Horny Toad guesthouses. **Amenities:** none. **Best for:** solitude, swimming, walking. ⊠ *Simpson Bay.*

FRENCH SIDE

Almost all the French-side beaches, whether busy Baie Orientale or less busy Baie des Pères (Friar's Bay), have beach clubs and restaurants. For about $25 a couple you get two chaises (*transats*) and an umbrella (*parasol*) for the day, not to mention chair-side service for drinks and food. Only some beaches have bathrooms and showers, so if that is your preference, inquire.

Anse Heureuse (*Happy Bay*). Not many people know about this romantic, hidden gem. Happy Bay has powdery sand, gorgeous luxury villas, and stunning views of Anguilla. The snorkeling is also good. To get here, turn left on the rather rutted dead-end road to Baie des Péres (Friars Bay). The beach itself is a 10- to 15-minute walk from the last beach bar. **Amenities:** none. **Best for:** solitude, walking, swimming, snorkeling. ⊠ *Happy Bay.*

Baie de Grand Case. Along this skinny stripe of a beach bordering the culinary capital of Grand Case, the old-style gingerbread architecture sometimes peeps out between the bustling restaurants. The sea is calm, and there are tons of fun lunch options from bistros to beachside barbecue stands (called *lolos*). Several of the restaurants rent chairs and umbrellas; some include their use for lunch patrons. In between there is a bit of shopping, certainly for beach necessities but also for the same kinds of handcrafts found in the Marigot market. **Amenities:** food and drink, toilets. **Best for:** swimming, walking. ⊠ *Grand Case.*

Baie des Péres (*Friars Bay*). This quiet cove close to Marigot has beach grills and bars, with chaises and umbrellas, calm waters, and a lovely view of Anguilla. Kali's Beach Bar, open daily for lunch and (weather permitting) dinner, has a Rasta vibe and color scheme—it's the best place to be on the full moon, with music, dancing, and a huge bonfire, but you can get lunch, beach chairs, and umbrellas there in any moon phase. Friar's Bay Beach Café is a French bistro on the sand. Its open from breakfast to sunset. To get to the beach, take National Road 7 from Marigot, go toward Grand Case to the Morne Valois hill, and turn left on the dead-end road at the sign. **Amenities:** food and drink, toilets. **Best for:** partiers, swimming, walking. ⊠ *Friar's Bay.*

Baie Longue (*Long Bay*). Though it extends over the French Lowlands, from the cliff at La Samanna to La Pointe des Canniers, the island's longest beach has no facilities or vendors. It's the perfect place for a romantic walk. But car break-ins are a particular problem here. To get here, take National Road 7 south of Marigot. The entrance marked "La Samanna" is the first entrance to the beach. For a splurge, lunch at the resort, or sunset drinks are a must. **Amenities:** none. **Best for:** solitude, walking. ⊠ *Baie Longue.*

★ **Fodor's Choice Baie Orientale** (*Orient Bay*). Many consider this the island's most beautiful beach, but its 2 miles (3 km) of satiny white sand, underwater marine reserve, variety of water sports, beach clubs, and hotels also make it one of the most crowded. Lots of "naturists" take advantage of the clothing-optional policy, so don't be shocked. Early-morning nude beach walking is de rigueur for the guests at Club Orient, at the southeastern end of the beach. Plan to spend the day at one of the clubs; each bar has different color umbrellas, and all boast terrific restaurants and lively bars. You can have an open-air massage, try any sea toy you fancy, and stay until dark. To get to Baie Orientale from Marigot, take National Road 7 past Grand Case, past the Aéroport de L'Espérance, and watch for the left turn. **Amenities:** food and drink, parking, toilets, water sports. **Best for:** partiers, nudists, swimming, walking, windsurfing. ⊠ *Baie Orientale.*

Baie Rouge (*Red Bay*). At this home to a couple of beach bars, complete with chaises and umbrellas, you can bask with the millionaires renting the big-ticket villas in the "neighborhood" and take advantage of the gorgeous beach they came for. Baie Rouge and its salt ponds make up a

Baie Orientale, widely considered St. Martin's best beach

nature preserve, the location of the oldest habitations in the Caribbean. This area is widely thought to have the best snorkeling beaches on the island. You can swim the crystal waters along the point and explore a swim-through cave. The beach is fairly popular with gay men in the morning and early afternoon. There are two restaurants here; only Chez Raymond is open every day, and cocktail hour starts when the conch shell blows, so keep your ears open. There is a sign and a right turn after you leave Baie Nettlé. **Amenities:** food and drink, toilets. **Best for:** snorkeling, swimming, walking. ⊠ *Baie Rouge*.

Ilet Pinel. A protected nature reserve, this kid-friendly island is a five-minute ferry ride from French Cul de Sac ($7 per person round-trip). The ferry runs every half hour from midmorning until dusk. The water is clear and shallow, and the shore is sheltered. If you like snorkeling, don your gear and paddle along both coasts of this pencil-shaped speck in the ocean. You can rent equipment on the island or in the parking lot before you board the ferry for about $10. Plan for lunch any day of the week at the water's edge at a palm-shaded beach hut at Karibuni (except in September, when it's closed) for the freshest fish, great salads, tapas, and drinks—try the frozen mojito for a treat. **Amenities:** food and drink. **Best for:** swimming, snorkeling. ⊠ *Ilet Pinel*.

Ⓒ **Le Galion.** A coral reef borders this quiet beach, part of the island's nature preserve, which is paradise if you are traveling with children. The water is calm, clear, and quite shallow, so it's a perfect place for families with young kids. It's a full-service place, with chair rentals, restaurants, and water-sports operators. Kite-boarders and windsurfers like the trade winds at the far end of the beach. On Sunday there are always groups picnicking and partying. To get to Le Galion, follow the signs to the unmissable Butterfly Farm and continue toward the water. **Amenities:** food and drink, parking, toilets, water sports. **Best for:** partiers, swimming, windsurfing. ✉ *Quartier d'Orléans*.

WHERE TO EAT

Although most people come to St. Maarten/St. Martin for sun and fun, they leave praising the cuisine. On an island that covers only 37 square miles (96 square km), there are more than 400 restaurants from which to choose. You can sample the best dishes from France, Thailand, Italy, Vietnam, India, Japan, and, of course, the Caribbean.

Many of the best restaurants are in Grand Case (on the French side), but you should not limit your culinary adventures to that village. Great dining thrives throughout the island, from the bistros of Marigot to the hopping restaurants of Cupecoy to the low-key eateries of Simpson Bay. Whether you enjoy dining on fine china in one of the upscale restaurants or off a paper plate at the island's many lolos (roadside barbecue stands), St. Maarten/St. Martin's culinary options are sure to appeal to every palate. Loyalists on both "sides" will cheerfully try to steer you to their own favorites, and it's common to cite high euro prices to deter exploration, but some restaurants still offer a one-to-one exchange rate between dollars and euros if you use cash, and main-course portions are often large enough to be shared.

During high season, it's essential to make reservations, and making them a month in advance is advisable for some of the best places. Dutch-side restaurants sometimes include a 15% service charge, so check your bill before tipping. On the French side, service is always included, but it is customary to leave 5% to 10% extra in cash for the server. Don't count on leaving tips on your credit card—it's customary to tip in cash. A taxi is probably the easiest solution to the parking problems in Grand Case, Marigot, and Philipsburg. Grand Case has two lots—each costs $4—at each end of the main boulevard, but they're often packed.

BEST BETS FOR DINING

Fodor's Choice★
Bacchus, Mario's Bistro, La Cigale, L'Astrolabe, Le Pressoir, Le Tastevin, Talk of the Town, Temptation, Bamboo

MOST ROMANTIC
Antoine, Le Pressoir, Sol é Luna, La Samanna, Le Domaine de Lonvilliers, Temptation, La Marrakesh

BEST VIEW
Sol é Luna, La Cigale, Taloula Mango's

BEST LOCAL FOOD
Chesterfield's, Claude Mini-Club

BEST FOR FAMILIES
Taloula Mango's, Lolos

BEST FOR A SPECIAL OCCASION
La Samanna (especially the wine dinner in the cellar)

HIP AND YOUNG
Treelounge/Hidden Forest Café, Palm Beach, Temptation, Karakter, Bamboo, Calmos Café

What to Wear: Although appropriate dining attire ranges from swimsuits to sport jackets, casual dress is usually appropriate everywhere on the island. For men, a jacket and khakis or jeans will take you anywhere; for women, dressy pants, a skirt, or even fancy shorts are usually acceptable. Jeans are fine in the less formal eateries.

DUTCH SIDE

COLE BAY

$$$ **Fodor's Choice ✕ Peg Leg Pub.** *Steakhouse.* This place is a cross between your typical beach bar and an English pub, albeit one where steaks make up the heart of the menu. Lunch options include deli-style sandwich platters at much more moderate prices than you'll find at dinner (most options are under $10). By night, red meat rules the menu, though seafood, kebabs, and pastas shouldn't be overlooked. Good news for beer lovers: Peg Leg Pub serves more than 35 different brews. Best of all, appetizers are half price during happy hour; try the bacon-wrapped shrimp, jalapeño cheese poppers, or the coconut shrimp. There's entertainment on Wednesday and Friday nights as well as a Sunday buffet that starts at 4 pm. [$] *Average main: $30* ✉ *Port de Plaisance, Cole Bay* ☎ *721/544–5859* 🌐 *www.peglegpub.com* ⏲ *No lunch Sun.*

2

CUPECOY

$$$ ✕ **La Gondola.** *Italian.* Owner Davide Foini started out by selling just his homemade pasta, which proved to be so popular that he opened this authentic trattoria that has found its way onto many "best bets" lists of island regulars. The kitchen still rolls out the dough for the dozens of pasta dishes on the encyclopedic Italian menu, which also includes favorites like veal parmigiana, chicken piccata in marsala sauce, and osso buco Milanese. Save room for desserts like the *fantasia di dessert del Carnevale di Venezia* (a warm chocolate tart and frozen nougat served with raspberry sauce) or tiramisu. The service is professional and high-tech—the waiters take orders with earpieces and handheld computers. [$] *Average main: $28* ✉ *Atlantis World Casino, Rhine Rd. 106, Cupecoy* ☎ *721/544–3938* 🌐 *www.lagondola-sxm.com* 🕒 *No lunch.*

$$$$ ✕ **Rare.** *Steakhouse.* Within an intimate, clubby setting, a guitarist provides background music while carnivores delight in chef Dino Jagtiani's creative menu. The focus is steak: certified Angus prime cuts topped with chimichurri, béarnaise, horseradish, peppercorn, or mushroom sauce. Not into red meat? You can also choose from seafood, pork, lamb, or veal. Sample some delicious sides like truffled mashed potatoes or cultivated mushroom sauté (a tasty fungi variety). Luscious desserts will make you forget that you will want to look good in your bathing suit tomorrow morning. Check the restaurant's website for specials. [$] *Average main: $54* ✉ *Atlantis World Casino, Rhine Rd. 106, Cupecoy* ☎ *721/545–2254* 🌐 *ww.rareandtemptation.com* ✍ *Reservations essential* 🕒 *Closed Sept. and Mon. June–Oct. No lunch.*

$$$$ ★ ✕ **Temptation.** *Eclectic.* Supercreative chef Dino Jagtiani, who trained at the Culinary Institute of America, is the mastermind behind dishes like seared foie gras PB and J (melted foie gras accented with peanut butter and homemade port-wine fig jam) and herb-crusted Chilean sea bass. The chef, who compares dessert to lovemaking ("both intimate, and not to be indulged in lightly"), offers a crème brûlée tasting, as well as Granny Smith apple tempura with cinnamon ice cream and caramel sauce for the sweet tooth. The wine list is extensive, and features a number of reasonably priced selections. There are also many inventive cocktails, such as the St. Maartini—a refreshing blend of coconut rum, guava puree, passion-fruit juice, and peach schnapps. The dining room is pretty and intimate, in spite of its location behind the casino. There's outdoor seating as well.

$ *Average main: $36* ✉ *Atlantis Casino Courtyard, Rhine Rd. 106, Cupecoy* ☎ *721/545–2254* 🌐 *www.chefdino.com* ✍ *Reservations essential* ⏱ *Closed Sun. June–Oct. No lunch.*

MAHO

★ $$$ **Fodor's Choice** 🍴 **Bamboo.** *Asian.* This dramatic and hip addition to the top level of the Maho central shopping area features red lacquer walls, lounging tables, Indonesian art, a first-rate bar, and electro-house tunes. You can get terrific sushi and sashimi, both the classic Japanese varieties and the Americanized ones (California roll, for example). All are good, as are the Asian hot appetizers and bartender Viktor's exotic cocktails like the Tranquillity (citrus vodka and smoky oolong tea). If you're not into Asian fare, try the salmon, ribs, or beef. The young crowd keeps this place hopping way past midnight. If you're solo, you will have a great time hanging and even dining at the bar. There is a sake and sushi happy hour from 5 to 7 nightly. $ *Average main: $20* ✉ *Sonesta Maho Beach Resort & Casino, 1 Rhine Rd., Maho* ☎ *721/545–3622* 🌐 *www.bamboobernies.net* ⏱ *No lunch weekdays.*

$$$ 🍴 **Big Fish.** *Seafood.* A chic, white interior, fresh-caught fish, and friendly, if sometimes relaxed, service, are the draw at this Oyster Pond restaurant. The location is convenient whether you are staying in Oyster Pond or Dawn Beach. Stick with whatever was most recently in the sea, and you will be happy with your food. If offered, grouper in curry-coconut is a yummy option, and the hurricane shrimp is a local favorite. The owners also run a fishing-charter outfit, and they will happily cook up your daily catch here, too. $ *Average main: $28* ✉ *14 Emerald Merrit Rd., Oyster Pond, St. Maarten* ☎ *721/586–1961.*

$$$ 👶 🍴 **Pizza Pasta Trattoria Italiana.** *Italian.* Tucked away on a quiet street near Casino Royale, this Italian eatery is extremely popular with locals. The menu includes favorites like penne Bolognese and eggplant Parmesan, but the real winners are the thin-crust pizzas. The freshly brewed iced tea is great on a hot day. With its laid-back atmosphere and friendly staff, this is a cozy spot for families with small children or a place where you just run in and grab a quick bite. $ *Average main: $22* ✉ *Maho Shopping Plaza, Maho* ☎ *721/545–4034* ⏱ *No lunch Sun.*

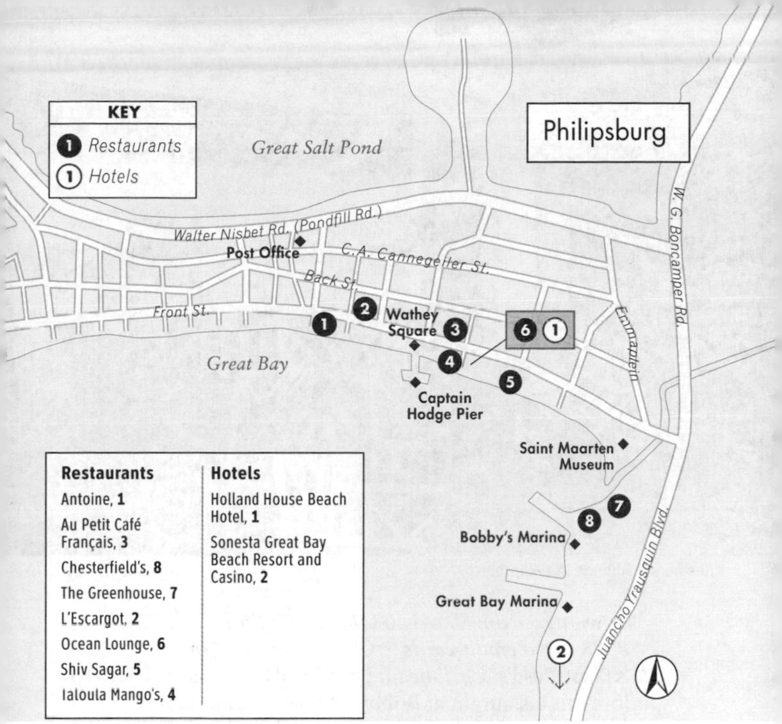

KEY
Restaurants
Hotels
Philipsburg
Great Salt Pond
Walter Nisbet Rd. (Pondfill Rd.)
Post Office
C.A. Cannegeiter St.
Back St.
Front St.
Wathey Square
W. G. Boncamper Rd.
Emmaplein
Great Bay
Captain Hodge Pier
Saint Maarten Museum
Bobby's Marina
Great Bay Marina
Juancho Yrausquin Blvd.
Restaurants
Antoine, 1
Au Petit Café Français, 3
Chesterfield's, 8
The Greenhouse, 7
L'Escargot, 2
Ocean Lounge, 6
Shiv Sagar, 5
Ialoula Mango's, 4
Hotels
Holland House Beach Hotel, 1
Sonesta Great Bay Beach Resort and Casino, 2

PHILIPSBURG

$$$$ 🍴 **Antoine.** *French.* You'd be hard-pressed to find a more enjoyable evening in Philipsburg. Owner Jean Pierre Pomarico's warmth shines through as he greets guests and ushers them into the comfy seaside restaurant. Low-key, blue-accented decor, white bamboo chairs, watercolors lining the walls, and candles—along with the sound of the nearby surf—create a relaxing atmosphere. The lobster thermidor (a succulent tail oozing with cream and Swiss cheese) is a favorite, but other specialties include lobster bisque, seafood linguine, and a beef fillet with béarnaise sauce. The prix-fixe menu is a great deal. [$] *Average main: $32* ✉ *119 Front St., Philipsburg* ☎ *721/542–2964* 🌐 *www.antoinerestaurant.com* ✍ *Reservations essential.*

$ 🍴 **Au Petit Café Français.** *French.* This tiny bistro is found in the quaint shopping area just off Front Street. Although there are only a small number of tables (both indoor and out), you should still stop by for a quick, inexpensive snack or for a freshly ground cup of coffee. Watching employees make crepes is half the fun; eating them is the other half. You can also order hearty salads, pizza, and hot or cold sandwiches on fresh bread. It is open from 8 am to 4:30 pm.

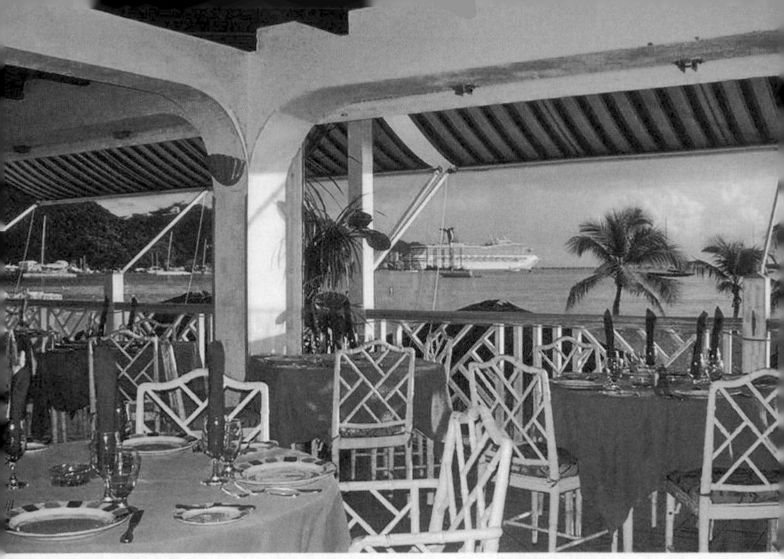

Restaurant Antoine in Philipsburg

$ *Average main: $9* ✉ *120 Old St., Philipsburg* ☎ *721/552–8788* 💳 *No credit cards* ⏰ *Closed Sun. No dinner.*

$$ 🍴 **Chesterfield's.** *Caribbean.* Both locals and tourists seem to love this restaurant at Bobby's Marina. Seafood is the main focus, but steaks, burgers, pasta, and poultry are all on the dinner menu, and you can also get breakfast and lunch. If you love sophisticated cuisine, look elsewhere, but the portions are big and the prices reasonable. Happy hour is every night from 5 to 7. $ *Average main: $19* ✉ *Great Bay Marina, Philipsburg* ☎ *721/542–3484* 🌐 *www.chesterfields-restaurant.com.*

$$ 🍴 **The Greenhouse.** *Eclectic.* The famous happy hour is just one of the reasons people flock to the Greenhouse. This waterfront restaurant balances a relaxed atmosphere, reasonable prices, and popular favorites like burgers, prime rib, and steaks. If you're seeking something spicy, try the creole shrimp. The daily specials, like the Friday-night Lobster Mania, are widely popular. $ *Average main: $21* ✉ *Bobby's Marina, Philipsburg* ☎ *721/542–2941* 🌐 *www.thegreenhouserestaurant.com.*

$$$ 🍴 **L'Escargot.** *French.* The wraparound verandah, the bunches of grapes hanging from the chandeliers, and the Toulouse-Lautrec–style murals add to the colorful atmosphere of this restaurant in a 150-year-old, gingerbread, Creole house. As the name suggests, snails are a specialty, and are offered several ways. But the menu also includes many other French standards like onion soup, crispy duck, and veal cordon

bleu. There's a Friday night cabaret show, complete with cancan in the tradition of *La Cage aux Folles.* $ *Average main: $28* ✉ *96 Front St., Philipsburg* ☎ *721/542–2483* ⊕ *www.lescargotrestaurant.com* ⊙ *Closed Sun. June–Oct. No lunch weekends.*

$$$ ✕ **Ocean Lounge.** *Eclectic.* An airy modern veranda perched on the Philipsburg boardwalk gives Ocean Lounge its distinct South Beach vibe. You'll want to linger over fresh fish and steaks, as you watch the scene with tourists of all varieties passing by two-by-two on romantic evening strolls, or determined cruise-ship passengers surveying the surrounding shops by day. The daily tasting menu (one option includes two glasses of good wine) offers a chance to sample the cuisine. $ *Average main: $30* ✉ *Holland House Beach Hotel, 43 Front St., Philipsburg* ☎ *721/542–2572* ⊕ *www.hhbh.com.*

$$ ✕ **Shiv Sagar.** *Indian.* The colors of India—notably yellow and green—enliven this second-floor restaurant in Philipsburg. What it lacks in decor it more than makes up for in flavor. The menu emphasizes northern Indian specialties, including marvelous tandooris and curries, but try one of the less familiar dishes such as *madrasi machi* (red snapper with hot spices) or *saag gosht* (lamb sautéed with spinach). $ *Average main: $14* ✉ *20 Front St., opposite First Caribbean International Bank, Philipsburg* ☎ *721/542–2299* ⊕ *www.shivsagarsxm.com* ⊙ *No dinner Sun.*

$$ ✕ **Taloula Mango's.** *Eclectic.* Ribs are the specialty at this casual beachfront restaurant, but the jerk chicken and thin-crust pizza, not to mention a few vegetarian options like the tasty falafel, are not to be ignored. On weekdays lunch is accompanied by live music; every Friday during happy hour a DJ spins tunes. In case you're wondering, the restaurant got its name from the owner's golden retriever. $ *Average main: $17* ✉ *Sint Rose Shopping Mall, off Front St. on beach boardwalk, Philipsburg* ☎ *721/542–1645* ⊕ *www. taloulamango.com.*

SIMPSON BAY

$$ ✕ **The Boathouse.** *Seafood.* Sitting on Simpson Bay's waterfront, this eatery now has new owners, a fresh look, and a revised menu. Still featured are seafood dishes like coconut shrimp and red snapper stuffed with crabmeat, but now it caters more to carnivores. Steaks and burgers are more succulent than ever. The bar is a great place to catch live music throughout the week. It's open for lunch and dinner, but if you'd rather, just hang out at the bar. $ *Average main: $15* ✉ *74 Airport Rd., Simpson Bay* ☎ *721/544–5409.*

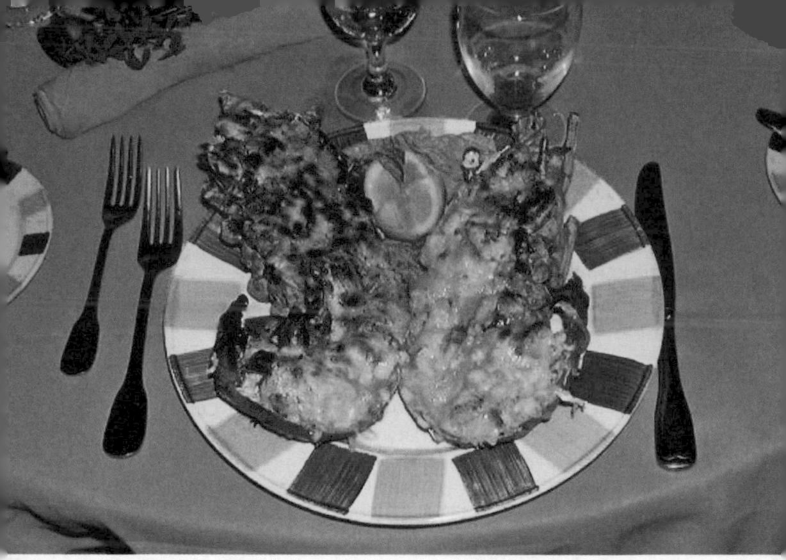

Caribbean lobster, a popular luxury in St. Maarten/St. Martin

$$ ✕ **Karakter Beach Lounge.** *Eclectic.* Karakter, a funky and ★ charming modern beach bar, is right behind the airport, serving up fun, great music, relaxation, and a lot of style. The vibe is more like St-Tropez than St. Maarten. Open from 10 am till sunset, the restaurant serves up healthy and tasty choices for any appetite: fresh fruit smoothies, tropical cocktails, fresh fruit salads, healthy sandwiches, and tapas. A sign near the shower/bathhouse invites guest to "come hang out here and shower before you go to the airport." So this is a place to keep in mind in case your flight is delayed or if you have a layover between flights, or if you just want to spend every last second of your vacation on the sand. *Average main: $14* *121 Simpson Bay Rd., Simpson Bay, St. Maarten* *721/523–9983* *www.karakterbeach.com.*

$$ ✕ **Pineapple Pete.** *Seafood.* This popular, casual, and fun place is well located, with a game room that includes seven pool tables, four dart boards, an arcade, and flat-screen TVs tuned to sports. A friendly, efficient staff will serve you burgers, seafood, and ribs, but for a real treat try one of the specialties like the tasty crab-stuffed shrimp appetizer. Follow it up with succulent, herb-crusted rack of lamb. There's free Wi-Fi and live entertainment Tuesday through Sunday. Its an easy choice for a bite near the airport, and open nonstop from 11 am through closing. *Average main: $20* *56 Welfare Rd., Simpson Bay* *721/544–6030* *www.pineapplepete.com* *Reservations essential.*

2

$$$ ✕ **Saratoga.** *Eclectic.* At Simpson Bay Yacht Club you can choose to be inside or on the waterside terrace. The menu changes daily, but you can never go wrong with one of chef John Jackson's fish specialties, including red snapper with white wine reduction or yellowfin tuna "filet mignon" with miso-roasted veggies. You might start with oysters flown in from France, or sesame seaweed salad. The wine list includes 150 different bottles, including many by the glass. [$] *Average main: $27* ✉ *Simpson Bay Yacht Club, 68 Welfare Rd., Simpson Bay* ☎ *721/544–2421* 🌐 *www.sxmsaratoga.com* ✍ *Reservations essential* ⏲ *Closed Sun. Closed Aug.–Sept. No lunch.*

$ ✕ **Top Carrot.** *Vegetarian.* Open from 7 am to 6 pm, this café and juice bar is a popular breakfast and lunch stop. It features vegetarian entrées, sandwiches, salads, homemade pastries, and, more recently, fresh fish. Favorites include a pastry stuffed with pesto, avocado, red pepper, and feta cheese, or a cauliflower, spinach, and tomato quiche. The house-made granola and yogurt are local favorites, but folks also drop in just for espresso and the large selection of teas. Many also come for the free Wi-Fi service. Adjacent to the restaurant is a gift shop with Asian inspired items and spiritual books. [$] *Average main: $8* ✉ *Airport Rd., near Simpson Bay Yacht Club, Simpson Bay* ☎ *721/544–3381* ⏲ *Closed Sun. No dinner.*

$ ✕ **Zee Best.** *Café.* This friendly bistro serves one of the best breakfasts on the island. There's a huge selection of fresh-baked pastries—try the almond croissants—plus sweet and savory crepes, omelets, quiches, and freshly baked croissants and other treats from the oven. Specialties include the St. Maarten omelet, filled with ham, cheese, mushrooms, onions, green peppers, and tomatoes. Best of all, breakfast is served from 7:30 am until 2 pm. Lunch includes sandwiches, salads, and the chef's famous spaghetti Bolognese. Grab a table in the dining room or on the terrace; it's a good place to relax with a newspaper and a cup of cappuccino. ■ **TIP→** There are also locations near the Airport, and at Port de Plaisance. [$] *Average main: $8* ✉ *Plaza del Lago, Simpson Bay* ☎ *721/544–2477* ▭ *No credit cards.*

FRENCH SIDE

BAIE NETTLÉ

★ **$$$$** **Fodor'sChoice** ✕ **La Cigale.** *French.* On the edge of Baie Nettlé, La Cigale has wonderful views of the lagoon from its dining room and its open-air patio, but the charm of the restaurant comes from the devoted attention of adorable owner Olivier, helped by his mother and brother, and various cousins, too. Stephane Istel's delicious food is edible sculpture: ravioli of lobster with wild mushrooms and foie gras is poached in an intense lobster bisque, and house-smoked swordfish and salmon are garnished with goat cheese and seaweed salad drizzled with dill-lime vinaigrette. Ⓢ *Average main: €37* ⊠ *101 Laguna Beach, Baie Nettlé* ☎ *599/87–90–23* ⊕ *www.restaurant-lacigale.com* ⚆ *Reservations essential* ☉ *Closed Sun. in Sept. and Oct. No lunch.*

$$ ✕ **Les Boucaniers.** *Caribbean.* Dine here, and you can enjoy
ⓒ good creole and French food and still wriggle your toes in the sand. The creole "assortment" offers a mini-culinary education of *accras* (codfish balls), avocado mousse, *boudin noir* (blood sausage), and stuffed crab. Dessert features the most delicious Valrhona chocolate *pot de crème*—its not your grandma's chocolate pudding! There's also a kid's menu. Ⓢ *Average main: €19* ⊠ *501 Route des Terres Basse, Baie Nettlé* ☎ *0590/29–21–75.*

$$$ ✕ **Ma Ti' Beach.** *French.* Here's a great choice for a casual
ⓒ beach bar with better-than-average food, right across from the Mercure Resort on the road to Marigot. Open for lunch and dinner, it offers great views across the turquoise water to Anguilla. You can always get fresh lobster from the tank, and the excellent traditional French onion soup with a cheesy crust. Prices are happily modest, but some major construction work is going on next door. Ⓢ *Average main: €23* ⊠ *Anse Margot, across the road from the Mercure Resort, Baie Nettlé* ☎ *590/87–01–30* ☉ *Closed Tues.*

BAIE ORIENTALE

$$$$ ✕ **L'Astrolabe.** *French.* Chef Stephan Decluseau gets raves for his modern interpretations of classic French cuisine served around the pool at this cozy, relaxed restaurant in the Esmeralda Resort. Corn soup; foie gras terrine with apricot and quince jam; an amazing roast duck with pineapple-ginger sauce; and deliciously fresh fish dishes are just some of the offerings. There are lots of choices for vegetarians, a three-course prix fixe, a children's menu, and a lobster party with live music every Friday night. Ⓢ *Average main: €26* ⊠ *Esmeralda Resort, Baie Orientale* ☎ *0590/87–11–20* ⊕ *www.esmeralda-resort.com* ⚆ *Reservations essential* ☉ *No lunch. No dinner Wed.*

$$$ ✕ **Palm Beach.** *American.* One of the newer additions to
★ the Baie Orientale beach clubs is as stylish as its Florida namesake. Balinese art and furniture, big comfy chaises on the beach, and an active bar set the stage. Pretty girls are

the decor. There are three big tree-house-like lounges for lunch or if you are looking for a place to spend the afternoon. The menu of salads, grills, and brochettes is served in a pavilion shaded by sail-like awnings. Take the exit to BooBoo Jam after the gas station. The Sunday night beach party is the place to be for locals and guests alike. [$] *Average main: €24* ✉ *Baie Orientale* ☎ *690/35–99–06* 🌐 *www.palmbeachsxm.net* ⏲ *No dinner.*

$$$ 🍴 **Waikiki Beach.** *Eclectic.* Sit at a picnic table, or on a lounge–bed and enjoy the food and great people-watching. If there's a big cruise-ship group, however, you may just want to head down to the beach. During the Christmas holiday season, top DJs are brought in for partying into the night, and there is a lobster buffet lunch on Saturdays. [$] *Average main: €25* ✉ *5 Baie Orientale, Baie Orientale* ☎ *590/87–43–19* 🌐 *www.waikikibeachsxm.com.*

FRIAR'S BAY

$$ 🍴 **Friar's Bay Beach Café.** *Bistro.* There is a sophisticated vibe at this quiet, rather elegant beach club that may make patrons feel as if they are on a private beach. The decor is not as funky as at some of the other beach-club restaurants, but look out for the red and black signs on the road between Grand Case and Marigot so you'll know where to turn. Drive slow, because the road is rough. You can rent lounge chairs and umbrellas and spend the whole day relaxing, drinking, and dining. The restaurant is open from breakfast through the spectacular sunset, offering a menu reminiscent of a French bistro's. Be sure to look at the specials on the blackboard, but carpaccios of meat and fish are sparklingly fresh, and the salads are terrific. Plus, you'll also find French standbys such as tomato and goat cheese tartlets, as well as "international" ones like burgers and sandwiches. On Sunday evenings there is live music until 9 pm. [$] *Average main: €18* ✉ *Friar's Bay Rd., Friar's Bay* ☎ *590/49–16–87* ▬ *No credit cards.*

FRENCH CUL DE SAC

$$$ 🍴 **Sol é Luna.** *Caribbean.* Charming and romantic, this restaurant puts its best tables on the balcony, from which you can best appreciate the great views. Begin your meal with an appetizer like curry tuna carpaccio, monkfish spring rolls, or roasted vegetables with goat cheese; then move on to an entrée such as fresh pasta with mixed seafood or beef tenderloin flamed with Cognac. Don't be surprised if you see a proposal or two during your meal, as this is one of the most romantic restaurants on the island. ■ **TIP→** Before

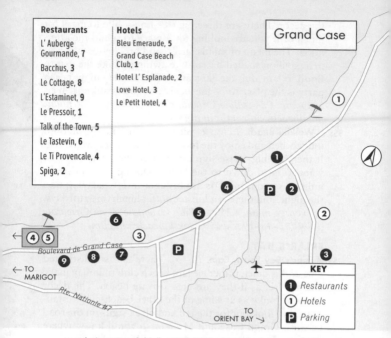

Restaurants	Hotels
L' Auberge Gourmande, 7	Bleu Emeraude, 5
Bacchus, 3	Grand Case Beach Club, 1
Le Cottage, 8	Hotel L' Esplanade, 2
L'Estaminet, 9	Love Hotel, 3
Le Pressoir, 1	Le Petit Hotel, 4
Talk of the Town, 5	
Le Tastevin, 6	
Le Ti Provencale, 4	
Spiga, 2	

Grand Case

Boulevard de Grand Case

← TO MARIGOT

Rte. Nationle #7

TO ORIENT BAY →

KEY
1 Restaurants
1 Hotels
P Parking

ordering one of the "specials," ask about the prices; sometimes they can be surprisingly high compared to regular menu items. $ *Average main: €21* ⊠ *61 Rte. de Mont Vernon, French Cul de Sac* ☎ *590/29–08–56* ⊕ *www.solelunarestaurant.com* ⊘ *Closed mid-June–early July and Sept.–early Oct.*

GRAND CASE

★ **Fodor's**Choice ✕**Bacchus.** *French.* If you want to lunch with
$$ the savviest locals, you have to scrape yourself from the beach and head into the industrial park outside Grand Case, where Benjamin Laurent, the best wine importer in the Caribbean, has built this lively, deliciously air-conditioned reconstruction of a wine cellar. He serves up first-rate starters, salads, and main courses made from top ingredients brought in from France, lovingly prepared by top chefs. Shop here for gourmet groceries for your villa, or hang in the new cigar–rum lounge. The wines are sublime, and you will get an amazing education along with a great lunch. You won't mind eating indoors here—just think of it as the perfect sunblock. Enter at the "Hope Estate" sign in the roundabout across from the road that leads to the Grand Case Airport. $ *Average main: €20* ⊠ *18–19 Hope Estate,*

Grand Case Rd., Grand Case ☎ *0590/87–15–70* 🌐 *www.bacchussxm.com* 🕒 *No dinner. Closed Sun.*

$$$ 🍴 **L'Auberge Gourmande.** *French.* A fixture of Boulevard Grand Case, L'Auberge Gourmande is in one of the oldest Creole houses in St. Maarten/St. Martin. The formal dining room is framed by elegant arches. The light Provençal cuisine is a delight, with menu choices like roasted rack of lamb with an herb crust over olive mashed potatoes, Dover sole in lemon butter, and pork filet mignon stuffed with apricots and walnuts. There are vegetarian options, a kids' menu, and a good selection of wines. Ask for an outside table. [$] *Average main: €21* ✉ *89 bd. de Grand Case, Grand Case* ☎ *590/87–73–37* 🌐 *www.laubergegourmande.com* 🕒 *Closed Sept. No lunch.*

$$$ ★ 🍴 **Le Cottage.** *French.* Inventive, beautiful, French cuisine is prepared with a light touch and presented with flair, and perhaps a bit of humor here. On the "fooding-tasting" menus, you can create your own selection from a tempting list of beautifully-plated mini-servings. Or try a prix-fixe meal. Huge portions of hearty French food are served by a genial staff to a lively community gathered on the street-front porch. Don't miss the caramel dessert tasting, which features a perfect soufflé, or the house-made salted caramel meringues. [$] *Average main: €27* ✉ *97 bd. de Grand Case, Grand Case* ☎ *590/29–03–30* 🌐 *www.restaurantlecottage.com* ✍ *Reservations essential.*

WORD OF MOUTH. "You should not visit St. Martin without enjoying at least one dinner at Le Pressoir (we chose to eat there twice on our last visit). Each course was outstanding, and the wine list is superb. Though the menu is a bit pricey, the food, service, and charm of the place make it worth every penny." —AddieLangdon

★ $$$ **Fodor'sChoice** 🍴 **Le Pressoir.** *French.* In a carefully restored West Indian house painted in brilliant reds and blues, Le Pressoir has charm to spare. The name comes from the historic salt press that sits opposite the restaurant, but the thrill comes from the culinary creations of chef Franc Mear and the hospitality of his beautiful wife Melanie. If you are indecisive, or just plain smart, try any (or all) of the degustations (tastings) of four soups, four foie gras preparations, or four fruit desserts, each showcasing sophisticated preparations with adorable presentations. Foie gras is served in a dollhouse-size terrine, with a teensy glass of Sauternes. [$] *Average main: €30* ✉ *30 bd. de Grand Case, Grand Case* ☎ *590/87–76–62* 🌐 *www.lepressoir-sxm.com*

✍ Reservations essential ⊗ Closed mid-Sept.–mid-Oct. and Sun. in May–Dec. No lunch.

$$$ 🍴 **L'Estaminet.** *French.* The name of this restaurant is an old-fashioned word for "tavern" in French, but the food is anything but archaic. The creative, upscale cuisine served in this modern, clean space is fun and surprising, utilizing plenty of molecular gastronomy. This means that intense liquid garnishes might be inserted into your goat-cheese appetizer or perhaps given to you in a tiny toothpaste tube, or even a plastic syringe. The bright flavors, artistic plating, and novelty make for a lively meal that will be remembered fondly. Under no circumstances should you pass up the chocolate tasting for dessert. [$] *Average main: €23* ✉ *139 bd. de Grand Case, Grand Case* ☎ *590/29–00–25* 🌐 *www.estaminet-sxm.com* ⊗ *Closed Mon. in June–Nov.*

$$$ 🍴 **Le Tastevin.** *French.* In the heart of Grand Case, Le Tastevin is on everyone's list of favorites. The attractive wood-beamed room is the "real" St. Martin style, and the tasty food is enhanced by Joseph, the amiable owner, who serves up lunch and dinner every day on a breezy porch over a glittering blue sea. Salads and simple grills rule for lunch; at dinner, try one of the two tasting menus, either a "brasserie" style menu or a more expensive "gourmet" menu that includes excellent wines. [$] *Average main: €29* ✉ *86 bd. de Grand Case, Grand Case* ☎ *590/87–55–45* 🌐 *www.letastevin-restaurant.com* ✍ *Reservations essential* ⊗ *Closed mid-Aug.–Sept.*

$$$ 🍴 **Le Ti Provençale.** *French.* Its always a good idea to follow the French locals for the best food in St. Martin; chef Hervé Sageot has won the gold medal as the chef of the year in the local Taste of St. Martin festival several times. In a new location, right on the water, you'll find a full blackboard of daily specials, which invariably focus on seafood. The day's catch is brought to your table for you to "meet" and for you to discuss its preparation. This offers a great opportunity to learn about local seafood. The fish soup is made from rouget (red mullet) and served with the traditional garlicky rouille. But the restaurant does serve more than just fish; there are good pastas and lamb and steaks if your preferences aren't fishy. The restaurant is open for both lunch and dinner, and there is a little beach club, too. [$] *Average main: €27* ✉ *140 bd. de Grand Case, Grand Case* ☎ *590/87–02–31* 🌐 *letiprovencal.com* ⊗ *Closed Sun.*

$$$ 🍴 **Spiga.** *Italian.* In a beautifully restored Creole house, Spiga's tasty cuisine fuses Italian and Caribbean ingredients and cooking techniques. Appetizers are tasty and

2

ample. Follow with one of the excellent pasta dishes or a main course featuring fresh fish or meat such as the delicious pesto-crusted rack of lamb. Save room for the lemon-ricotta cake and try the selection of grappas. $ *Average main: €23* ⊠ *4 Rte. de L'Esperance, Grand Case* ☎ *590/52–47–83* ⊕ *www.spiga-sxm.com* ⚍ *Reservations essential* ☉ *Closed mid-Sept.–late Oct. and Tues. in June–mid-Sept. No lunch Sun.*

★ **Fodor's**Choice ✕ **Talk of the Town.** *Caribbean.* Although St.
$ Martin is known for its upscale dining, each town has its roadside barbecue stands, called lolos, including the island's culinary capital of Grand Case. They are open from lunchtime until evening, but earlier in the day you'll find fresher offerings. Locals flock to the square of a half-dozen stands in the middle of Grand Case, on the water side. Not to say that these stands offer haute or fine cuisine, but they are fun, relatively cheap, and offer an iconic St. Martin meal. Talk of the Town is one of the most popular. With plastic utensils and paper plates, it couldn't be more informal. The menu includes everything from succulent grilled ribs to stewed conch, fresh snapper, and grilled lobster at the most reasonable price on the island. Don't miss the johnnycakes and side dishes like plantains, curried rice, beans, and coleslaw that come with your choice. The service is friendly, if a bit slow, but sit back with a beer and enjoy the experience. On weekends there is often live music. **Sky's the Limit** is another iconic lolo, just two picnic tables over. At this writing the lolos are still offering a one-to-one exchange between euros and dollars. $ *Average main: €10* ⊠ *Bd. de Grand Case, Grand Case* ☎ *590/29–63–89* ⚍ *Reservations essential* ⊟ *No credit cards.*

MARIGOT

$$$ ✕ **Bistrot Nu.** *French.* It's hard to top the authentic French fare and reasonable prices you can find at this intimate restaurant tucked in a Marigot alley. Traditional French dishes like steak au poivre, sweetbreads with mushroom sauce, and sole meuniere are served in a friendly, intimate dining room, which is now air-conditioned. The prix-fixe menu is a very good value. The place is popular, and the tables are routinely packed until it closes at midnight. It can be difficult to park here, so take your chances at finding a spot on the street—or try a taxi. $ *Average main: €24* ⊠ *Allée de l'Ancienne Geôle, Marigot* ☎ *590/87–97–09* ⊕ *www. bistronu.com* ⚍ *Reservations essential* ☉ *Closed Sun.*

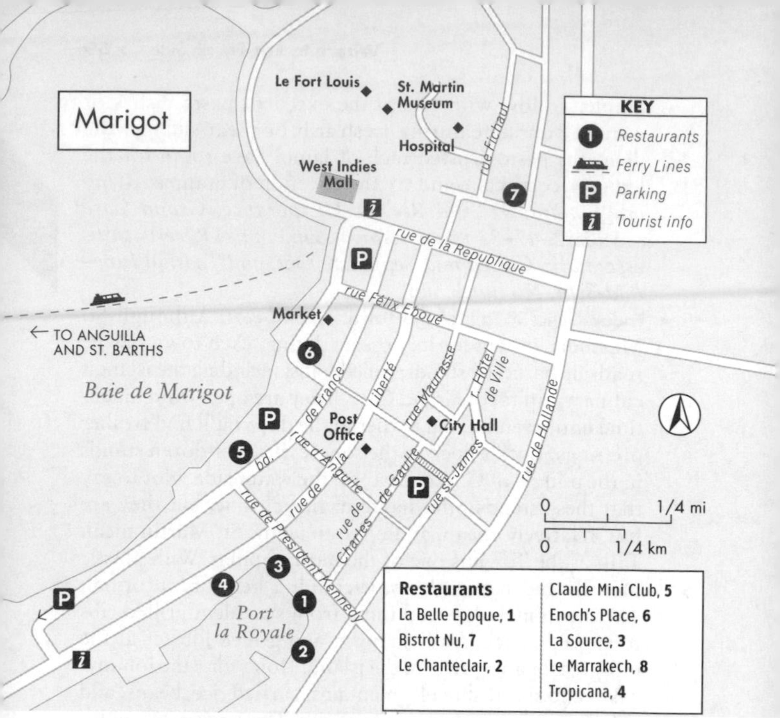

$$$ 🍴 Claude Mini-Club. *Caribbean.* An island institution, Claude Mini-Club has delighted patrons with its blend of creole and French food since 1969, but it now has new owners and a fresh paint job. The whole place is built tree-house style around the trunks of coconut palms, and the lofty perch means you have great views of Marigot Harbor. The dinner buffet on Wednesday and Saturday nights is legendary. It includes more than 30 dishes, often including conch soup, grilled lobster, roast leg of lamb, Black Angus roast beef, and roast pig. The prix-fixe menus are something of a bargain. There's live music for dancing on Fridays. [$] *Average main: €24* ✉ *49 bd. de France, Marigot* ☎ *590/87–50–69* 🌐 *www.restaurantminiclub.com* 🕒 *Closed Sun.*

$$ 🍴 Enoch's Place. *Caribbean.* The blue-and-white-striped awning on a corner of the Marigot Market makes this place hard to miss. But Enoch's cooking is what draws the crowds. Specialties include garlic shrimp, fresh lobster, and rice and beans (like your St. Martin mother used to make). Try the saltfish and fried johnnycake—a great breakfast option. The food more than makes up for the lack of decor, and chances are you'll be counting the days until you can return. [$] *Average main: €13* ✉ *Marigot Market, Front de*

Mer, Marigot ☎ *590/29–29–88* 🌐 *www.enochsplace.com* ✍ *Reservations not accepted* 💳 *No credit cards* ⏰ *Closed Sun. No dinner.*

$$ 🍴 **La Belle Epoque.** *Eclectic.* A favorite among locals, this brasserie is a good choice at the Marigot marina. Whether you stop for a drink or a meal, you'll soon discover that it's a great spot for boat- and people-watching. The menu has a bit of everything: big salads, pizza, and seafood are always good bets. There's also a good wine list. And it's open nonstop seven days a week for breakfast through late dinner. [$] *Average main: €16* ✉ *Marina de la Port Royale, Marigot* ☎ *590/87–87–70* 🌐 *www.belle-epoque-sxm.com.*

$$ 🍴 **La Source.** *Contemporary.* Somewhat hidden behind the boutiques in Marina La Royale (look near Vilbrequin), this tiny new "healthy" restaurant features a French seasonal menu as well as sandwiches, salads, soups, fair-trade coffee and teas, and organic pastries. A bargain lunch special includes the special of the day and a drink, and the organic pasta dishes are delicious and inventive. The light choices, which include crab tartare with seaweed, and organic-chicken salad, are terrific. Even the pastries are organic. [$] *Average main: €11* ✉ *Port La Royale Marina, Marigot* ☎ *590/27–17–27.*

$$$ 🍴 **Le Chanteclair.** *French.* Dinner in Marigot's Marina Port La Royale, with its string of pleasant restaurants wrapping around the harbor filled with gleaming boats, is a St. Martin must. This family-run restaurant is a favorite, serving French dishes with an inventive Caribbean twist in a sunshine-yellow room. In high season you'll have to reserve ahead. The fixed-price *assiettes dégustations* (tasting plates) set the meal around theme ingredients such as foie gras or lobster; there are usually cheaper and more expensive options. However, you can also order à la carte. The desserts are just as creative, especially the *l'innommable au chocolat,* the "unnamable" dessert made with chocolate and vanilla ice cream. The menu proudly proposes its philosophy: "The good food is the foundation of true happiness." Not the best English, perhaps, but a worthy observation. [$] *Average main: €28* ✉ *Marina Port La Royale, Marigot* ☎ *590/87–94–60* 🌐 *www.lechanteclair.com* ✍ *Reservations essential* ⏰ *Closed Sun. mid-Sept.–mid-Oct.*

$$$ ★ 🍴 **Le Marrakech.** *Moroccan.* Some twenty years ago, the charming owners renovated this beautifully historic St. Martin *case.* After several other restaurant ventures, they have returned to the original cottage to serve up delicious, authentic Moroccan cusine in a beautiful and romantic

Breakfast overlooking Maho Bay at the Sonesta Maho Beach Resort

space with an open garden that feels just like Morocco. And it should feel authentic; the decor was created by a Moroccan architect. The food is fragrant and delicious, with portions so huge you will have enough lunch for the next day. The couscous and tagines are authentically spiced and served with professional friendliness by an affable staff in Moroccan serving pieces. The mixed appetizers (*meze*) are delectable, and the royal couscous is justly popular. Kabobs and tajines are a great change of pace from the usual Caribbean and French fare. Lounge in the tented courtyard after dinner—and don't be surprised to be entertained by a talented belly-dancer. The restaurant is on Marigot's main road across from the stadium. $ *Average main: €24* ⊠ *169 rue de Hollande, Marigot* ☎ *590/27–54–48* ⚜ *Reservations essential* ⊙ *Closed Sun.*

$$ ✕ **Tropicana.** *French.* This bustling bistro at the Marina Port La Royale is busy all day long, thanks to a varied menu, (relatively) reasonable prices, and friendly staff. Salads are a must for lunch, especially the salad Niçoise with medallions of crusted goat cheese. Dinner includes some exceptional steak and seafood dishes. The wine list is quite extensive. Desserts are tasty, and you'll never be disappointed with old standbys like the crème brûlée. You can dine outside or inside along the yacht-filled waterfront, which is busy with shoppers during the day. $ *Average main: €21* ⊠ *Marina de la Port Royale, Marigot* ☎ *590/87–79–07.*

2

PIC DU PARADIS

★ **Fodor'sChoice ✕ Hidden Forest Café.** *Caribbean.* Schedule your
$$ trip to Loterie Farm to take advantage of the lovely tree-house pavilions where lunch or dinner has a safari vibe and where the yummy, locally sourced food is inventive and fresh. New in 2012 is L'Eau Lounge, a giant spring-fed pool with Jacuzzis, lounge-cabanas, and a St. Barth-meets-Wet 'n' Wild atmosphere. Curried-spinach chicken with banana fritters is a popular pick, but there are great choices for vegetarians, too, including cumin lentil balls; those with stouter appetites dig into the massive Black Angus tenderloin. Loterie Farm's other eatery, Treelounge, features great cocktails and tapas, is open Monday through Saturday, and stays open late with frequent live music. [$] *Average main: €20* ✉ *Loterie Farm, Pic Paradis 103, Rambaud* ☎ *590/87–86–16* 🌐 *www.loteriefarm.com* 🕓 *Closed Mon.*

SANDY GROUND

★ **Fodor'sChoice ✕ Mario's Bistro.** *Eclectic.* Don't miss dinner at
$$$$ this romantic eatery, a perennial favorite for its ravishing cuisine, romantic ambience, and most of all the marvelously friendly owners. Didier Gonnon and Martyne Tardif are out front, while chef Mario Tardif is in the kitchen creating ravishing dishes such as bouillabaisse with green Thai curry, a duet of grilled lamb chops and braised lamb shank shepherd pie, and sautéed jumbo scallops with crab mashed potatoes and leek tempura. Leave room for the heavenly upside-down banana coconut tart with caramel sauce and coconut ice cream. The restaurant is rather strict about reservations for large groups, so be sure to call and get the details. [$] *Average main: €31* ✉ *48 Rue Morne Rd, at the Sandy Ground Bridge, Sandy Ground* ☎ *590/87–06–36* 🌐 *www.mariosbistro.com* ✍ *Reservations essential* 🕓 *Closed Sun., Aug., and Sept. No lunch.*

WHERE TO STAY

St. Maarten/St. Martin accommodations range from modern megaresorts such as the Radisson and the Westin St. Maarten to condos and small inns. On the Dutch side many hotels cater to groups, and although that's also true to some extent on the French side, you can find a larger collection of intimate accommodations there. ■ **TIP→** Off-season rates (April through the beginning of December) can be as little as half the high-season rates.

St. Maarten vs. St. Martin

If this is your first trip to St. Maarten/St. Martin, you're probably wondering which side will better suit your needs. That's hard to say, because in some ways the difference between the two can seem as subtle as the hazy boundary line dividing them. But there are some major differences.

St. Maarten, the Dutch side, has the casinos, more nightlife, and bigger hotels. St. Martin, the French side, has no casinos, less nightlife, and hotels that are smaller and more intimate.

Many have kitchenettes, and most include breakfast. There are many good restaurants on the Dutch side, but if fine dining makes your vacation, the French side rules.

The biggest difference might be currency—the Netherlands Antilles guilder (also called the florin) on the Dutch side, the euro on the French side. And the relative strength of the euro can translate to some expensive surprises. Many establishments on both sides (even the French) accept U.S. dollars.

TIME-SHARE RENTALS

Time-share properties are scattered around the island, mostly on the Dutch side. There's no reason to buy a share, as these condos are rented out whenever the owners are not in residence. If you stay in one, be prepared for a sales pitch. Most rent by the night, but there are often substantial savings if you secure a weekly rate. Not all offer daily maid service, so make sure to ask before you book. As some properties are undergoing renovations at this writing, be sure to ask about construction conditions, and in any case, ask for a recently renovated unit.

PRIVATE VILLAS

Villas are a great lodging option, especially for families who don't need to keep the kids occupied, or groups of friends who just like hanging out together. Since these are for the most part freestanding houses, their greatest advantage is privacy. These properties are scattered throughout the island, often in gated communities or on secluded roads. Some have bare-bones furnishings, whereas others are over-the-top luxurious, with gyms, theaters, game rooms, and several different pools. There are private chefs, gardeners, maids, and other staffers to care for both the villa and its occupants.

Villas are secured through rental companies. They offer properties with weekly prices that range from reasonable to more than many people make in a year. Check around, as prices for the same property vary from agent to agent. Because of the economy, many villas are now offered by the night rather than by the week, so it's often possible to book for less than a full week's stay. Rental companies usually provide airport transfers and concierge service, and for an extra fee will even stock your refrigerator.

For expanded reviews, facilities, and current deals, visit Fodors.com.

RENTAL CONTACTS

French Caribbean International. French Caribbean International offers rental properties on the French side of the island. ☎ *800/322–2223 in the U.S.* ⊕ *www.frenchcaribbean.com.*

Island Hideaways. Island Hideaways, the island's oldest rental company, rents villas on both sides. ☎ *800/832–2302 in the U.S., 703/378–7840* ⊕ *www.islandhideaways.com.*

Island Properties. Island Properties has properties scattered around the island. ✉ *62 Welfare Rd., Simpson Bay, St. Maarten* ☎ *599/544–4580, 866/978–5852 in the U.S.* ⊕ *www.remaxislandproperties.com.*

Jennifer's Vacation Villas. Jennifer's Vacation Villas rents villas on both sides of the island. ✉ *Plaza Del Lago, Simpson Bay Yacht Club, Simpson Bay, St. Maarten* ☎ *631/546–7345 in New York, 721/544–3107 in St. Maarten* ⊕ *www.jennifersvacationvillas.com.*

Pierrescaraïbes. Pierrescaraïbes, owned by American Leslie Reed, has been renting and selling upscale St. Martin villas to satisfied clients for more than a decade. The company's well-designed website makes it easy to get a sense of the first-rate properties available in all sizes and prices. The company is associated with Christie's Great Estates. ✉ *Plaza Caraibes, rue Kennedy, Bldg. A, Marigot, St. Martin* ☎ *590/51–02–85 in St. Martin* ⊕ *www.pierrescaraibes.com.*

Romac Southeby's International Realty. Romac Southeby's International Realty rents luxury villas, many in gated communities. ✉ *54 Simpson Bay Rd., Simpson Bay, St. Maarten* ☎ *877/537–9282 in the U.S.* ⊕ *www.caribbean-bestrealestate.com.*

Hot Deals in High Season

The most expensive time to visit St. Maarten/St. Martin is the high season, which runs from mid-December to April. But this shouldn't deter bargain hunters. Finding good deals takes perseverance, patience, and flexibility. When you're booking a room, call the hotel directly and ask about special offers. Even the most upscale resorts offer discount rates for certain rooms and certain days of the week even in high season. Also, there is often a big difference between accommodations even within the same property, especially if there is renovation going on. Be sure to ask if you have special requests or concerns about smoking, accessibility, and amenities. Packages with special themes like water sports or spas can also save you money. Check out deals where kids stay free, you get a free night when you book a certain number of nights, or packages include meals. Some of the hotels are getting more relaxed about minimum stays.

There's a lot of competition at the island's shops and boutiques. You can always try bargaining, especially in the jewelry stores. You can sometimes get as much as 25% off. Ask "is this your best price?" They will let you know if they're in the mood to deal. Very low prices on "designer" items, however, should be greeted with skepticism, as fakes abound. Casinos are always giving something away—chips, drinks, limo service. At restaurants, the prix-fixe lunch or dinner is usually the better deal. On slower nights like Monday and Tuesday, many restaurants offer specials. Look for special offers at the local tourism board and in the local newspaper, the *Daily Herald*.

Villas of Distinction. Villas of Distinction is one of the oldest villa-rental companies on the French side of the island. Check their website for special deals. ☎ *800/289–0900 in the U.S.* ⊕ *www.villasofdistinction.com.*

WIMCO. WIMCO has more hotel, villa, apartment, and condo listings in the Caribbean than just about anyone else. ☎ *401/849–8012 in Rhode Island, 866/449–1553 in the U.S.* ⊕ *www.wimco.com.*

DUTCH SIDE

CUPECOY

$$$ **The Cliff at Cupecoy Beach.** *Rental.* The Cliff at Cupecoy Beach, offers luxurious, high-rise condos, rented out when the owners are not in residence. **Pros:** great views; good for families; close to Maho casinos and restaurants; tight security. **Cons:** it's apartment living, so if you're looking for resort-y or beachy, this is not your place; there is a concierge, but no other hotel services. [$] *Rooms from: $425* ✉ *Rhine Rd., Cupecoy* ☎ *866/978–5839, 721/546–6633* 🌐 *www.cliffsxm.com* ⇨ *72 apartments.*

2

LITTLE BAY

$$ **Belair Beach.** *Rental.* This time-share complex has an unbeatable location on Little Bay Beach, one of St. Maarten's nicest and least crowded stretches of sand. **Pros:** close to Philipsburg; away from the crowds. **Cons:** no full-service restaurant; some rooms are dated. [$] *Rooms from: $319* ✉ *Little Bay Beach Rd., Little Bay* ☎ *599/542–3366* 🌐 *www.belairbeach.com* ⇨ *72 suites* 🍴 *No meals.*

$ **Divi Little Bay Beach Resort.** *Resort.* Bordering the lovely but sparsely populated Little Bay, this renovated property is well located and is awash with water sports. **Pros:** good location; lovely beach, kids stay and eat free. **Cons:** ongoing renovations; pool areas not great. [$] *Rooms from: $219* ✉ *Little Bay Rd., Little Bay* ☎ *721/542–2333, 800/367–3484 in the U.S.* 🌐 *www.divilittlebay.com* ⇨ *218 rooms* 🍴 *No meals.*

MAHO

$$ **Royal Islander Club La Terrasse.** *Rental.* This smaller and nicer sister resort to the Royal Island Club La Plage is right across the street and shares many of the same amenities, including the larger resort's beach. **Pros:** in a hip area, near restaurants and bars. **Cons:** not on the beach; because this is a time-share rooms can be hard to book during peak periods. [$] *Rooms from: $245* ✉ *1 Rhine Rd., Maho* ☎ *721/545–2388* 🌐 *royalislander.com* ⇨ *67 units* ⊗ *Closed 1st 2 wks in Sept.* 🍴 *No meals.*

$$ **Sonesta Maho Beach Resort and Casino.** *Resort.* The island's largest hotel, which is on Maho Beach, isn't luxurious or fancy, but this full-service resort offers everything right on the premises at reasonable rates, and it is located very close to the airport. **Pros:** huge resort complex; lots of shopping; nonstop nightlife. **Cons:** resort is aging; not the place for a personal, quiet getaway, limited dining choices

BEST BETS FOR LODGING

Fodor's Choice ★
L'Esplanade, Blue Pelican,
the Horny Toad, La Samanna,
Palm Court, Westin St.
Maarten Dawn Beach Resort
& Spa

BEST FOR ROMANCE
La Samanna, Le Domaine
de Lonvilliers, Palm Court,
Princess Heights

BEST BEACHFRONT
The Horny Toad, La Samanna,
Le Domaine de Lonvilliers,

Esmeralda, Radisson Blu
St. Martin

BEST POOL
Radisson Blu St. Martin, Westin St. Maarten Dawn Beach
Resort & Spa

BEST SERVICE
La Samanna, Le Domaine de
Lonvilliers

BEST FOR KIDS
Alamanda Resort, Divi Little
Bay Beach Resort, Radisson
Blu St. Martin, Royal Islander

on the all-inclusive plan. Ⓢ *Rooms from: $289* ✉ *1 Rhine Rd., Box 834, Maho* ☎ *721/545–2115, 800/223–0757, 800/766–3782* ⊕ *www.sonesta.com/mahobeach* ⇝ *537 rooms* ⏏ *No meals.*

OYSTER POND

$ ⚄ **Oyster Bay Beach Resort.** *Resort.* Jutting out into Oys-
☺ ter Bay, this happening, newly renovated condo resort sits on Dawn Beach. **Pros:** lots of activities; nightly entertainment; comfortable accommodations. **Cons:** isolated location; need a car to get around; older units are plain. Ⓢ *Rooms from: $275* ✉ *10 Emerald Merit Rd., Oyster Pond* ☎ *721/543–6040* ⊕ *www.oysterbaybeachresort.com* ⇝ *157 units* ⏏ *No meals.*

$$ ⚄ **Princess Heights.** *Rental.* Perched on a hill 900 feet above
★ Oyster Bay, newly renovated, spacious suites offer privacy, luxury, and white-balustrade balconies with a smashing view of St. Barth. **Pros:** away from the crowds; friendly staff, lovely accommodations; gorgeous vistas. **Cons:** not on the beach; numerous steps to climb; not easy to find; need a car to get around; no restaurant; tiny gym. Ⓢ *Rooms from: $275* ✉ *156 Oyster Pond Rd., Oyster Pond* ☎ *599/543–6906, 800/441–7227 in the U.S.* ⊕ *www.princessheights. com* ⇝ *51 suites* ⏏ *No meals.*

★ **Fodor's** Choice ⚄ **Westin St. Maarten Dawn Beach Resort & Spa.**
$$ *Resort.* Straddling the border between the Dutch and
☺ French sides, the modern Westin sits on one of the island's best beaches. **Pros:** on Dawn Beach; plenty of activities; no

smoking allowed. **Cons:** very big; a bit off the beaten track; time-share sales people can be bothersome. [$] *Rooms from: $322* ✉ *144 Oyster Pond Rd., Oyster Pond* ☎ *599/543–6700, 800/228–3000 in the U.S.* 🌐 *www.westinstmaarten.com* ⇨ *310 rooms, 15 suites, 99 1-, 2-, and 3-bedroom condo units* 🍴 *No meals.*

PELICAN KEY

$ 🏨 **Atrium Beach Resort.** *Rental.* Lush tropical foliage in the glassed-in lobby—hence the name—makes a great first impression. **Pros:** family-friendly environment; short walk to restaurants. **Cons:** rooms lack private balconies; neighborhood is crowded; taxes and service charges add a whopping 25% to basic rates. [$] *Rooms from: $205* ✉ *6 Billy Folly Rd., Pelican Key* ☎ *721/544–2126* 🌐 *atriumbeachstmaarten.com* ⇨ *87 rooms* 🍴 *No meals.*

★ **Fodor's Choice** 🏨 **Blue Pelican.** *Rental.* The 13 brand-new apartment units hidden in this private enclave in Pelican Key were built by the owners of Hotel L'Esplanade and Le Petit Hotel on the French side. **Pros:** gorgeous new residences; great pool; excellent management and security. **Cons:** residence, not a resort; not on the beach; definitely need a car to get around since there is no restaurant. [$] *Rooms from: $290* ✉ *Billy Folly Rd., Pelican Key, St. Maarten* ☎ *590–690/50–60–20* 🌐 *www.bluepelicansxm.com* ⇨ *13 apartments* 🍴 *No meals.*

$$

$$ 🏨 **Diamond Resort International Flamingo Beach.** *Rental.* There are so many activities at this resort that you might not return to your room before bedtime. **Pros:** close to a variety of restaurants and nightlife; lots of activities. **Cons:** area gets crowded; small beach. [$] *Rooms from: $300* ✉ *6 Billy Folly Rd., Pelican Key* ☎ *721/544–3900, 800/438–2929 in the U.S.* 🌐 *www.diamondresorts.com* ⇨ *240 units* 🍴 *No meals.*

PHILIPSBURG

$ 🏨 **Holland House Beach Hotel.** *Hotel.* An ideal location for shoppers and sun worshippers, this historic hotel faces the Front Street pedestrian mall; to the rear are the boardwalk and a long stretch of Great Bay Beach. **Pros:** excellent location; free Wi-Fi; young, engaging management. **Cons:** in a busy, downtown location; no pool, not very resort-y. [$] *Rooms from: $175* ✉ *43 Front St., Philipsburg* ☎ *721/542–2572* 🌐 *www.hhbh.com* ⇨ *48 rooms, 6 suites* 🍴 *Multiple meal plans.*

$ 🏨 **Sonesta Great Bay Beach Resort and Casino.** *Resort.* Location, location, location. Away from the docks that are usually crawling with cruise ships, but only a 10-minute walk from

DID YOU KNOW?

French hotelier Christophe Leroy, owner of La Table du Marché in Saint-Tropez and Marrakech, has taken over Le Domaine de Lonvilliers.

downtown Philipsburg, this resort is well positioned even if it doesn't offer the height of luxury. **Pros:** good location; nice beach and pool; enough activities to keep you busy. **Cons:** hallways are white and bare, giving them a hospital-like feel; Wi-Fi is expensive; although it's beautiful, pollution can be a problem at the beach. [$] *Rooms from: $135* ✉ *19 Little Bay Rd., Philipsburg* ☎ *721/542–2446, 800/223–0757 in the U.S.* 🌐 *www.sonesta.com/greatbay* 🛏 *257 rooms* 🍴 *Multiple meal plans.*

SIMPSON BAY

★ **Fodor's Choice** 🏨 **The Horny Toad.** *B&B/Inn.* Because of its stupendous view of Simpson Bay and the simple, but immaculate and comfortable rooms with creative decor, this lovely guesthouse is widely considered the best on this side of the island. **Pros:** tidy rooms; friendly vibe; beautiful beach is usually deserted. **Cons:** rooms are very basic; need a car to get around; no kids under seven allowed; no pool. [$] *Rooms from: $218* ✉ *2 Vlaun Dr., Simpson Bay* ☎ *721/545–4323, 800/417–9361 in the U.S.* 🌐 *www.thtgh.com* 🛏 *8 rooms* 🍴 *No meals.*

$

$ 🏨 **La Vista.** *Rental.* Hibiscus and bougainvillea line brick walkways that connect the 32 wood-frame bungalows and beachfront suites of this intimate and friendly, family-owned time-share resort perched at the foot of Pelican Key. **Pros:** close to restaurants and bars. **Cons:** no-frills furnishings; not the best beach. [$] *Rooms from: $180* ✉ *53 Billy Folly Rd., Simpson Bay* ☎ *721/544–3005, 888/790–5264 in the U.S.* 🌐 *www.lavistaresort.com* 🛏 *50 suites, penthouses, and cottages* 🍴 *No meals.*

$ 🏨 **Mary's Boon Beach Plantation.** *Hotel.* A shaded courtyard welcomes guests at this quirky, informal guesthouse on a 3-mile-long stretch of Simpson Bay. **Pros:** small and intimate; interesting history. **Cons:** need a car; charge for Internet; because of airport proximity, it can be quite noisy; mosquitoes abound year-round. [$] *Rooms from: $150* ✉ *117 Simpson Bay Rd., Simpson Bay* ☎ *721/545–7000* 🌐 *www.marysboon.com* 🛏 *37 rooms* 🍴 *No meals* ☞ *6-night min. late Dec.–mid-Mar.*

$ 🏨 **Royal Turtle Inn.** *B&B/Inn.* This tiny property appeals to those who like small inns with simple surroundings and a lagoon view, and who don't mind a three-minute walk to the beach. **Pros:** low rates; close to airport. **Cons:** faces a very busy street; rooms are very basic. [$] *Rooms from: $89* ✉ *114 Airport Rd., Simpson Bay* ☎ *721/545–2563* 🌐 *www.theroyalturtle.net/* 🛏 *8 rooms* 🍴 *Breakfast.*

The casino at the Sonesta Maho Beach Resort

FRENCH SIDE

ANSE MARCEL

$$ ★ [H] **Hotel Le Marquis.** *Hotel.* If you crave spectacular vistas and intimate surroundings and don't mind heights or steep walks, this is a fun property, with a funky St. Barth vibe. **Pros:** romantic honeymoon destination; doting staff; amazing views. **Cons:** not on the beach; no restaurant; on a steep hill. [$] *Rooms from: €245* ✉ *Pigeon Pea Hill, Anse Marcel* ☎ *590/29–42–30* 🌐 *www.hotel-marquis.com* ⇨ *17 rooms* 🍴 *Breakfast.*

★ **Fodor'sChoice** [H] **Le Domaine de Lonvilliers by Christophe Leroy.** $$$$ *Resort.* International sophisticates are excited to see what the chic restaurateur-chef of St-Tropez's Table du Marché and superluxe vacation properties in Marrakech and Avoriaz will make of this classic property on 148 acres of lush gardens bordering the exceptionally beautiful and secluded beach in Anse Marcel. **Pros:** excellent restaurant; chic atmosphere; lovely gardens; beachfront setting, great breakfast buffet. **Cons:** some rooms have round bathtubs right in the middle of the room; you will need a car to get around; beach is shared with the busy Radisson Blu. [$] *Rooms from: €470* ✉ *Anse Marcel* ☎ *590/52–35–35* 🌐 *www.hotel-le-domaine.com* ⇨ *124 rooms, 5 suites* ⏲ *Closed Sept.* 🍴 *Breakfast.*

Westin St. Maarten Dawn Beach Resort & Spa

★ **Fodor's Choice** 🏨 **Radisson Blu St. Martin Resort, Marina and Spa.**
$$$ *Resort.* A $10 million renovation in 2011 has brought a new level of service, design, and comfort to this family-friendly resort with 18 prime acres on one of the island's prettiest beachy coves. **Pros:** newly refurbished resort; attentive service; activities galore; great beach; excellent breakfast buffet. **Cons:** need a car to get around; lots of families at school-vacation times; beach can be busy. [$] *Rooms from: €371* ✉ *BP 581 Marcel Cove, Anse Marcel* ☎ *590/87–67–09, 800/333–3333 in the U.S.* 🌐 *www.radissonblu.com/resort-stmartin* ⇐ *189 rooms, 63 suites* 🍴 *Breakfast.*

BAIE LONGUE

★ **Fodor's Choice** 🏨 **La Samanna.** *Resort.* A long stretch of pretty,
$$$$ white-sand beach borders this venerable resort. **Pros:** great beach; convenient location; romantic; attentive service; excellent spa. **Cons:** rather pricey for standard rooms; small pools; ongoing renovations in some areas. [$] *Rooms from: €995* ✉ *Baie Longue* ☎ *590/87–64–00, 800/854–2252 in the U.S.* 🌐 *www.lasamanna.com* ⇐ *27 rooms, 54 suites* ⊗ *Closed Sept. and Oct.* 🍴 *Breakfast.*

BAIE ORIENTALE

$$$ 🏨 **Alamanda Resort.** *Resort.* One of the few resorts directly on the white-sand beach of Orient Bay, this hotel has a funky feel and spacious, colonial-style suites with terraces that overlook the pool, beach, or ocean. **Pros:** pleasant property; friendly staff; right on Orient Beach. **Cons:** some rooms

CLOSE UP

Condo Rentals

Condo rentals are another lodging option. They appeal to travelers who aren't interested in the one-size-fits-all activities offered by the resorts. Condos are much cheaper than villas, but you get many of the same amenities, including kitchens, and save money by cooking your own meals. To rent a condo, contact the rental company or the individual owner.

The Cliff at Cupecoy Beach., offers luxurious, high-rise condos, rented out when the owners are not in residence. Depending on the owner's personal style, they can be downright fabulous. For extra privacy, separate elevators serve only two apartments on every floor. All units have large living and dining rooms plus fully equipped kitchens with stainless-steel appliances and granite countertops. All have sweeping vistas, but upper-level residences showcase Anguilla, Simpson Bay, and Basses Terres. The fitness center boasts a gym with sauna, whirlpool, and both indoor and outdoor pools. The megachic Dior Spa overlooks the huge indoor swimming pool. **Pros:** great views; good for families; close to Maho casinos and restaurants; tight security. **Cons:** it's apartment living, so if you're looking for resort-y or beachy, this is not your place; there is a concierge, but no other hotel services; no restaurant. ✉ *Rhine Rd., Cupecoy* ☎ *866/978-5839 or 599/546-6633* 🌐 *www.cliffsxm.com.*

Jennifer's Vacation Villas rents condos near Simpson Bay Beach. ☎ *631/546-7345 or 011/599-54-43107* 🌐 *www.jennifersvacationvillas.com.*

Sint Maarten Condos rents several condos on Pelican Key. ☎ *501/984-2483* 🌐 *www.stmaartencondos.com.*

2

are noisy; could use some updating. [$] *Rooms from: €375* ✉ *Baie Orientale* ☎ *590/52-87-40, 800/622-7836* 🌐 *www.alamanda-resort.com* 🛏 *42 rooms* 🍴 *Breakfast.*

★ **Fodor's Choice** 🏨 **Caribbean Princess.** *Rental.* These 12 large, newly decorated, well-equipped, and updated two- and three-bedroom condos have big kitchens and living rooms, lovely balconies over Orient Beach (a few steps away), new furniture, and share a pretty pool. **Pros:** the comforts of home; nice interior design; direct beach access. **Cons:** not a full-service resort. [$] *Rooms from: €500* ✉ *C5 Parc de la Baie Orientale, Baie Orientale* ☎ *0590/52-94-94* 🌐 *www.hotelcaribbeanprincess.com/* 🛏 *12 condos* ⊗ *Closed Sept.* 🍴 *Breakfast.*

$$$$

👶

DID YOU KNOW?

La Samanna, which was built by James Frankel and opened in 1974, overlooks Baie Longue on the French side of St. Martin.

$ 🏨 **Club Orient Resort.** *Resort.* For something rather different, consider letting it all hang out at this clothing-optional hotel on Baie Orientale. **Pros:** nice location; on-site convenience store. **Cons:** no TVs; a bit pricey; rooms are the bare minimum. [$] *Rooms from: $225* ✉ *1 Baie Orientale, Baie Orientale* ☎ *590/87–33–85, 877/456–6833 in the U.S.* 🌐 *www.cluborient.com* 🛏 *137 rooms* 🍴 *No meals.*

$$ 👪 ★ 🏨 **Esmeralda Resort.** *Hotel.* Almost all of these traditional Caribbean-style, kitchen-equipped villas, which can be configured to meet the needs of different groups, have their own private pool, and the fun of Orient Beach, where the hotel has its own private beach club, is a two-minute walk away. **Pros:** beachfront location; private pools; plenty of activities; frequent online promotions. **Cons:** need a car to get around; iffy Wi-Fi service. [$] *Rooms from: €300* ✉ *Baie Orientale* ☎ *590/87–36–36, 800/622–7836* 🌐 *www.esmeralda-resort.com* 🛏 *65 rooms* 🕓 *Closed Sept. and Oct.* 🍴 *Breakfast.*

$$$$ 🏨 **Green Cay Village.** *Rental.* Surrounded by five acres of lush greenery high above Baie Orientale, these villas are perfect for families or groups of friends who are looking for privacy and the comforts of home. **Pros:** beautiful setting; near Baie Orientale; perfect for families with teens or older kids. **Cons:** need a car to get around; beach is a five-minute walk; need to be vigilant about locking doors, as there have been reports of crime in the area. [$] *Rooms from: €660* ✉ *Parc de la Baie Orientale, Baie Orientale* ☎ *590/87–38–63* 🌐 *www.greencay.com* 🛏 *9 villas* 🍴 *Breakfast.*

$ 🏨 **Hotel La Plantation.** *Hotel.* Perched high above Orient Bay, this colonial-style hotel is a charmer, and guests give high marks to the recent renovations. **Pros:** relaxing atmosphere; eye-popping views. **Cons:** small pool; beach is a 10-minute walk away. [$] *Rooms from: €205* ✉ *C5 Parc de La Baie Orientale, Baie Orientale* ☎ *590/29–58–00* 🌐 *www.la-plantation.com* 🛏 *52 rooms* 🕓 *Closed Sept.–mid-Oct.* 🍴 *Breakfast.*

★ $$$ **Fodor's Choice** 🏨 **Palm Court.** *Hotel.* The romantic beachfront units of this *hotel de charme* are steps from the fun of Orient Beach yet private, quiet, and stylishly up-to-date. **Pros:** big rooms; fresh and new; nice garden. **Cons:** across from, but not on the beach. [$] *Rooms from: €360* ✉ *Parc de la Baie Orientale, Baie Orientale* ☎ *590/87–41–94* 🌐 *www.sxm-palm-court.com* 🛏 *24 rooms* 🕓 *Closed Sept.* 🍴 *Breakfast.*

Palm Court Hotel, St. Martin

FRENCH CUL DE SAC

★ **Fodor's Choice** 🏨 **Karibuni Lodge.** *B&B/Inn.* Lovely in every way, this new, super-chic, yet reasonably-priced, enclave of spacious suites surrounded by gorgeous tropical gardens offer stunning views of tiny Pinel Island. **Pros:** stylish; new; eco-friendly; lushly comfortable; amazing views. **Cons:** removed from the action; definitely need a car; not a resort, and not on the beach. $ *Rooms from: €255* ✉ *29 Terrasses de Cul de Sac, French Cul de Sac* ☎ *690/64–38–58* 🌐 *www.lekaribuni.com* ➪ *6 suites* 🍴 *Breakfast.*

$$

GRAND CASE

$$$$ 🏨 **Bleu Emeraude.** *Rental.* The 11 spacious apartments in this tidy complex sit right on a sliver of Grand Case Beach. **Pros:** brand-new; walk to restaurants; attractive decor. **Cons:** it's not resort-y at all. $ *Rooms from: €400* ✉ *240 bd. de Grand Case, Grand Case* ☎ *0590/87–27–71* 🌐 *www.bleuemeraude.com* ➪ *4 studios, 6 1-bedroom apartments, 1 2-bedroom apartment* 🍴 *Breakfast.*

$$ 🏨 **Grand Case Beach Club.** *Resort.* This beachfront property on a cove at the east end of Grand Case has a friendly staff and spectacular sunset views. **Pros:** reasonably priced; comfortable rooms; walking distance to restaurants. **Cons:** small beach; dated decor and buildings; need a car to explore island. $ *Rooms from: €335* ✉ *21 rue de Petit Plage, at north end of bd. de Grand Case, Box 339, Grand*

Case ☎ *590/87–51–87, 800/344–3016 in the U.S.* 🌐 *www.grandcasebeachclub.com* ⇨ *72 apartments* 🍴 *Breakfast.*

★ Fodor's Choice 🏨 **Hôtel L'Esplanade.** *Hotel.* Enthusiasts return
$$$ again and again to the classy, loft-style suites in this immac-
👶 ulate boutique hotel. **Pros:** attentive management; very clean; updated room decor; family-friendly feel. **Cons:** lots of stairs to climb; not on the beach. [$] *Rooms from: €425* ✉ *Grand Case* ☎ *590/87–06–55, 866/596–8365 in the U.S.* 🌐 *www.lesplanade.com* ⇨ *24 units* 🍴 *No meals.*

$$$ 🏨 **Le Petit Hotel.** *Hotel.* Surrounded by some of the best
👶 restaurants in the Caribbean, this beachfront boutique
★ hotel, sister hotel to Hotel L'Esplanade, oozes charm and has the same caring, attentive management. **Pros:** walking distance to everything in Grand Case; friendly staff; clean, updated rooms. **Cons:** many stairs to climb; no pool. [$] *Rooms from: €390* ✉ *248 bd. de Grand Case, Grand Case* ☎ *590/29–09–65* 🌐 *www.lepetithotel.com* ⇨ *9 rooms, 1 suite* 🍴 *Breakfast.*

$ 🏨 **Love Hotel.** *B&B/Inn.* This cozy, seven-room guesthouse right on Grand Case Beach was renovated by the young owners themselves. **Pros:** young, fun vibe; in-town location. **Cons:** pretty basic rooms; ongoing construction; staff not always helpful; hotel can be noisy or hopping depending on your definition. [$] *Rooms from: €133* ✉ *140 bd. de Grand Case, Grand Case* ☎ *0590/29–87–14* 🌐 *www.love-sxm.com* ⇨ *7 rooms* 🍴 *No meals.*

OYSTER POND

$ 🏨 **Captain Oliver's Resort.** *Hotel.* This cluster of pink bungalows is perched high on a hill above a lagoon. **Pros:** restaurant is reasonably priced; ferry trips leave from the hotel. **Cons:** not on the beach; not fancy or modern. [$] *Rooms from: €241* ✉ *Oyster Pond* ☎ *590/87–40–26* 🌐 *www.captainolivers.com* ⇨ *50 suites* ⏲ *Closed Sept. and Oct.* 🍴 *Breakfast.*

NIGHTLIFE

St. Maarten has lots of evening and late-night action. To find out what's doing on the island, pick up *St. Maarten Nights, St. Maarten Quick Pick Guide,* or *St. Maarten Events,* all of which are distributed free in the tourist office and hotels. The glossy *Discover St. Martin/St. Maarten* magazine, also free, has articles on island history and on the newest shops, discos, and restaurants. Or buy a copy of Thursday's *Daily Herald* newspaper, which lists all the

Gambling, the most popular indoor activity in St. Maarten

week's entertainment. Insiders will tell you to head to Maho, go first to Bamboo for cocktails and sushi, hit Sky Beach, then finally, go to Tantra.

The island's casinos—all 13 of them—are found only on the Dutch side. All have craps, blackjack, roulette, and slot machines. You must be 18 years or older to gamble. Dress is casual (but excludes bathing suits or skimpy beachwear). Most casinos are found in hotels, but there are also some independents.

DUTCH SIDE

COLE BAY

CASINOS

Princess Casino. One of the island's largest gaming halls, Princess Casino has a wide array of restaurants and entertainment options. ✉ *Port de Plaisance, 155 Union Rd, Cole Bay* ☎ *721/544-4311* ⊕ *www.princessportdeplaisance.com.*

CUPECOY

CASINOS

Atlantis World Casino. With some of the best restaurants on the island, Atlantis World is a popular destination even for those who don't gamble. It has more than 500 slot machines and gaming tables offering roulette, baccarat, three-card poker, Texas Hold'em poker, and Omaha high poker, not to mention some of the best restaurants on the Dutch side of the island. ⊠ *106 Rhine Rd., Cupecoy* ☎ *721/545–4601* ⊕ *www.atlantisworld.com.*

MAHO

BARS AND CLUBS

Bamboo. Bamboo is a sophisticated club-restaurant with soft techno music. ⊠ *Sonesta Maho Beach Resort & Casino, 1 Rhine Rd., Maho* ☎ *721/545–3622* ⊕ *www.bamboobernies.net.*

Bliss. The open-air nightclub and lounge, which is good for dancing, rocks till late. ⊠ *Caravanserai Resort, Maho* ☎ *721/544–3410* ⊕ *www.bliss-sxm.com.*

Cheri's Café. Across from Maho Beach Resort and Casino, Cheri's (you can't miss it—look for pink) features Sweet Chocolate, a lively band that will get your toes tapping and your tush twisting. Snacks and hearty meals are available all day long on a cheerful veranda decorated with thousands of inflatable beach toys. It's closed Tuesdays. ⊠ *45 Rhine Rd., Maho* ☎ *721/545–3361* ⊕ *www.cheriscafe.com.*

★ **Fodor's**Choice **Sky Beach.** The Sky Beach Rooftop Beach and Lounge is perfect for visitors who don't want to leave the beach vibe after the sun goes down. The elegant rooftop pulses with techno and house music while guests lounge on beds in cabanas. There is sand volleyball for fun and great cocktails at the happening bar. Great views and stargazing come with the territory. In-the-know clubbers come here after a bite of sushi at Bamboo but before Tantra starts to wake up after midnight. Open Wednesday through Sunday til late. There is live jazz on weekends and outdoor movies on Thursdays. ⊠ *Sonesta Maho Resort & Casino, 1 Rhine Rd., Maho, St. Maarten* ☎ *721/545–3547* ⊕ *www.theskybeach.com.*

Soprano's. Starting each night at 8, the pianist at Soprano's takes requests for oldies, romantic favorites, or smooth jazz. Come for Happy Hour from 8 to 9 pm with a full menu that includes pizza. the bar is open until 3 am nightly. ⊠ *Sonesta Maho Beach Resort & Casino, 1 Rhine Rd., Maho* ☎ *721/545–2485* ⊕ *www.sopranospianobar.com.*

Sunset Beach Bar. This popular spot offers a relaxed, anything-goes atmosphere. Enjoy live music Wednesday through Sunday as you watch planes from the airport next door fly directly over your head. Bring your camera for stunning photos. ⊠ *Maho Beach, Maho* ☎ *721/545–3998* ⊕ *www.sunsetsxm.com.*

2

Tantra Nightclub & Sanctuary. This is definitely the hottest nightclub at the Sonesta Maho. Come late—things don't really get going until after 1 am. On Wednesday nights ladies drink champagne for free, and drinks are $2 for everyone on Fridays. Celebrity DJs spin on Saturdays. Feel free to dress up. ⊠ *Sonesta Maho Beach Resort & Casino, 1 Rhine Rd., Maho Bay* ☎ *721/545–2861* ⊕ *www.tantrasxm.com.*

CASINOS

Casino Royale. Casino Royale at the Sonesta Maho Beach Resort & Casino is the largest on the island, with some 1,300 square meters of gaming and a full theater with 750 seats for events and shows. There are 30 tables for gaming, including roulette (American and French), craps, blackjack, and poker (3-card and Caribbean). The 400 slot machines include a variety of classics and modern video slots. *Sonesta M* ⊠ *Maho Beach Resort & Casino, 1 Rhine Rd., Maho* ☎ *721/545–2590* ⊕ *www.playmaho.com.*

OYSTER POND

CASINOS

Westin Casino. The Westin Casino is somewhat more sedate than other island casinos. If you ever get tired of the slot machines and gaming tables, beautiful Dawn Beach is just outside the door. ⊠ *Westin Dawn Beach Resort and Spa, 144 Oyster Pond Rd., Oyster Pond* ☎ *721/543–6700* ⊕ *www.westinstmaarten.com.*

PHILIPSBURG

BARS AND CLUBS

Axum Art Café and Gallery. This 1960s-style coffee shop offers local cultural activities as well as live jazz and reggae. It's open daily, 11:30 am until the wee hours. ⊠ *7L Front St., Philipsburg* ☎ *721/542–0547.*

Ocean Lounge. Ocean Lounge is the quintessential people-watching venue. Sip a guavaberry colada and point your chair toward the boardwalk. ⊠ *Holland House Hotel, 43 Front St., Philipsburg* ☎ *721/542–2572.*

CASINOS

Beach Plaza Casino. Beach Plaza Casino, in the heart of the shopping area, has more than 180 slots and multi-game machines with the latest in touch-screen technology. Because of its location, it is popular with cruise-ship passengers. ⊠ *Front St., Philipsburg* ☎ *721/543–2031* ⊕ *www.atlantisworld.com.*

Coliseum Casino. The Coliseum is popular with fans of slots, blackjack, poker, or roulette. ⊠ *Front St., Philipsburg* ☎ *721/543–2101* ⊕ *www.coliseumsxm.com.*

Diamond Casino. Diamond Casino has 250 slot machines, plus the usual tables offering games like blackjack, roulette, and three-card poker. The casino is in the heart of Philipsburg. ⊠ *1 Front St., Philipsburg* ☎ *721/543–2583* ⊕ *www. diamondcasinosxm.com.*

Golden Casino. The Sonesta Great Bay's casino is on the small side. But fans say the 84 slots machines and tables with Caribbean poker, blackjack, and roulette are more than enough. ⊠ *Great Bay Beach Hotel, Little Bay Rd., Great Bay* ☎ *721/542–2446* ⊕ *www.sonesta.com/greatbay.*

Jump-Up Casino. The Jump-Up is on the main shopping street in Phillipsburg and near the cruise-ship pier, so it attracts lots of day-trippers. ⊠ *1 Emmaplein, Philipsburg* ☎ *721/542–0862* ⊕ *www.jumpupcasino.com.*

PELICAN KEY

CASINOS

Hollywood Casino. Centrally located to the Simpson Bay area, one of the island's entertainment hotspots is Pelican Key, where you'll find the Hollywood Casino. This attractive casino lets you play table games and slots, while enjoying the Hollywood star themeTheme. ⊠ *Pelican Resort, 37 Billy Folly Rd., Pelican Key* ☎ *721/544–4463* ⊕ *www. casinosxm.com.*

SIMPSON BAY

BARS AND CLUBS

Buccaneer Bar. Buccaneer Bar is the place to enjoy a BBC (Bailey's banana colada), a slice of pizza, and a nightly bonfire. It's family-friendly and conveniently located. ⊠ *Behind Atrium Beach Resort, 10 Billy Folly Rd., Simpson Bay* ☎ *721/522–9700* ⊕ *www.buccaneerbeachbar.com.*

Pineapple Pete. At Pete's you can groove to live music or visit the game room for a couple of rounds of pool. ⊠ *Airport Rd., Simpson Bay* ☎ *721/544–6030* ⊕ *www. pineapplepete.com.*

Red Piano. The Red Piano has terrific live music and great cocktails every night. ⊠ *Hollywood Casino, Billy Folly Rd., Simpson Bay* ☎ *721/580–1841* ⊕ *www.theredpianosxm.com.*

CASINOS

Paradise Plaza Casino. Paradise Plaza has 250 slots and multigame machines. Betting on sporting events is a big thing here, which explains the 20 televisions tuned to whatever game happens to be on at the time. ⊠ *69 Welfare Rd, Simpson Bay* ☎ *721/543–4721* ⊕ *www.paradisecasinosxm.com.*

FRENCH SIDE

BAIE DES PÈRES

BARS AND CLUBS

★ **Kali's Beach Bar.** On the French side, Kali's Beach Bar Restaurant is a happening spot with live music late into the night, and has been since the late 1980s. On the night of the full moon and on every Friday night, the beach bonfire and late-night party here is the place to be, but its a great place to hang out all day long on the chaises you can rent for the day. The Rasta-theme restaurant serves lunch and dinner on bright yellow and red picnic tables shaded by palm-fronds. You can rent a beach kayak and paddle the secluded, relatively tranquil bay. Be sure to ask Kali for some tastes of his homemade fruit-infused rum. ⊠ *Baie des Pères* ☎ *690/49–06–81.*

BAIE ORIENTALE

BARS AND CLUBS

Boo Boo Jam. This beach club on Orient Bay is a jumping joint with a mix of calypso, meringue, salsa, and other beats with parties on Friday and Sunday nights, and every day for lunch. △ As at other beach venues, don't leave any belongings at all in your car. ⊠ *Baie Orientale* ☎ *690/75–21–66.*

GRAND CASE

BARS AND CLUBS

★ **Calmos Café.** Calmos Café draws a young local crowd. Just walk through the boutique and around the back to the sea and pull up a beach chair or park yourself at a picnic table. It's open all day, but the fun really begins at the cocktail hour, when everyone enjoys tapas. The little covered deck at the end is a perfect for romance. On Thursday and Sunday there is often live reggae on the beach. ⊠ *40 bd. de Grand Case, Grand Case* ☎ *590/29–01–85* ⊕ *lecalmoscafe.com.*

La Noche. La Noche may tempt you during your after-dinner stroll in Grand Case; consider continuing your evening at this sexy lounge decorated in red, where the house music starts at 11 (or later) and continues until the last reveler quits. The dress code is "chic and sexy." ✉ *147 bd. de Grand Case, Grand Case* ☎ *590/29–72–89.*

SHOPPING

It's true that the island sparkles with its myriad outdoor activities—diving, snorkeling, sailing, swimming, and sunning—but shopaholics are drawn to the sparkle in the jewelry stores. The huge array of such stores is almost unrivaled in the Caribbean. In addition, duty-free shops can offer substantial savings—about 15% to 30% below U.S. and Canadian prices—on cameras, watches, liquor, cigars, and designer clothing. It's no wonder that many cruise ships make Philipsburg a port of call. Stick with the big vendors that advertise in the tourist press, and you will be more likely to avoid today's ubiquitous fakes and replicas. On both sides of the island, be alert for idlers. They can snatch unwatched purses. Just be sure to know the U.S. prices of whatever you plan on buying in St. Maarten so you know if you're getting a deal or just getting dealt a bad hand.

Prices are in dollars on the Dutch side, in euros on the French side. As for bargains, there are more to be had on the Dutch side; prices on the French side may sometimes be higher than those you'll find back home, and the fact that prices are in euros doesn't help affordability. Merchandise may not be from the newest collections, especially with regard to clothing, but there are items available on the French side that are not available on the Dutch side. Finally, remember the important caveat about shopping anywhere: if it sounds too good to be true, it usually is.

DUTCH SIDE

MAHO

You'll find a moderately good selection of stores in Maho Plaza, near the Sonesta resort in Maho. Many Americans prefer to shop here since they can pay in U.S. dollars and get better deals than on the French side.

CLOTHING

Hip Up. Hip Up has a terrific selection of swimsuits, cute cover-ups, and beach accessories like rhinestone-studded flip-flops at this outpost of the popular French retailer. Many of the swimsuits are sold as separates—you pick the top and the bottom in the size and style that suits. There

Marigot's waterfront market

is another branch in Marigot. ⊠ *Maho Plaza, Maho, St. Maarten* ☎ *721/545–4011* ⊕ *www.hipup.com.*

PHILIPSBURG

Philipsburg's **Front Street** has reinvented itself. Now it's mall-like, with a redbrick walk and streets, palm trees lining the sleek boutiques, jewelry stores, souvenir shops, and outdoor restaurants, and the old reliables, such as McDonald's and Burger King. Here and there a school or a church appears to remind visitors there's more to the island than shopping. Back Street is where you'll find the **Philipsburg Market Place,** a daily open-air market where you can haggle for bargains on items such as handicrafts, souvenirs, and beachwear. **Old Street,** near the end of Front Street, has stores, boutiques, and open-air cafés offering French crepes, rich chocolates, and island mementos.

ART GALLERIES

Art Gallery Le Saint Geran. On the Dutch side of the Island, this gallery has a collection of more than 250 original works by Caribbean artists and artisans. There's also a selection of sculptures and ceramics. ⊠ *117 Front St., Philipsburg* ☎ *721/542–1023.*

CLOTHING

Liz Claiborne. Claiborne sells designer women's clothes. ⊠ *48A Front St., Philipsburg* ☎ *721/543–0380.*

Dutch architecture along Philipsburg's pedestrian mall

Polo Ralph Lauren. Polo Ralph Lauren has men's and women's sportswear in preppy styles. ✉ *31 Front St., Philipsburg* ☎ *721/543–0196.*

Tommy Hilfiger. This outlet sells sportswear in the designer's trademark colors. ✉ *28 Front St., Philipsburg* ☎ *721/542–6315.*

CRYSTAL AND CHINA
In addition to the stores listed here, both Little Europe and Little Switzerland carry china and crystal.

Divine. Divine has a sparkling array of Swarovski crystal and a timely selection of Swatches. ✉ *4 Sint Rose Arcade, 26 Front St., Philipsburg* ☎ *721/542–9955.*

Lalique. Lalique has a fine collection of French crystal. ✉ *13 Sint Rose Arcade, 26 Front St., Philipsburg* ☎ *721/542–0763.*

HANDICRAFTS
Guavaberry Emporium. Visitors to the Dutch side of the island come for free samples at the the small factory where the Sint Maarten Guavaberry Company makes its famous liqueur. You'll find a multitude of versions, including one made with jalapeño peppers. Check out the hand-painted bottles. The store also sells the Gourmet BBQ & Hot Sauce Collection and souvenir hats ✉ *8–10 Front St., Philipsburg* ☎ *721/542–2965* ⊕ *www.guavaberry.com.*

Shipwreck Shop. Shipwreck Shop has outlets all over the island that stock a little of everything: colorful hammocks, hand-made jewelry, and lots of the local guavaberry liqueur, but the main store on Front Street in Philipsburg has the largest selection of wares. ✉ *42 Front St., Philipsburg* ☎ *721/542–2962, 721/542–6710* ⊕ *www.shipwreckshops.com.*

JEWELRY AND GIFTS

Jewelry is big business on both the French and Dutch sides of the island, and many stores have outlets in both places. The so-called duty-free prices, however, may not give you much savings (if anything) over what you might pay at home, and sometimes prices are higher than you would pay at a shop back home. Compare prices in a variety of stores before you buy, and if you know you want to search for an expensive piece of jewelry or high-end watch, make sure you price your pieces at home and bargain hard to ensure you get a good deal.

Artistic Jewelers. Artistic Jewelers carries jewelry and watches by David Yurman, Breitling, Chanel, Chopard, Jaeger-Lecoultre, and others. ✉ *61 Front St., Philipsburg* ☎ *721/542–3456.*

Art of Time Jewelers. Art of Time, a sister store to Artistic Jewlers, specializes in watches, Montblanc pens, and jewelry by David Yurman, Chopard, and Mikimoto, among others. ✉ *26 Front St., Philipsburg* ☎ *721/542–2180* ⊕ *www.artoftimejewelers.com.*

Carat. Carat sells jewelry by Pomellato, watches by Bell & Ross, and other luxury brands. ✉ *73 Front St., Philipsburg* ☎ *721/542–2180.*

Cartier. The famous upscale jeweler has a lovely collection on sale here. ✉ *35 Front St., Philipsburg* ☎ *721/543–7700.*

Little Europe. Little Europe sells fine jewelry, crystal, and china in its two branches in Philipsburg. ✉ *80 Front St., Philipsburg* ☎ *721/542–4371* ⊕ *www.littleeuropejewellers.com* ✉ *2 Front St., Philipsburg* ☎ *721/542–4371* ⊕ *www.littleeuropejewellers.com.*

Little Switzerland. The large Caribbean duty-free chain sells watches, fine crystal, china, perfume, and jewelry. ✉ *52 Front St., Philipsburg* ☎ *721/542–2523* ⊕ *www.littleswitzerland.com* ✉ *Harbor Point Village, Pointe Blanche* ☎ *721/542–7785* ⊕ *www.littleswitzerland.com* ✉ *Westin Dawn Beach*

Resort & Spa, Dawn Beach ☎ *721/543–6451* ⊕ *www. littleswitzerland.com.*

Oro Diamante. Oro Diamante carries loose diamonds, jewelry, watches, perfume, and cosmetics. ✉ *62-B Front St., Philipsburg* ☎ *599/543–0342, 800/635–7950 in the U.S.* ⊕ *www.oro-diamante.com.*

PERFUME

Lipstick. Lipstick has an enormous selection of perfume and cosmetics. ✉ *31 Front St., Philipsburg* ☎ *721/542–6052.*

FRENCH SIDE

BAIE NETTLÉ

ART GALLERIES

Francis Eck. The brilliant oil paintings of Francis Eck are true to the primary colors and shapes of the Caribbean. ✉ *1104 Le Flamboyant, Baie Nettlé* ☎ *590/59–79–27* ⊕ *www.francis-eck.com.*

BAIE ORIENTALE

ART GALLERIES

Antoine Chapon. On the French side, the watercolor paintings of Antoine Chapon reflect the peaceful atmosphere of St. Martin and the sea surrounding it. Call for an appointment to view the work. ✉ *Terrasses de Cul-de-Sac, Baie Orientale* ☎ *590/52–93–75* ⊕ *www.chaponartgallery.com.*

COLOMBIER

ART GALLERIES

Minguet Art Gallery. The Minguet Gallery, between Marigot and Grand Case, is managed by the daughter of the late artist Alexandre Minguet. The gallery carries original paintings, lithographs, posters, and postcards depicting island flora and landscapes by Minguet, as well as original works by Robert Dago and Loic BarBotin. ✉ *Rambaud Hill* ☎ *590/87–76–06* ⊕ *www.minguet.com.*

GRAND CASE

ART GALLERIES

★ **Atelier des Tropismes.** Contemporary Caribbean artists, including Paul Elliot Thuleau, who is a master of capturing the unique sunshine of the islands, are showcased at Atelier des Tropismes. This is a serious gallery with some very good artists. And it's open late, so you can browse before dinner.

⊠ *107 bd. de Grand Case, Grand Case* ☎ *590/29–10–60* ⊕ *tropismesgallery.com.*

MARIGOT

On the French side, wrought-iron balconies, colorful awnings, and gingerbread trim decorate Marigot's smart shops, tiny boutiques, and bistros in the **Marina Port La Royale** complex and on the main streets, **Rue de la Liberté** and **Rue de la République**. Also in Marigot are the pricey **West Indies Mall** and the **Plaza Caraïbes**, which house designer shops, although some shops are closing in the economic downturn.

ART GALLERIES

Galerie Camaïeu. This gallery sells both originals and copies of works by Caribbean artists. ⊠ *8 rue de Kennedy, Marigot* ☎ *590/87–25–78* ⊕ *www.camaieu-artgallery.com.*

Gingerbread Galerie. This gallery on the far side of the marina specializes in Haitian art and sells both expensive paintings and more reasonably priced decorative pieces of folk art. ⊠ *Marina Port La Royale, Marigot* ☎ *590/51-94-95* ⊕ *www.gingerbread-gallery.com.*

Vou Deco. Shop here for beautiful modern home accessories with a French flair. ⊠ *Plaza Caraïbes, Rue du General de Gaulle, Marigot* ☎ *590/29–46–63.*

CLOTHING

On the French side, the best luxury-brand shops are found either in the modern, air-conditioned West Indies Mall or the Plaza Caraïbes center across from Marina Port La Royale in Marigot. There is also a small center in Grand Case, called La Petite Favorite, with four shops and a café.

Banana Moon. Find a terrific selection of bathing suits and other beachwear here on the Marina. There is a sister shop in Maho. ⊠ *Marina Port La Royale, Marigot* ☎ *590/87–87–15.*

Blue Glue. If you have the body they have the super-sexy bikini for it. ⊠ *12 Rue du Général de Gaulle, Marigot* ☎ *690/72–74–04* ⊕ *www.blue-glue.com.*

Lacoste. The preppy clothier has everything with the alligator logo for men, women, and children, and the offerings are generally the better-quality and more expensive. made-in-France items, not the made-in-Peru items usually available in the United States. ⊠ *West Indies Mall, Front de Mer, Marigot* ☎ *590/52–84–84.*

Max Mara. Max Mara has beautifully made, tailored women's clothes with an elegant attitude. ⊠ *6 rue du Kennedy, Marigot* ☎ *590/52–99–75.*

120% Lino. This store has nicely made and classy shirts and pants for men and women made of pure linen in pastel tones. ⊠ *21 Marina Port La Royale, Marigot* ☎ *590/87–25–43.*

Tuula. Tuula is another good boutique across from Marina Port La Royale, this one stocking an interesting selection of fashion-forward and one-of-a-kind apparel and accessories. ⊠ *Rue de President Kennedy, Marigot* ☎ *590/87–50–94.*

Vilebrequin St. Tropez. This shop on the marina has a vast selection of the brighly patterned status swim suits for men and boys. ⊠ *Marina de la Port Royale, Marigot* ☎ *590/29–13–09.*

JEWELRY AND GIFTS

Artistic Jewelers. Artistic Jewelers carries the work of David Yurman, among many others, as well as high-end designer watches, including Chanel, Baum & Mercier, Technomarine, and Chopard. ⊠ *8 rue du Général de Gaulle, Marigot* ☎ *590/52–24–80* ⊕ *www.artisticjewelers.com.*

Carat. Carat sells jewelry by Pomellato, watches by Bell & Ross, and other luxury brands. ⊠ *16 rue de la République, Marigot* ☎ *590/87–73–40.*

Cartier. Cartier has a lovely collection of fine jewelry. ⊠ *Rue du Général de Gaulle, Marigot* ☎ *590/52–40–02.*

Manek's. Manek's sells, on two floors, electronics, luggage, perfume, jewelry, Cuban cigars, duty-free liquors, and tobacco products. ⊠ *Rue de la République, Marigot* ☎ *590/87–54–91.*

LEATHER GOODS AND ACCESSORIES

Longchamp. This is the local outpost for the chic French leather-goods company, where you'll find an especially good selection of the Pliage line of foldable, durable, coated-zipper totes with leather handles. ⊠ *11 Rue du Général de Gaulle, Marigot* ☎ *590/87–92–76* ⊕ *www.longchamp.com.*

PERFUME

Lipstick. Lipstick has an enormous selection of perfume and cosmetics. ⊠ *Plaza Caraïbes, Rue du Kennedy, Marigot* ☎ *590/87–73–24.*

A Day in St. Eustatius

2

The Quill, St. Eustatius' dormant volcano

Unless you're a diver or a history buff, chances are you have never heard of St. Eustatius, or Statia, as it is often called. So many ships once crowded its harbor that it was tagged the Emporium of the Western World. That abruptly changed in 1776. With an 11-gun salute to the American *Andrew Doria*, Statia became the first country to recognize U.S. independence. Great Britain retaliated by economically devastating the island.

Fort Oranje, from where famous shots came, is a history buff favorite. In Oranjestad, it has protected the island beginning in 1636. Its courtyard houses the original Dutch Reformed Church (1776). Honen Dalim, one of the oldest synagogues in the Caribbean (1738), is on Synagogepad (Synagogue Path).

The island's interior is gorgeous. For hikers, the Quill is the challenge. The long and windy trail to the top of the 1,968-foot crater is lined with wild orchids, frilly ferns, elephant ears, and various other kinds of flora. Beaches, on the other hand, hold little attraction. There's no real sandy spot on the Caribbean shore, and the beaches on the Atlantic side are too rough for swimming.

Statia is a pleasant change from the bustle of St. Maarten. No matter how much time you spend on the island, locals will wave or beep at you in recognition. You never feel like a stranger.

Sailing is a popular activity in St. Maarten/St. Martin.

OYSTER POND

ART GALLERIES
Céramiques d'art Marie Moine. This shop sells ceramics that are unique and affordable. ✉ *76 rue de la Flibuste, Oyster Pond* ☎ *590/29–53–76.*

SPORTS AND ACTIVITIES

BIKING

Mountain biking is a great way to explore the island. Beginner and intermediate cyclists can ride the coastal trails from Cay Bay to Fort Amsterdam or Mullet Beach. More serious bikers can cruise the Bellevue Trail from Port de Plaisance to Marigot. Bring your bathing suit—along the way you can stop at Baie Rouge or Baie des Prunes for a dip. The bike trails to Fort Louis offer fabulous views. The most challenging ride is up Pic du Paradis. If you would feel better tackling this route with a guide, ask at one of the bike shops. Several locally known guides can help you make this trip.

DUTCH SIDE
TriSport. TriSport rents bikes that come with helmets, water bottle, locks, and repair kits. Rates are $17 per half day, $24 overnight, and $110 per week. Guided bicycle tours are offered. TriSport also rents kayaks and stand-up paddle

boards, and arranges hikes, outings, and even triathlons. ⊠ *14B Airport Rd., Simpson Bay* ☎ *721/545–4384* ⊕ *www. trisportsxm.com.*

FRENCH SIDE

Loterie Farm. Loterie Farm arranges mountain-biking tours around Pic du Paradis. ⊠ *Rte. de Pic du Paradis 103, Rambaud* ☎ *721/87–86–16, 721/57–28–55.*

BOATING AND SAILING

The island is surrounded by water, so why not get out and enjoy it? The water and winds are perfect for skimming the surf. It'll cost you around $1,200 to $1,500 per day to rent a 28- to 40-foot powerboat, considerably less for smaller boats or small sailboats. Drinks and sometimes lunch are usually included on crewed day charters.

DUTCH SIDE

Random Wind. Random Wind offers full-day sailing and snorkeling trips on a traditional 54-foot clipper. Charter prices depend on the size of the group and whether lunch is served. The regularly scheduled Paradise Daysail costs $95 per person ($50 for kids) and includes food and drink. Departures are on the Dutch side, from Skipjack's at Simpson Bay, at 8:30 am Tuesday through Friday. ⊠ *Ric's Place, Simpson Bay* ☎ *721/587–5742* ⊕ *www.randomwind.com.*

St. Maarten 12-Metre Challenge. Sailing experience is not necessary for the St. Maarten 12-Metre Challenge, one of the island's most popular activities. Participants compete on 68-foot racing yachts, including Dennis Connor's *Stars and Stripes* (the actual boat that won the America's Cup in 1987) and the *Canada II*. Anyone can help the crew grind winches, trim sails, and punch the stopwatch, or you can just sit back and watch everyone else work. The thrill of it is priceless, but book well in advance; this is the most popular shore excursion offered by cruise ships in the Caribbean. It's offered four times daily; the entire experience lasts about three hours. Only children over 12 are allowed. ⊠ *Bobby's Marina, Philipsburg* ☎ *721/542–0045* ⊕ *www.12metre.com.*

FRENCH SIDE

MP Yachting. MP Yachting rents boats of all sizes, with or without a crew, for short trips and long, and it's located conveniently at Marina Port La Royale in Marigot. ⊠ *Marina Port La Royale, Marigot* ☎ *690/53–37–40* ⊕ *www.mpyachting.com.*

Sun Evasion. Sun Evasion is a charter company with locations all over the world, including St. Martin. You can take a half- or full-day charter to Tintamarre, St. Barth, or Ilet Pinel on a mono- or multihull powerboat, available with or without a skipper. ⊠ *Marina Port La Royale, Marigot* ☎ *690/35–03–18* ⊕ *www.sun-evasion.com.*

FISHING

You can angle for yellowtail snapper, grouper, marlin, tuna, and wahoo on deep-sea excursions. Costs range from $150 per person for a half day to $250 for a full day. Prices usually include bait and tackle, instruction for novices, and refreshments. Ask about licensing and insurance.

DUTCH SIDE

Lee's Deepsea Fishing. Lee's Deepsea Fishing organizes excursions, and when you return, Lee's Roadside Grill will cook your tuna, wahoo, or whatever else you catch and keep. Rates start at $200 per person for a half day. ⊠ *82 Welfare Rd., Cole Bay* ☎ *721/544–4233* ⊕ *www.leesfish.com.*

Natalie Kate Adventures. Captain Paul enjoys helping beginners to catch big sailfish including white, striped, and blue marlin, from a 33-foot Bertram sport fishing vessel. The company also does private charters, transfers, and sunset cruises. ☎ *721/580–0800* ⊕ *www.nataliekateadventures.com.*

Rudy's Deep Sea Fishing. Rudy's Deep Sea Fishing has been around for years, and is one of the more experienced sport-angling outfits. A private charter trip for four people starts at $525 for a half-day excursion. ⊠ *14 Airport Rd., Simpson Bay* ☎ *721/545–2177* ⊕ *www.rudysdeepseafishing.com.*

FRENCH SIDE

Private Yacht Charter. Private Yacht Charter offers deep-sea fishing, snorkeling trips, and catamaran trips including snacks and drinks. ⊠ *Oyster Pond Great House Marina, 14 Emerald Merit Rd, Oyster Pond, St. Maarten* ☎ *690/83–53–05* ⊕ *www.privateyachtcharter-sxm.com.*

Horseback riding in the surf, St. Maarten

GOLF

DUTCH SIDE

Mullet Bay Golf Course. St. Maarten is not a golf destination. Nevertheless, there have been improvements to Mullet Bay Golf Course, on the Dutch side, which is now again an 18-hole course and the island's only choice. But it's still not a major draw or a must-play. ✉ *Airport Rd., north of airport, Mullet Bay* ☎ *721/545–3069.*

HORSEBACK RIDING

Island stables offer riding packages for everyone from novices to experts. A 90-minute ride along the beach costs $50 to $70 for group rides and $70 to $90 for private treks. Reservations are necessary. You can arrange rides directly or through most hotels.

FRENCH SIDE

Bayside Riding Club. Bayside Riding Club, on the French side, is a long-established outfit that can accommodate all levels of riders. Group beach rides of 1 to 1½ hours around a nature preserve are €65–€80 per person. Full moon rides get rave reviews. Other rides can be arranged with prior contact. ✉ *Galion Beach Rd., Baie Orientale* ☎ *590/87–36–64.*

KAYAKING

Kayaking is becoming very popular and is almost always offered at the many water-sports operations on both the Dutch and the French sides. Rental starts at about $15 per hour for a single and $19 for a double.

DUTCH SIDE

TriSports. TriSports organizes kayaking and snorkeling excursions in addition to its biking operation. ⊠ *Airport Rd. 14B, Simpson Bay* ☎ *721/545–4384* ⊕ *www.trisportsxm.com.*

FRENCH SIDE

Kali's Beach Bar. On the French side, kayaks are available at Kali's Beach Bar. ⊠ *Friar's Bay* ☎ *690/49–06–81* ⊕ *www. kali-beach-bar.com.*

Wind Adventures. Near Le Galion Beach, Wind Adventures offers rentals and instruction in kayaking, kitesurfing, windsurfing, Hobie cats, and stand-up paddle surfing. ⊠ *Baie Orientale* ☎ *590/29–41–57* ⊕ *www.wind-adventures.com.*

PARASAILING

FRENCH SIDE

Kontiki Watersports. Kontiki Watersports offers parasailing for $40 per half hour on Baie Orientale, giving you aerial views of Green Key, Tintamarre, Ilet Pinel, and St. Barth. You can also rent Jet Skis for $45 for a half hour. ⊠ *Northern beach entrance, Baie Orientale* ☎ *590/87–43–27* ⊕ *kontiki-sxm.com.*

SCUBA DIVING

Diving in St. Maarten/St. Martin is mediocre at best, but those who want to dive will find a few positives. The water temperature here is rarely below 70°F (21°C). Visibility is often 60 to 100 feet. The island has more than 30 dive sites, from wrecks to rocky labyrinths. Right outside of Philipsburg, 55 feet under the water, is the HMS *Proselyte,* once explored by Jacques Cousteau. Although it sank in 1801, the boat's cannons and coral-encrusted anchors are still visible.

Off the north coast, in the protected and mostly current-free Grand Case Bay, is **Creole Rock.** The water here ranges in depth from 10 feet to 25 feet. Other sites off the north coast include **Ilet Pinel,** with its good shallow diving; **Green Key,** with its vibrant barrier reef; and **Tintamarre,** with its

CLOSE UP

A Day in Saba

2

The Bottom, Saba.

Erupting out of the Caribbean, that 5-square-mi rock is called Saba (pronounced say-ba). The 14-minute flight from St. Martin has you landing on the world's smallest commercial runway— bordered on three sides by 100-foot cliffs. Arrive by boat and you will not see a beach. What little sand there is on this island comes and goes at the whim of the sea.

Hire a cab to navigate "The Road" and its 14 hairpin turns. The thoroughfare, under construction for 15 years, leads to the island towns of Windward-side, Hells Gate, and the Bottom (a funny name for a place that is about halfway up the mountain). Gingerbread-like cottages hang off the hillsides, making this island feel like a step back in time.

The Road may be a thrill ride, but most people visit Saba to do some hiking, diving, and relaxing. Its most famous trek is up the 1,064 steps to the summit of 2,855-foot Mt. Scenery. Goats occupy the snakelike Sulphur Mine Trail, which winds around to an abandoned mine with a colony of bats. Extraordinary underwater wonders attract divers. Saba National Marine Park, which circles the island, has a labyrinth formed by an old lava flow and various tunnels and caves filled with colorful fish.

The isle is renowned for its 151-proof rum, Saba Spice. The rum, along with lace and hand-blown glass are the most popular souvenirs.

Saba Tourist Office. For more information, contact the Saba Tourist Office. ☎ *599/416–2231, 599/416–2322* ⊕ *www. sabatourism.com.*

sheltered coves and geologic faults. On average, one-tank dives start at $55; two-tank dives are about $100. Certification courses start at about $400.

The Dutch side offers several full-service outfitters and SSI (Scuba Schools International) and/or PADI certification. There are no hyperbaric chambers on the island.

DUTCH SIDE

Dive Safaris. Dive Safaris has a shark-awareness dive on Friday where participants can watch professional feeders give reef sharks a little nosh. The company also offers a full PADI training program and can tailor dive excursions to any level. ⊠ *La Palapa Marina, Simpson Bay* ☎ 721/545–3213 ⊕ *www.divestmaarten.com.*

Ocean Explorers Dive Shop. Ocean Explorers Dive Shop is St. Maarten's oldest dive shop, and offers different types of certification courses. ⊠ *113 Welfare Rd., Simpson Bay* ☎ 721/544–5252 ⊕ *www.stmaartendiving.com.*

FRENCH SIDE

Neptune. Neptune is a PADI-certified outfit and very popular for its friendly owners Fabien and Sylvie, whose extensive experience thrills happy clients of reef, wreck, and cove dives. There is also an extensive program for beginners. ⊠ *Plage d'Orient Bay, Baie Orientale* ☎ 690/50–98–51 ⊕ *www.neptune-dive.com.*

Octopus. Octopus offers PADI diving certification courses and all-inclusive dive packages, using the latest equipment and a 30-foot power catamaran called *Octopussy.* The company also offers private and group snorkel trips starting at $40, including all necessary equipment. The dive shop also services regulators. ⊠ *15 bd. de Grand Case, Grand Case* ☎ 590/29–11–27 ⊕ *www.octopusdiving.com.*

SEA EXCURSIONS

DUTCH SIDE

♻ **Aqua Mania Adventures.** You can take day cruises to Prickly Pear Cay, off Anguilla, aboard the *Lambada,* or sunset and dinner cruises on the 65-foot sail catamaran *Tango* with Aqua Mania Adventures. The company also operates a floating playground called "Playstation 4 Kids" that kids love. ⊠ *Pelican Marina, Simpson Bay* ☎ 721/544–2640, 721/544–2631 ⊕ *www.stmaarten-activities.com.*

Ilet Pinel, St. Martin

Bluebeard II. This 60-foot custom-built day-sail catamaran is specially designed for maximum safety and comfort. *Bluebeard II* sails around Anguilla's south and northwest coasts to Prickly Pear Cay, where there are excellent coral reefs for snorkeling and powdery white sands for sunning. ⊠ *Simpson Bay* ☎ 721/587–5935 ⊕ *www.bluebeardcharters.com.*

Celine. For low-impact sunset and dinner cruises, try the catamaran *Celine.* ⊠ *Skip Jack's Restaurant, Simpson Bay* ☎ 721/526–1170, 721/552–1335 ⊕ *www.sailstmaarten.com.*

🕙 **Golden Eagle.** The sleek 76-foot catamaran *Golden Eagle* takes day-sailors to outlying islets and reefs for snorkeling and partying. ⊠ *Bobby's Marina, Philipsburg* ☎ 721/526–1170 ⊕ *www.sailingsxm.com.*

SNORKELING

Some of the best snorkeling on the Dutch side can be found around the rocks below Fort Amsterdam off Little Bay Beach, in the west end of Maho Bay, off Pelican Key, and around the reefs off Oyster Pond Beach. On the French side, the area around Orient Bay—including Caye Verte, Ilet Pinel, and Tintamarre—is especially lovely and is officially classified and protected as a regional underwater nature reserve. Sea creatures also congregate around Creole Rock at the point of Grand Case Bay. The average cost of an afternoon snorkeling trip is about $45 to $55 per person.

DUTCH SIDE

⟲ **Aqua Mania Adventures.** Aqua Mania Adventures offers a variety of snorkeling trips. The newest activity, called Rock 'n Roll Safaris, lets participants not only snorkel, but navigate their own motorized rafts. ⊠ *Pelican Marina, Simpson Bay* ☎ *721/544–2640, 721/544–2631* ⊕ *www.stmaarten-activities.com.*

Eagle Tours. Eagle Tours is geared more to cruise groups, but anyone can sign on for the four-hour power rafting or sailing trips that include snorkeling, a beach break, and lunch. The sailing trips are done aboard a 76-foot catamaran. Some cruises stop in Grand Case or Marigot for a bit of shopping. ⊠ *Bobby's Marina, Philipsburg* ☎ *721/542–3323* ⊕ *www.sailingsxm.com.*

FRENCH SIDE

Kontiki Watersports. Arrange equipment rentals and snorkeling trips through Kontiki Watersports. ⊠ *Northern beach entrance, Parc de la Baie Orientale, Baie Orientale* ☎ *590/87–46–89.*

SPAS

Spas have added a pampering dimension to several properties on both the French and Dutch sides of the island. Treatments and products vary depending on the establishment, but generally include several different massage modalities, body scrubs, facials, and mani-pedis; all the spas offer men's treatments, too. Be sure to phone to book in advance, however, as walk-ins are hardly ever accommodated. There are massage cabanas on some beaches, especially on the French side, and most of the beach clubs in Baie Orientale will have a blackboard where you can sign up or will give you the phone number for a massage therapist. Sometimes these beachside massages can be arranged on the spur of the moment. Hotels that don't have spas can usually arrange in-room treatments.

DUTCH SIDE

★ **Fodor's**Choice **Christian Dior Spa.** Christian Dior Spa, with its oceanfront setting, is undeniably dramatic, and the treatments are certainly creative. The Intense Youthfulness Treatment combines a 30-minute back massage with a facial cleansing therapy and shiatsu head massage. A two-hour Harmonizing Body Massage combines several techniques such as reflexology and shiatsu. Guests have all-day use of the pool, steam room, and sauna. A full line of Dior products is available for purchase. The spa is open weekdays 9 to 6 and Saturday 9 to 4. ✉ *The Cliff at Cupecoy Beach, Rhine Rd., Cupecoy* ☎ *721/546–6620* ⊕ *cliffsxm.com/spa.*

Good Life Spa. Good Life Spa offers aloe vera treatments (to combat sunburn) and a wide range of scrubs and wraps. There's also a fitness center. It's open weekdays from 8 to 8, Saturday from 8 to 6. ✉ *Sonesta Maho Beach Resort & Casino, 1 Rhine Rd., Maho* ☎ *721/545–2540, 721/545–2356* ⊕ *www.thegoodlifespa.com.*

Hibiscus Spa. Hibiscus Spa is an attractive facility offering the usual menu of facials, body treatment, and massages. The Hibiscus Expert Facial is formulated to benefit your skin type. It's open daily from 9 to 7. ✉ *Westin Dawn Beach Resort & Spa, 144 Oyster Pond Rd., Oyster Pond* ☎ *599/543–6700* ⊕ *www.starwoodcaribbean.com.*

FRENCH SIDE

★ **Fodor's**Choice **La Samanna Spa.** La Samanna Spa has one of the best spas on the island, and you don't have to be a guest at the famous hotel to enjoy a treatment or a day package at this heavenly retreat; just ring for an appointment and start to relax. In the lovely tropical garden setting, immaculate treatment rooms feature walled gardens with private outdoor showers. There are dozens of therapies for your body, face, hair, and spirit on the spa menu, and any can be customized to your desires or sensitivities. There are over a dozen different massage modalities offered, including Indian Ayurvedic, Thai, Japanese, and Chinese, and facials, scrubs, and soothing treatments for sunburn. The spa is open daily from 9 to 8. ✉ *La Samanna, Baie Longue* ☎ *590/87–65–69* ⊕ *www.lasamanna.orient-express.com.*

Le Spa. Le Spa, opened in 2009, offers a full menu of more than 40 services, including advanced skin-care therapies, integrative massages, exfoliation and body treatments, facials, and nail care performed by skilled Parisian-trained Carita therapists. Tropical ingredients are appropriate to the beach setting, so try the Lulur, Lotus, and Frangipani, a luxurious scrub that begins with a massage using rice, coconut powder, and flowers from Bali. ✉ *Radisson St. Martin Resort, Marina & Spa, Anse Marsel* ☎ *590/87–67–01* ⊕ *www.radissonblu.com.*

WATERSKIING

Expect to pay $50 per half hour for waterskiing, $40 to $45 per half hour for jet skiing.

FRENCH SIDE

Kontiki Watersports. On the French side, Kontiki Watersports offers rentals of windsurfing boards, Jet Skis, and WaveRunners, and also offers waterskiing, snorkling, banana boating, as well as instruction for all of these sports. ⊠ *Northern beach entrance, Park de la Baie Orientale, Baie Orientale* ☎ *590/87–46–89* ⊕ *kontiki-sxm.com.*

WINDSURFING

The best windsurfing is on Galion Bay on the French side. From November to May, trade winds can average 15 knots.

FRENCH SIDE

Wind Adventures. Wind Adventures offers rentals and lessons in both windsurfing and kitesurfing. One-hour lessons are about €40. The company offers a fun vacation package that works out to a terrific deal: two hours of activities each day for five days for €199. ⊠ *Northern beach entrance, Baie Orientale* ☎ *590/29–41–57* ⊕ *www.wind-adventures.com.*

Windy Reef. Windy Reef has offered windsurfing lessons and rentals since 1991. ⊠ *Galion Beach, past Butterfly Farm* ☎ *690/34–21–85* ⊕ *www.windyreef.com.*

St. Barthélemy

WORD OF MOUTH

"If you've been to France and like the culture then I'm sure you will enjoy St. Barth. It's France in the tropics."

—Sharona

By Elise
Meyer

ST. BARTHÉLEMY BLENDS THE RESPECTIVE ESSENCES of the Caribbean, France, and *Architectural Digest* in perfect proportions. A sophisticated but unstudied approach to relaxation and respite prevails: you can spend the day on a beach, try on the latest French fashions, and watch the sunset while nibbling tapas over Gustavia Harbor, then choose from nearly 100 excellent restaurants for an elegant or easy evening meal. You can putter around the island, scuba dive, windsurf on a quiet cove, or just admire the lovely views.

A mere 8 square miles (21 square km), St. Barth is a hilly island, with many sheltered inlets providing visitors with many opportunities to try out picturesque, quiet beaches. The town of Gustavia wraps itself around a modern harbor lined with everything from size-matters megayachts to rustic fishing boats to sailboats of all descriptions. Red-roofed villas dot the hillsides, and glass-front shops line the streets. Beach surf runs the gamut from kiddie-pool calm to serious-surfer dangerous, beaches from deserted to packed. The cuisine is tops in the Caribbean, and almost everything is tidy, stylish, and up-to-date. French *savoir vivre* prevails throughout the island.

Christopher Columbus discovered the island—called "Ouanalao" by its native Caribs—in 1493; he named it for his brother Bartolomé. The first group of French colonists arrived in 1648, drawn by the ideal location on the West Indian Trade Route, but they were wiped out by the Caribs, who dominated the area. Another small group from Normandy and Brittany arrived in 1694. This time the settlers prospered—with the help of French buccaneers, who took advantage of the island's strategic location and protected harbor. In 1784 the French traded the island to King Gustav III of Sweden in exchange for port rights in Göteborg. The king dubbed the capital Gustavia, laid out and paved streets, built three forts, and turned the community into a prosperous free port. The island thrived as a shipping and commercial center until the 19th century, when earthquakes, fires, and hurricanes brought financial ruin. Many residents fled for newer lands of opportunity, and Oscar II of Sweden decided to return the island to France. After briefly considering selling it to America, the French took possession of St. Barthélemy again on August 10, 1877.

Today the island is a free port, and in 2007 it became a Collectivity, a French-administered overseas territory outside of continental France. Arid, hilly, and rocky, St. Barth was

LOGISTICS

Getting to St. Barth: There are no direct flights to St. Barth (SBH). You must fly to another island and then catch a smaller plane for the hop over, or you can take a ferry. Most Americans fly first to St. Maarten, and then take the 10-minute flight to St. Barth, but you can connect through St. Thomas or San Juan as well.

Hassle Factor: Medium–high.

On the Ground: Many hotels offer free airport transfers; before you arrive, they will contact you for your arrival information. Otherwise, there's a taxi stand at the airport; unmetered taxis cost about €10 to €25 to reach most hotels. If you are renting a car, you may pick it up from the airport; if you have a reservation, rental agents will meet you at the ferry if you arrive by boat.

Getting Around the Island: Most people coming to St. Barth rent a car. Taxis are expensive, but some visitors are happy to let an experienced driver negotiate the roads at night. Any restaurant will be happy to call a cab back to your hotel after dinner. Otherwise, there is no other transportation option on the island. It's also possible to rent a motorbike, but steep roads can make driving a stressful experience if you aren't experienced.

3

unsuited to sugar production and thus never developed an extensive slave base. Some of today's 3,000 current residents are descendants of the tough Norman and Breton settlers of three centuries ago, but you are more likely to encounter attractive French twenty- and thirtysomethings from Normandy and Provence who are friendly, English speaking, and here for the sunny lifestyle.

PLANNING

WHEN TO GO

High season in St. Barth is typical for the Caribbean, from mid-December through mid-April (or until after Easter). During busy holiday periods prices can shoot up to the highest levels, but in the summer (particularly June and July), there are some remarkable bargains on the island, though some restaurants still close over the summer months, and hotels tend to do their annual maintenance during this time as well.

Gustavia's waterfront promenade

ACCOMMODATIONS

Most hotels on St. Barth are small (the largest has fewer than 70 rooms) and stratospherically expensive, but there are some reasonable options. About half of the accommodations on St. Barth are in private villas. Prices drop dramatically after March, and summer is a great time for a visit. Check hotel websites for updates of discounts and special offers that seem to be becoming more common with the current economy.

HOTEL AND RESTAURANT PRICES

Prices in the restaurant reviews are the average cost of a main course at dinner or, if dinner is not served, at lunch; taxes and service charges are generally included. Prices in the hotel reviews are the lowest cost of a standard double room in high season, excluding taxes, service charges, and meal plans (except at all-inclusives). Prices for rentals are the lowest per-night cost for a one-bedroom unit in high season.

EXPLORING ST. BARTHÉLEMY

With a little practice, negotiating St. Barth's narrow, steep roads soon becomes fun. Recent infrastructure upgrades and the prevalence of small, responsive cars have improved things a lot. Free maps are everywhere, roads are smooth and well marked, and signs will point the way. The tourist office has annotated maps with walking tours that highlight sights of interest. Parking in Gustavia is still a challenge, especially during busy vacation times.

☪ **Corossol.** Traces of the island's French provincial origins are evident in this two-street fishing village with a little rocky beach.

Inter Oceans Museum/Museum of Shells. Ingenu Magras's Inter Oceans Museum has more than 9,000 seashells and an intriguing collection of sand samples from around the world. You can buy souvenir shells. ✉ *Corossol* ☎ *0590/27–62–97* 💷 *€3* ⊗ *Tues.–Sun. 9–12:30 and 2–5.*

Gustavia. You can easily explore all of Gustavia during a two-hour stroll. Most shops close from noon to 3 or 4, so plan lunch accordingly, but stores stay open past 7 in the evening.

Tourist Office. A good spot to park your car is rue de la République, alongside the catamarans, yachts, and sailboats. The tourist office on the pier can provide maps and a wealth of information. During busier holiday periods the office may be open all day. ✉ *Rue de la République, Gustavia* ☎ *0590/27–87–27* ⊕ *www.saintbarth-tourisme.com* ⊗ *Mon. 8:30–12:30, Tues.–Fri. 8–noon and 2–5, Sat. 9–noon*

Le musée territorial de Saint Barthélemy. On the far side of the harbor known as La Pointe is the charming Municipal Museum, where you can find watercolors, portraits, photographs, and historic documents detailing the island's history, as well as displays of the island's flowers, plants, and marine life. ✉ *La Pointe, Gustavia* ☎ *590/29–71–55* 💷 *€2* ⊗ *Mon., Tues., Thurs., and Fri. 8:30–12:30 and 2:30–6, Sat. 9–12:30. Closed July 26–August 31.*

Lorient. Site of the first French settlement, Lorient is one of the island's two parishes; a restored church, a school, and a post office mark the spot. Note the gaily decorated graves in the cemetery.

Le Manoir. One of St. Barth's secrets is Le Manoir, a 1610 Norman manor, now a guesthouse, which was painstakingly shipped from France and reconstructed in Lorient in 1984. Look for the entrance by the Ligne de St. Barth building. ✉ *Lorient* ☎ *0590/27–79–27.*

St-Jean. There is a monument at the crest of the hill that divides St-Jean from Gustavia. Called *The Arawak,* it symbolizes the soul of St. Barth. A warrior, one of the earliest

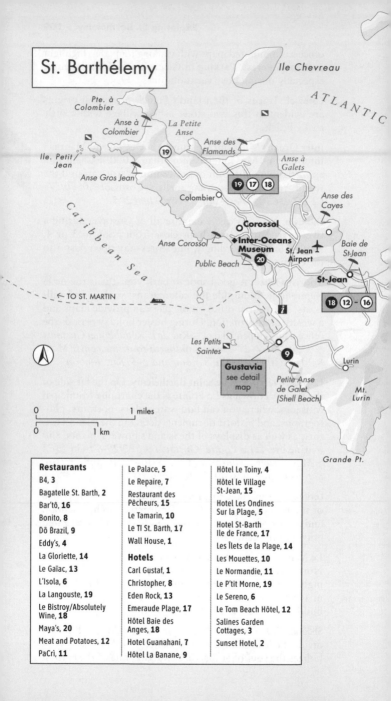

St. Barthélemy

Ile Chevreau

ATLANTIC

Pte. à Colombier

La Petite Anse

Anse à Colombier

Anse des Flamands

Anse à Galets

Ile. Petit Jean

Anse Gros Jean

19

Colombier

19 **17** **18**

Anse des Cayes

Caribbean Sea

Anse Corossol

Corossol

◆**Inter-Oceans Museum**

Public Beach

20

St. Jean Airport

Anse des Cayes

Baie de St-Jean

St-Jean

18 **12** – **16**

← TO ST. MARTIN

ℹ

Les Petits Saintes

Gustavia see detail map

9

Petite Anse de Galet (Shell Beach)

Lurin

Mt. Lurin

Grande Pt.

0 ————— 1 miles
0 ————— 1 km

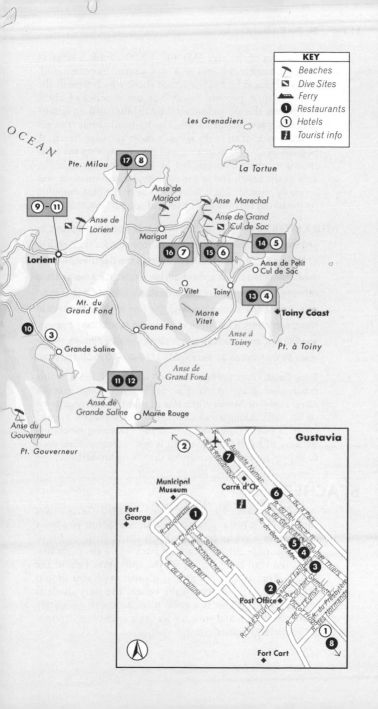

inhabitants of the area (AD 800–1,800), holds a lance in his right hand and stands on a rock shaped like the island; in his left hand he holds a conch shell, which sounds the cry of nature; perched beside him are a pelican (which symbolizes the air and survival by fishing) and an iguana (which represents the earth). The half-mile-long crescent of sand at St-Jean is the island's most popular beach. A popular activity is watching and photographing the hair-raising airplane landings, but be sure to not stand in the area at the beach end of the runway, where someone was seriously injured. You'll also find some of the best shopping on the island here, as well as several restaurants. ⊠ *St-Jean*.

NEED A BREAK? If you find yourself in St-Jean and need a picnic or just want some food to take home to your villa for later, stop in at **Maya's To Go**, which can be found in the Galeries de Commerce shopping center across from the airport. It's a more casual offering from the owners of the Gustavia favorite and is open daily from 7 to 7 (except Monday), has free Wi-Fi on the deck in front, and offers a full menu of prepared foods, baked goods, sandwiches, and salads for beach picnics or villa dinners. ⊠ *Galeries de Commerce, St-Jean* ☎ *0590/29–83–70* ⊗ *Closed Mon.*

Toiny Coast. Over the hills beyond Grand Cul de Sac is this much-photographed coastline. Stone fences crisscross the steep slopes of Morne Vitet, one of many small mountains on St. Barth, along a rocky shore that resembles the rugged coast of Normandy. Nicknamed the "washing machine" because of its turbulent surf, it is not recommended even to expert swimmers because of the strong undertow.

BEACHES

Anse à Colombier. The beach here is the least accessible, thus the most private, on the island; to reach it you must take either a rocky footpath from Petite Anse or brave the 30-minute climb down (and back up) a steep, cactus-bordered trail from the top of the mountain behind the beach. Appropriate footgear is a must, and you should know that once you get to the beach, the only shade is a rock cave. But this is a good place to snorkel. Boaters favor this beach and cove for its calm anchorage. ⊠ *Anse à Colombier, Colombier*.

DID YOU KNOW?

Every one of St. Barth's twenty-some white-sand beaches is open to the public, whether or not it's the home of a tony resort.

Anse de Grand Cul de Sac. The shallow, reef-protected beach is nice for small children, fly-fishermen, kayakers, and wind-surfers—and for the amusing pelicanlike frigate birds that dive-bomb the water fishing for their lunch. There is a good dive shop. You needn't do your own fishing; you can have a wonderful lunch at one of the excellent restaurants, and use their lounge chairs for the afternoon. ⊠ *Grand Cul de Sac.*

★ Fodor'sChoice **Anse de Grande Saline.** Anse de Grande Saline.
☾ Secluded, with its sandy ocean bottom, this is just about everyone's favorite beach and is great for swimmers, too. Without any major development (although there is some talk of developing a resort here), it's an ideal Caribbean strand. However, there can be a bit of wind here, so you can enjoy yourself more if you go on a calm day. In spite of the prohibition, young and old alike go nude. The beach is a 10-minute walk up a rocky dune trail, so be sure to wear sneakers or water shoes, and bring a blanket, umbrella, and beach towels. Although there are several good restaurants for lunch near the parking area, once you get here the beach is just sand, sea, and sky. The big salt ponds here are no longer in use, and the place looks a little desolate when you approach, but don't despair. ⊠ *Grande Saline.*

Anse de Lorient. This beach is popular with St. Barth families and surfers, who like its rolling waves and central location. Be aware of the level of the tide, which can come in very quickly. Hikers and avid surfers like the walk over the hill to Point Milou in the late afternoon sun when the waves roll in. ⊠ *Lorient.*

Anse des Flamands. This is the most beautiful of the hotel beaches—a roomy strip of silken sand. Come here for lunch and then spend the afternoon sunning, taking a long beach walk, and swimming in the turquoise water. From the beach, you can take a brisk hike along a paved side-walk to the top of the now-extinct volcano believed to have given birth to St. Barth. ⊠ *Anse des Flamands, Flamands.*

★ **Anse du Gouverneur.** Because it's so secluded, this beach is
☾ a popular place for nude sunbathing. It is truly beautiful, with blissful swimming and views of St. Kitts, Saba, and St. Eustatius. Venture here at the end of the day and watch the sun set behind the hills. The road here from Gustavia also offers spectacular vistas. Legend has it that pirates' treasure is buried in the vicinity. There are no restaurants or other services here, so plan accordingly. ⊠ *Anse du Gouverneur, Gouverneur.*

☻ **Baie de St-Jean.** Like a mini–Côte d'Azur—beachside bistros, terrific shopping, bungalow hotels, bronzed bodies, windsurfing, and day-trippers who tend to arrive on BIG yachts—the reef-protected strip is divided by Eden Rock promontory. Except when the hotels are filled to capacity you can rent chaises and umbrellas at La Plage restaurant or at Eden Rock, where you can lounge for hours over lunch. ⊠ *Baie de St-Jean, St-Jean.*

3

WHERE TO EAT

Dining on St. Barth compares favorably to almost anywhere in the world. Varied and exquisite cuisine, a French flair in the decor, sensational wine, and attentive service make for a wonderful epicurean experience in almost any of the more than 80 restaurants. On most menus, freshly caught local seafood mingles on the plate with top-quality provisions that arrive regularly from Paris. Interesting selections on the Cartes de Vins are no surprise, but don't miss the sophisticated cocktails whipped up by island bartenders. They are worlds away from cliché Caribbean rum punches with paper umbrellas.

Most restaurants offer a chalkboard full of daily specials that are usually a good bet. But even the pickiest eaters will find something on every menu. Some level of compliance can be paid to dietary restrictions within reason, and especially if explained in French; just be aware that French people generally let the chef work his or her magic. Expect your meal to be costly; however, you can dine superbly and somewhat economically if you limit pricey cocktails, watch wine selections, share appetizers or desserts, and pick up snacks and picnic meals from one of the well-stocked markets. Or you could follow the locals to small *crêperies,* cafés, sandwich shops, and pizzerias in the main shopping areas. Lunch is usually less costly than dinner. *Ti Creux* means "snack" or "small bite."

Lavish publications feature restaurant menus and contacts. Ask at your hotel or look on the racks at the airport for current issues. Reservations are strongly recommended and, in high season, essential. Lots of restaurants now accept reservations by email. Check websites and social media. Except during the Christmas–New Year's season it's not usually necessary to book far in advance. A day's—or even a few hours'—notice is usually sufficient. At the end of the meal, as in France, you must request the bill. Until you do, you can feel free to linger at the table and enjoy the complimentary vanilla rum that's likely to appear.

Check restaurant bills carefully. A *service compris* (service charge) is always added by law, but you should leave the server 5% to 10% extra in cash. You'll usually come out ahead if you charge restaurant meals on a credit card in euros instead of paying with American currency, as your credit card might offer a better exchange rate than the restaurant (though since most credit cards nowadays have conversion surcharges of 3% or more, the benefit of using plastic is rapidly disappearing). Many restaurants serve locally caught *langouste* (lobster); priced by weight, it's usually the most expensive item on a menu and, depending on its size and the restaurant, will range in price from $40 to $60. *In menu prices below, it has been left out of the range.*

What to Wear: A bathing suit and *gauzy top or shift* is acceptable at beachside lunch spots, but not really in Gustavia. Jackets are never required and are rarely worn by men, but most people do dress fashionably for dinner. Casual chic is the idea; women wear whatever is hip, current, and sexy. You can't go wrong in a tank dress or anything clingy and ruffly with white jeans and high sandals. The sky is the limit for high fashion at nightclubs and lounges in high season, when you might (correctly) think everyone in sight is a model. Nice shorts (not beachy ones) at the dinner table may label a man *américain,* but many locals have adopted the habit, and nobody cares much. Wear them with a pastel shirt to really fit in (never tucked in). Pack a light sweater or shawl for the occasional breezy night.

BACK UP FERRY. Even if you are planning to fly to St. Barth, it's a good idea to keep the numbers and schedules for the three ferry companies handy in case your flight is delayed. An evening ferry could save you having to scramble for a hotel room in St. Maarten. If you are planning to spend time in St. Maarten before traveling on to St. Barth, the ferry is half the cost and somewhat more reliable than the puddle-jumper, and you can leave from Marigot, Oyster Pond, or Philipsburg. Check at the brand-new St. Barth Tourist Information counter at Princess Juliana Airport for specifics if things didn't go according to your plan.

Le Gaïac restaurant by candlight

ANSE DE TOINY

★ **Fodor's Choice** 🍴 **Le Gaïac.** *Modern French.* Chef Stéphane Mazières is the only person in the Caribbean to share the Grand Chef designation of the Relais & Châteaux organization with the likes of Daniel Boulud and Thomas Keller. The new management of Hôtel Le Toiny (which includes Francophile Lance Armstrong) has fine-tuned the dramatic, tasteful, cliff-side dining porch to showcase his gastronomic art, and this is one dinner that you won't want to miss. Less stuffy than you might remember from seasons past, the food is notable for its innovation and extraordinary presentation, and the warm but consummately professional service sets a glorious standard. Rare ingredients and unique preparations delight: gossamer sheets of beet encase tuna tartare "cannelloni"; tender roasted Iberian pork is served in a potato crust and a piquant sauce; venison medallions come with tender chestnut blinis. A greenhouse has even been installed on this former pineapple field to grow organic produce for the restaurant, and you can think of it while you savor saffron candied pineapple. The menu changes frequently, evolving and refining ideas. On Tuesday's special Fish Market Night, you choose your own fish to be grilled; there's a €43 buffet brunch on Sunday. This is one restaurant that is a true hedonistic experience, but you're on vacation, after all. [$] *Average main: €36* ✉ *Hôtel Le Toiny, Anse à Toiny* ☎ *0590/29–77–47* 🌐 *www.letoiny.com* ✍ *Reservations essential* ⊗ *Closed Sept.–mid-Oct.*

$$$$

FLAMANDS

$$$ 🍴 **La Langouste.** *Seafood.* This tiny beachside restaurant in the pool courtyard of Hôtel Baie des Anges is run by Anny, the hotel's amiable, ever-present proprietor. It lives up to its name by serving fantastic, fresh-grilled lobster at a price that is somewhat gentler than at most other island venues. Simple, well-prepared fish, pastas, and an assortment of refreshing cold soups, including a corn-and-coconut soup perfumed with lemongrass, are also available. Be sure to try the warm goat cheese in pastry served on a green salad with a fruity salsa. [$] *Average main: €25* ✉ *Hôtel Baie des Anges, Anse des Flamands* ☎ *0590/27–63–61* 🌐 *www.hotelbaiedesanges.fr* ✍ *Reservations essential* ⏲ *Closed May–Oct.*

GRAND CUL DE SAC

$$$$ 🍴 **Bar'tô.** *Italian.* The pretty restaurant in the gardens of the Guanahani hotel showcases the refined cuisine of chef Philippe Masseglia presented beautifully from a menu that ranges from seared sea scallops in a light curry sauce to baby veal with purple artichokes. There is a €75 tasting menu if the whole table is adventurous. Don't miss the amazing soft coconut cake served with a luscious sauce of spiced passion fruit. [$] *Average main: €35* ✉ *Hotel Guanahani, Grand Cul de Sac* ☎ *590/27–66–60* ⏲ *Closed Mon. and Tues.*

$$$ 🍴 **La Gloriette.** *Caribbean.* For a beachside lunch with your toes in the sand, La Gloriette is a dream. Picnic tables under the cocoloba trees are shady, and everyone is having a great time. Longtime visitors will remember the original creole restaurant here, and will be happy to know that the *accras* (salt-cod fritters with spicy sauce) are as good as ever. There are huge, fresh salads and many daily specials on the blackboard. Super-fresh grilled fish is a great choice, and the sushi-style tatakis are light and delicious. At dinner there are good pizzas for dining in or taking back to your villa. Don't miss the artisanal, island-flavored rums offered after your meal, and available at the tiny shop. [$] *Average main: €23* ✉ *Plage de Grand Cul de Sac, Grand Cul de Sac* ☎ *690/29–85–71* ⏲ *Closed Wed.*

$$$$ ★ 🍴 **Restaurant des Pêcheurs.** *Seafood.* From fresh, morning beachside brioche to a final evening drink in the sexy lounge, you can dine all day in this soaring thatch pavilion that is the epitome of chic. The restaurant at Le Sereno, like the Christian Liaigre–designed resort, is serenity itself. Each menu item is a miniature work of art, beautifully arranged and amiably served. Each day there is a different

€44 three-course menu. "Authentic" two-course bouil-labaisse *à l'ancienne,* the famous French seafood stew, is served every Friday, and the chef even gives a class in its preparation, but the menu also lists daily oceanic arrivals from Marseille and Quiberon on France's Atlantic coast: roasted, salt-crusted, or grilled to your personal perfection. Fans of Provence will love the aioli special on Wednesday, and Sunday is paella night. This—and sand between your toes—is heaven. $ *Average main: €32* ⊠ *Le Sereno, Grand Cul de Sac* ☎ *0590/29–83–00* ⊕ *www.lesereno.com* ⚓ *Reservations essential.*

GRANDE SALINE

$$$ ✕ **Le Tamarin.** *French.* A leisurely lunch here en route to
★ Grande Saline beach is a St. Barth *must.* But new management makes it tops for dinner too. Sit on one of the licorice-colored Javanese couches in the lounge area and nibble excellent sushi, or settle at a table under the wondrous tamarind tree for which the restaurant is named. A unique cocktail each day, ultrafresh fish provided by the restaurant's designated fisherman, and gentle prices accommodate local residents as well as the holiday crowd. The restaurant is open year-round. $ *Average main: €21* ⊠ *Grande Saline* ☎ *0590/27–72–12* ⊘ *Closed Tue.*

$$$ ✕ **Meat and Potatoes.** *Steakhouse.* If you think that St. Barth is sometimes too "girly," you will love this new restaurant at the end of the road to Saline Beach. The white interior is lined with banquettes heaped with red, black, and gray pillows; there are almost a dozen different cuts of steak, from tenderloins to T-bones, at least a dozen starchy sides, and some vegetables for good measure. There is also fresh fish for the red-meat averse. Don't miss the Provençal *pommes ratte,* wedges of potatoes cooked in duck fat, fresh rosemary, and sea salt. The wine list is full of complementary bottles, heavy on Bordeaux's best. $ *Average main: €30* ⊠ *Grande Saline* ☎ *590/51–15–98.*

$$$$ ✕ **PuCri.** *Italian.* Recently moved to the Manapany Hotel,
★ an adorable young husband-and-wife team (she is the chef) serve delicious, huge portions of house-made pasta, wood-oven pizza (at lunch only), and authentic Italian main courses, including chicken Milanese, and fresh local fish carpaccios on a breezy open terrace in Anse de Cayes, a popular surfing beach. The menu—handwritten on a chalkboard—changes daily. Don't miss the softball-size hunk of the best artisanal mozzarella you've ever had, flown in from

Puglia, Italy, and garnished with prosciutto or tomato and basil. The eggplant Parmesan appetizer is delicious and more than enough for a meal. Like the pastas, the bread and the desserts are made in-house, and the authentic tiramisu is only one of the winners. [$] *Average main: €33* ✉ *Anse de Cayes* ☎ *0590/27–66–55* 🌐 *www.pacristbarth.com* ✍ *Reservations essential.*

GUSTAVIA

$$ ✕ **B4.** *French.* Pronounced *before,* this lounge-restaurant occupies the central former location of longtime St. Barth mainstay Le Sapotillier. In addition to enjoying lighter French cuisine, wok stir-frys, generous salads, pizzas, and traditional raclette, you can hang out in the lounge with music, bar, and flat-screen TVs. The restaurant is great to fill up the pocket time after dinner and *before* you head to your other late-night activities. [$] *Average main: €19* ✉ *13 rue Samuel Fahlberg, Gustavia* ☎ *590/52–45–31* 🕓 *Closed Tue.*

$$$$ ✕ **Bagatelle St. Barth.** *Bistro.* New in 2012, the sophisticated St. Tropez–inspired interior, right on the harbor, is a pretty place to watch big boats and enjoy a menu of classic French bistro favorites such as truffled roast chicken, pastis-flamed shrimp, and steak tartare. There are platters of charcuterie and fromage for sharing, and a great wine list. Fans of the popular sister establishments in New York's Meatpacking District and Los Angeles will recognize the friendly service and lively atmosphere, and the great music provided by resident DJs. [$] *Average main: €32* ✉ *Rue Samuel Fahlberg, Gustavia* ☎ *590/27–51–51.*

★ **Fodor's Choice** ✕ **Bonito.** *Latin American.* The former Mandala
$$$$ space has been completely transformed into a chic beach house, with big, white, canvas couches in the center, tables around the sides, an open kitchen, and three bar areas. The young Venezuelan owners go to great lengths to see that guests are having as much fun as they are. The specialty is ceviche with eight different varieties, in combos that are prettily arrayed on poured-glass platters for culinary experimentation. Try octopus and shrimp, or wahoo garnished with sweet potatoes and popcorn. Traditionalists might like the fricassee of escargots, or foie gras served with mango, soy, and preserved lemon. Carnivores will love the rack of lamb. [$] *Average main: €32* ✉ *Rue de la Sous-Préfecture, Gustavia* ☎ *590/27–96–96* 🌐 *www.ilovebonito.com* ✍ *Reservations essential* 🕓 *Closed Mon. No lunch.*

$$$$ ✕ **Dõ Brazil.** *Eclectic.* This restaurant is open every day for lunch and dinner and offers live music for sundown cocktail hour on Thursday, Friday, and Saturday evenings, as well as top DJs spinning the latest club mixes for evening events, which are listed in the local papers. Right on Gustavia's Shell Beach, you'll find tasty light fare like chilled soups, fruit-garnished salads with tuna, shrimp, and chicken, plus sandwiches, burgers, pastas, and grilled fresh fish for lunch. Everyone loves the Dõ Brazil hot pot: mahimahi, shrimps and sea scallops in a sauce of lemongrass and coconut milk. At dinner there is also a €35 three-course prix fixe and some reasonable soups and salads, which can help keep the bill in line. The extensive cocktail menu tempts, but at €12 each, your bar bill can quickly exceed the price of dinner. There is a €20 children's menu. [$] *Average main: €33* ✉ *Shell Beach, Gustavia* ☎ *0590/29–06–66* 🌐 *www.dobrazil.com.*

$$$ ✕ **Eddy's.** *Asian.* By local standards, dinner in the pretty, open-air, tropical garden here is reasonably priced. The cooking is French-creole-Asian. Fish specialties, especially the sushi tuna sampler, are fresh and delicious, and there are always plenty of notable daily specials. Just remember some mosquito repellent for your ankles. [$] *Average main: €24* ✉ *Rue du Centenaire, Gustavia* ☎ *0590/27–54–17* ✍ *Reservations not accepted* ⏲ *Closed Sun. No lunch.*

$$$ ✕ **Le Palace.** *Caribbean.* Tucked into a tropical garden, this
★ popular in-town restaurant known for its barbecued ribs, beef fillet, and rack of lamb is consistently one of our absolute favorites. Fish-market specialties like red snapper cooked in a banana leaf or grilled tuna are good here, as are grilled duck with mushroom sauce and a skewered surf-and-turf with a green curry sauce. The blackboard lists daily specials that are usually a great choice, like a salad of tomato, mango, and basil. [$] *Average main: €23* ✉ *Rue Général-de-Gaulle, Gustavia* ☎ *0590/27–53–20* ✍ *Reservations essential* ⏲ *Closed Sun. and mid-June–July.*

$$ ✕ **Le Repaire.** *Eclectic.* This friendly brasserie overlooks
👶 Gustavia's harbor, and is a popular spot from its opening
★ at noon to its late-night closing. The flexible hours are great if you arrive midafternoon and need a substantial snack before dinner. Grab a cappuccino, pull a captain's chair up to the street-side rail, and watch the pretty girls. The menu ranges from cheeseburgers, which are served only at lunch along with the island's best fries, to simply grilled fish and meat, pastas, and risottos. The composed salads always please. Wonderful ice-cream sundaes round out the menu.

ⓈAverage main: €19 ⊠Quai de la République, Gustavia ☎0590/27–72–48 ⊙ Closed Sun. in June.

★ **Fodor's**Choice ✕ **L'Isola.** *Italian.* St. Barth's chic sister to the
$$$ Santa Monica (California) favorite, Via Veneto, is packing in happy guests for Italian classic dishes, dozens of house-made pasta dishes, prime meats, and the huge, well-chosen wine list. Restaurateur Fabrizio Bianconi wants it all to feel like a big Italian party, and with all the celebrating you can hear at dinner in this pretty and romantic room it sure sounds like he succeeded. Favorite dishes include a hearty veal chop in a sage-butter sauce, and supernal risot-tos, with wild mushrooms or wild boar, depending on how wild you like it. ⓈAverage main: €27 ⊠Rue du roi Oscar II, Gustavia ☎590/51–00–05 ⊕www.lisolastbarth.com ⚄Reservations essential ⊙ Closed Sep. and Oct.

$$$$ ✕ **Maya's.** *French.* New Englander Randy Gurley and his wife Maya (the French-born chef) provide a warm welcome and a very pleasant dinner on their cheerful dock deco-rated with big, round tables and crayon-colored canvas chairs, all overlooking Gustavia Harbor. A market-inspired menu of good, simply prepared and garnished dishes like stir-fry scallops and shrimp, and pepper-marinated beef fillet changes daily, assuring the ongoing popularity of a restaurant that seems to be on everyone's list of favorites. ⓈAverage main: €39 ⊠Public, Gustavia ☎0590/27–75–73 ⊕www.mayas-stbarth.com ⚄Reservations essential.

★ **Fodor's**Choice ✕ **Wall House.** *Eclectic.* The food is excellent—
$$$$ and the service is always friendly—at this restaurant on the far side of Gustavia Harbor. The light-as-air gnocci with pesto are legendary, and the rotisserie duck marinated in honey from the rotisserie is a universal favorite. Local businesspeople crowd the restaurant for the bargain €11 prix-fixe lunch menu, with classic dishes like duck-leg con-fit. For €18 the menu includes the main dish or salad of the day, coffee and petits fours, and a glass of wine or beer. An old-fashioned dessert trolley showcases some really yummy sweets—the sugar topping for your crème brûlée is blazed with a mini-torch tableside. ⓈAverage main: €33 ⊠La Pointe, Gustavia ☎0590/27–71–83 ⊕www.wallhouseres-taurant.com ⚄Reservations essential ⊙ No lunch Sun.

POINTE MILOU

★ **Fodor's**Choice ✕ **Le Ti St. Barth Caribbean Tavern.** *Eclectic.* Chef-
$$$$ owner Carole Gruson captures the funky, sexy spirit of the island in her wildly popular hilltop hot spot. We always come here to dance to great music with the attractive crowd

lingering at the bar, lounge at one of the pillow-strewn banquettes, or chat on the torch-lighted terrace. By the time your appetizers arrive, you'll be best friends with the next table. Top-quality fish and meats are cooked on the traditional charcoal barbecue; big spenders will love the Angus beef filet Rossini with truffles, but there are lighter options like wok shrimp with Chinese noodles, and seared tuna with caviar. Provocatively named desserts, such as Nymph Thighs (airy lemon cake with vanilla custard), Daddy's Balls (passion-fruit sorbet and ice cream), and Sweet Thai Massage (kiwi, pineapple, mango, and lychee salad) end the meal on a fun note. Around this time someone is sure to be dancing on top of the tables. There's an extensive wine list. The famously raucous full-moon parties, cabarets, and Monday "Plastic Boots" Ladies' Night are all legendary. ⓢ *Average main: €47* ✉ *Pointe Milou* ☎ *0590/27–97–71* ⊕ *www.letistbarth.com* ⚓ *Reservations essential.*

ST-JEAN

★ **Fodor's**Choice ✕ **Le Bistroy/Absolutely Wine.** *Wine Bar.* A bit of
$$$ Bordeaux came to St. Barth in 2012. Sit at a shaded communal table at this lively, modern gastro-pub/wine bar/wine school in St-Jean's Villa Creole shopping enclave any time of the day. Come for first-rate sharing platters of charcuterie, pâté, artisanal cheeses, choose-your-ingredient salads, and fabulous wines. An affable young female sommelier gives daily wine courses and hosts tastings in the wine cellar . . . delightful! The on-site market sells delicacies to take back to your villa or hotel. ⓢ *Average main: €19* ✉ *La Villa Créole, St-Jean* ☎ *590/52–20–96* ⊕ *www.absolutely-wine.com.*

WHERE TO STAY

There's no denying that hotel rooms and villas on St. Barth carry high prices. You're paying primarily for the privilege of staying on the island, and even at $800 a night the bedrooms tend to be small. Still, if you're flexible—in terms of timing and in your choice of lodgings—you can enjoy a holiday in St. Barth and still afford to send the kids to college.

The most expensive season falls during the holidays (mid-December to early January), when hotels are booked far in advance, may require a 10- or 14-day stay, and can be double the high-season rates. At this writing, some properties are reconsidering minimum stays, and there are concessions to the current *crise* (economic downturn).

Getting a massage on a private deck at Le Sereno

A 5% government tourism tax on room prices (excluding breakfast) is in effect; be sure to ask if it is included in your room rate or added on.

When it comes to booking a hotel on St. Barth, the reservation manager can be your best ally. Rooms within a property can vary greatly. It's well worth the price of a phone call or the time investment of an email correspondence to make a personal connection, which can mean a lot when it comes to arranging a room that meets your needs or preferences. Details of accessibility, views, recent redecorating, meal options, and special package rates are topics open for discussion. Most quoted hotel rates are per room, not per person, and include service charges and airport transfers. Bargain rates found on Internet booking sites can sometimes yield unpleasant surprises in terms of the actual room you get. Consider contacting the hotel about a reservation and mentioning the rate you found. Often they will match it, with a better room.

For expanded reviews, facilities, and current deals, visit Fodors.com.

VILLAS AND CONDOMINIUMS
On St. Barth the term *villa* is used to describe anything from a small cottage to a luxurious, modern estate. Today almost half of St. Barth's accommodations are in villas, and we recommend considering this option, especially if you're

CLOSE UP

St. Barth's Spas

Visitors to St. Barth can enjoy more than the comforts of home by taking advantage of any of the myriad spa and beauty treatments that are available on the island. The major hotels, the Isle de France, the Guanahani, and the Carl Gustav, have beautiful, comprehensive, on-site spas. Others, including the Hôtel le Village St-Jean, Le Sereno, and Le Toiny, have added spa cottages, where treatments and services can be arranged on-site. Depending on availability, all visitors to the island can book services at all of these. In addition, scores of independent therapists will come to your hotel room or villa and provide any therapeutic discipline you can think of, including yoga, Thai massage, shiatsu, reflexology, and even manicures, pedicures, and hairdressing. You can get up-to-date recommendations at the tourist office in Gustavia.

3

traveling with friends or family. Ever more advantageous to Americans, villa rates are usually quoted in dollars, thus bypassing unfavorable euro fluctuations. Most villas have a small private swimming pool and maid service daily except Sunday. They are well furnished with linens, kitchen utensils, and such electronic playthings as CD and DVD players, satellite TV, and broadband Internet. Weekly in-season rates range from $1,400 to "oh-my-gosh." Most villa-rental companies are based in the United States and have extensive websites that allow you to see pictures or panoramic videos of the place you're renting; their local offices oversee maintenance and housekeeping and provide concierge services to clients. Just be aware that there are few beachfront villas, so if you have your heart set on "toes in the sand" and a cute waiter delivering your Kir Royale, stick with the hotels or villas operated by hotel properties.

VILLA RENTAL CONTACTS

Marla. Marla is a local St. Barth villa-rental company that represents more than 100 villas, many of which are not listed with other companies. ☎ 0590/27–62–02 ⊕ www.marlavillas.com.

St. Barth Properties, Inc. St. Barth Properties, Inc., owned by American Peg Walsh—a regular on St. Barth since 1986—represents more than 120 properties here and can guide you to the perfect place to stay. Weekly peak-season rates range from $1,400 to $40,000, depending on the property's size, location, and amenities. The excellent website offers virtual tours of most of the villas and even details of availability. An office in Gustavia can take care of any problems you may have and offers some concierge-type services. ☎ *508/528–7727, 800/421–3396* 🌐 *www.stbarth.com.*

Wimco. Wimco, which is based in Rhode Island, oversees bookings for more than 230 properties on St. Barth. Rents range from $2,000 to $10,000 for two- and three-bedroom villas; larger villas rent for $7,000 per week and up. Properties can be previewed and reserved on Wimco's website (which occasionally lists last-minute specials), or you can obtain a catalog by mail. The company will arrange for babysitters, massages, chefs, and other in-villa services for clients, as well as private air charters. ☎ *800/932–3222* 🌐 *www.wimco.com.*

ANSE DE TOINY

★ $$$$ **Fodor's Choice** 🏨 **Hôtel Le Toiny.** *Hotel.* Privacy and serenity are the mission here, but so is sustainability, with features such as a water-treatment plant, organic cleaning products, and moves toward using solar energy. **Pros:** extremely private; luxurious rooms; flawless service; environmental awareness. **Cons:** not on the beach; isolated (at least half an hour's drive from town). $ *Rooms from: €1,280* ✉ *Anse de Toiny* ☎ *0590/27–88–88* 🌐 *www.letoiny.com* 🛏 *14 1-bedroom villas, 1 3-bedroom villa* ⏲ *Closed Sept.–late Oct.* 🍴 *Breakfast.*

COLOMBIER

$$ 🏨 **Le P'tit Morne.** *B&B/Inn.* Each of the modestly furnished but freshly decorated and painted mountainside studios has a private balcony with panoramic views of the coastline. **Pros:** reasonable rates; great area for hiking. **Cons:** rooms are basic; remote location. $ *Rooms from: €195* ✉ *Colombier* ☎ *0590/52–95–50* 🌐 *www.timorne.com/fr* 🛏 *14 rooms* 🍴 *Breakfast.*

FLAMANDS

$$$ 👶 ★ 🏨 **Hôtel Baie des Anges.** *Hotel.* Everyone is treated like family at this casual retreat with 10 clean, spacious rooms. **Pros:** on St. Barth's longest beach; family-friendly; excellent value. **Cons:** the area is a bit remote from the town areas, necessitating a car. $ *Rooms from: €385* ✉ *Anse des Flamands* ☎ *0590/27–63–61* 🌐 *www.hotelbaiedesanges.fr* 🛏 *10 rooms* ⏲ *Closed Sept.* 🍴 *No meals.*

★ $$$$ **Fodor's Choice** 🏨 **Hotel St-Barth Isle de France.** *Resort.* An obsessively attentive management team ensures that this intimate, casual, refined resort remains among the very best accommodations in St. Barth—if not the entire Caribbean. **Pros:** prime beach location; terrific management; great spa; excellent restaurant. **Cons:** garden rooms—though large—can be dark; you will definitely want a car to get around; unfortunately, the day will come when you will have to leave this paradise. [$] *Rooms from: €695* ✉ *B.P. 612, Baie des Flamands* ☎ *0590/27–61–81* 🌐 *www.isle-de-france.com* ➡ *32 rooms, 2 villas* ⏲ *Closed Sept.–mid-Oct.* 🍴 *Breakfast.*

GRAND CUL DE SAC

★ $$$$ 👶 **Fodor's Choice** 🏨 **Hotel Guanahani and Spa.** *Resort.* The largest full-service resort on the island has lovely rooms and suites (14 of which have private pools) and impeccable personalized service, not to mention one of the island's only children's programs (though it's more of a nursery). **Pros:** fantastic spa; beach-side sports; family-friendly; great service. **Cons:** lots of walking all around the property, and a steep walk to beach. [$] *Rooms from: €646* ✉ *Grand Cul de Sac* ☎ *0590/27–66–60* 🌐 *www.leguanahani.com* ➡ *35 suites, 32 rooms* ⏲ *Closed Sept.* 🍴 *Breakfast.*

$$ 👶 ★ 🏨 **Hotel Les Ondines Sur La Plage.** *Rental.* Right on the beach of Grand Cul de Sac, this reasonably priced, intimate gem comprises modern, comfortable apartments with room to really spread out. **Pros:** spacious beachfront apartments; close to restaurants and water sports; pool; airport transfers. **Cons:** not a resort; beach is narrow in front of the property; will need a car to get around. [$] *Rooms from: €350* ✉ *Grand Cul de Sac* ☎ *590/27–69–64* 🌐 *www.stbarthlesondineshotel.com* ➡ *6 rooms* 🍴 *Breakfast.*

★ $$$$ **Fodor's Choice** 🏨 **Le Sereno.** *Resort.* Those seeking a restorative, sensous escape will discover true nirvana at the quietly elegant, aptly named Le Sereno. **Pros:** romantic rooms; beach location; superchic comfort; friendly atmosphere; handicap accessible. **Cons:** no a/c in bathrooms; some construction planned for this part of the island over the next few years. [$] *Rooms from: €690* ✉ *B.P. 19 Grand-Cul-de-Sac, Grand Cul de Sac* ☎ *0590/29–83–00* 🌐 *www.lesereno.com* ➡ *37 suites and villas* 🍴 *Breakfast.*

Fodor's Choice ★

Hotel St-Barth Isle de France

Guanahani Spa

Hotel Guanahani and Spa

Le Sereno

3

GRANDE SALINE

$ **Salines Garden Cottages.** *Rental.* Budget-conscious beach lovers who don't require a lot of coddling need look no further than these petite garden cottages, a short stroll from what is arguably St. Barth's best beach. **Pros:** only property walkable to Salines Beach; quiet; reasonable rates. **Cons:** far from town; not very private; strict cancellation policy. [$] *Rooms from: €140* ✉ *Grand Saline* ☎ *0590/51–04–44* 🌐 *www.salinesgarden.com* 🛏 *5 cottages* 🕓 *Closed mid-Aug.–mid-Oct.* 🍴 *Breakfast.*

GUSTAVIA

★ **Fodor's Choice** **Carl Gustaf.** *Hotel.* This sophisticated hotel
$$$$ right in Gustavia is the last word in luxury, and it's within walking distance of everything in town if you don't mind climbing the hill. **Pros:** luxurious decor; in-town location; loads of in-room gadgets; excellent restaurant; beautiful spa. **Cons:** not on the beach; outdoor space limited to your private plunge pool. [$] *Rooms from: €995* ✉ *Rue des Normands, Gustavia* ☎ *0590/29–79–00* 🌐 *www.hotelcarlgustaf.com* 🛏 *14 suites* 🕓 *Closed May–Oct.* 🍴 *Breakfast.*

$ **Sunset Hotel.** *Hotel.* Ten simple, utilitarian rooms (one can accommodate three people) right in Gustavia sit across from the harbor and offer an economical and handy, if not luxurious option for those who want to stay in town. **Pros:** reasonable rates; in town. **Cons:** no elevator; not resortlike in any way. [$] *Rooms from: €110* ✉ *Rue de la Républic, Gustavia* ☎ *590/27–77–21* 🌐 *www.saint-barths.com/sunset-hotel/* 🛏 *10 rooms* 🍴 *No meals.*

LORIENT

$$$ **Hotel La Banane.** *B&B/Inn.* Starting in 2012, the nine high-
★ style rooms in this small complex are available to groups who reserve at least three units, making it a great choice for a destination wedding. **Pros:** short walk to beach; friendly and social atmosphere at pool areas; great baths. **Cons:** just for weekly group rentals; rooms are small; location of entrance through parking lot is not attractive. [$] *Rooms from: €485* ✉ *Baie de Lorient, Lorient* ☎ *0590/52–03–00* 🌐 *www.labanane.com* 🛏 *9 rooms* 🕓 *Closed Sept.–Oct. 15* 🍴 *Breakfast.*

$ **Le Normandie.** *B&B/Inn.* The immaculate rooms here are
★ small but stylish, and there's nothing on the island at this price range compares. **Pros:** friendly management; pleasant

atmosphere; good value. **Cons:** tiny rooms, small bathrooms. [$] *Rooms from: €155* ✉ *Lorient* ☎ *0590/27–61–66* 🌐 *www.normandiehotelstbarts.com* 🛏 *8 rooms (7 double, 1 single)* 🍴 *Breakfast.*

$ 🏨 **Les Mouettes.** *Rental.* This guesthouse offers clean, simply
✋ furnished, and economical bungalows that open directly onto the beach. **Pros:** right on the beach; family-friendly. **Cons:** rooms are basic; right near the road; requirement of 30% prepayment 3 months in advance, which can only be cancelled one month in advance of reservation. No pool, no TV. [$] *Rooms from: €150* ✉ *Lorient Beach* ☎ *0590/27–77–91* 🌐 *lesmouetteshotel.com* 🛏 *7 bungalows* 💳 *No credit cards* 🍴 *No meals.*

POINTE MILOU

$$$ 🏨 **Christopher.** *Resort.* This longtime St. Barth favorite of
✋ European families is hosted by an experienced manage-
★ ment team that delivers a high standard of courteous professionalism and personalized service. **Pros:** comfortable elegance; family-friendly; reasonable price; updated rooms. **Cons:** resort is directly on the water but not on a beach, three-night minimum stay. [$] *Rooms from: €450* ✉ *Pointe Milou* ☎ *590/27–63–63* 🌐 *www.hotelchristopher.com* 🛏 *42 rooms* 🕓 *Closed Sept.–mid-Oct.* 🍴 *Breakfast.*

ST-JEAN

★ **Fodor's Choice** 🏨 **Eden Rock.** *Resort.* St. Barth's first hotel opened
$$$$ in the 1950s on the craggy bluff that splits Baie de St-Jean,
✋ and it's evolved into one of the island's top properties. **Pros:** chic clientele; beach setting; great restaurants; can walk to shopping and restaurants. **Cons:** some suites are noisy because of proximity to street. [$] *Rooms from: €695* ✉ *Baie de St-Jean, St-Jean* ☎ *0590/29–79–99, 877/563–7015 in U.S.* 🌐 *www.edenrockhotel.com* 🛏 *32 rooms, 2 villas* 🕓 *Closed Aug. 29 to Oct. 17* 🍴 *Breakfast.*

$$$ 🏨 **Emeraude Plage.** *Hotel.* Right on the beach of Baie de
✋ St-Jean, this petite resort consists of small but immacu-
★ late bungalows and villas with modern, fully equipped outdoor kitchenettes on small patios; nice bathrooms add to the comfort. **Pros:** beachfront and in-town location; good value; cool kitchens on each porch. **Cons:** smallish rooms. [$] *Rooms from: €385* ✉ *Baie de St-Jean, St-Jean* ☎ *0590/27–64–78* 🌐 *www.emeraudeplage.com* 🛏 *28 bungalows* 🕓 *Closed Sept.–mid-Oct.* 🍴 *No meals.*

Carl Gustaf

Eden Rock

Hôtel le Village St-Jean

★ Fodor'sChoice ⊞ **Hôtel le Village St-Jean.** *Hotel.* You get the
$ advantages of a villa and the services of a hotel at Hôtel
☺ Le Village, where for two generations the Charneau family
has offered friendly service and reasonable rates, making
guests feel like a part of the family. **Pros:** great value; convenient location; wonderful management, friendly clientele.
Cons: A walk up a steep hill to the hotel; can be noisy,
depending on how close your room is to the street below.
Ⓢ *Rooms from: €225* ⊠ *Baie de St-Jean, St-Jean* ☎ *0590/27–
61–39, 800/651–8366* ⊕ *www.villagestjeanhotel.com* ⊅ *5
rooms, 20 cottages, 1 3-bedroom villa, 2 2-bedroom villas*
⊺⊙⊺ *Breakfast.*

$$$ ⊞ **Les Îlets de la Plage.** *Rental.* On the far side of the airport,
☺ tucked away at the far corner of Baie de St-Jean, these well-
priced, comfortably furnished island-style one-, two-, and
three-bedroom bungalows (four right on the beach, seven
up a small hill) have small kitchens, pleasant open-air sitting
areas, and comfortable bathrooms. **Pros:** beach location;
apartment conveniences; front porches. **Cons:** no TV (unless
requested), a/c only in bedrooms; right next to the airport,
extra charge for Internet. Ⓢ *Rooms from: €450* ⊠ *Plage de
St-Jean, St-Jean* ☎ *0590/27–88–57* ⊕ *www.lesilets.com* ⊅ *11
bungalows* ⊘ *Closed Sept.–Nov. 1* ⊺⊙⊺ *No meals.*

$$$ ⊞ **Le Tom Beach Hôtel.** *Hotel.* This chic but casual boutique
hotel right on busy St-Jean beach is fun for social types,
and the nonstop house party often spills out onto the terraces and lasts into the wee hours. **Pros:** party central at
beach, restaurant, and pool; in-town location. **Cons:** trendy
social scene is not for everybody, especially light sleepers.
Ⓢ *Rooms from: €450* ⊠ *Plage de St-Jean, St-Jean* ☎ *0590/27–
53–13* ⊕ *www.tombeach.com* ⊅ *12 rooms* ⊺⊙⊺ *Breakfast.*

NIGHTLIFE

WORD OF MOUTH. "We've seen up and down nightlife in Gustavia
and St-Jean in March and April, better experiences in June, late
Sept./Oct., and Nov. Depends who and what fancy boats are in
dock and whether the jet set are partying publicly or privately.
Some nights the bars can be a snooze, other times packed and
Bohemian." —Mathieu

Most of the nightlife in St. Barth is centered in Gustavia,
though there are a few places to go outside of town. "In"
clubs change from season to season, so you might ask
around for the hot spot of the moment, but none really get

going until about midnight. Theme parties are the current trend. Check the daily *St. Barth News* or *Le Journal de Saint-Barth* for details. A late (10 pm or later) reservation at one of the club-restaurants will eventually become a front-row seat at a party. *Saint-Barth Leisures* contains current information about sports, spas, nightlife, and the arts.

GUSTAVIA

Bar de l'Oubli. This is where young locals gather for drinks. Bring cash, they don't accept plastic. ✉ *Rue du Roi Oscar II, Gustavia* ☎ *0590/27–70–06.*

Victoria's Restaurant at the Carl Gustaf. This hotel lures a more sedate crowd, namely those in search of quiet conversation and views of the sunset. The pretty room has tasty bar snacks, and the bartender whips up the best Planter's Punch on the island, digging into the hotel's stash of "Old Rums" from all over the Caribbean. ✉ *Hotel Carl Gustaf, Rue des Normands, Gustavia* ☎ *0590/27–82–83.*

Le Repaire. This restaurant lures a crowd for cocktail hour and its pool table. ✉ *Rue de la République, Gustavia* ☎ *0590/27-72 48.*

★ **Le Sélect.** This is St. Barth's original hangout, commemorated by Jimmy Buffett's song, "Cheeseburger in Paradise." The boisterous garden is where the barefoot boating set gathers for a cold Carib beer, at prices somewhat lower than the usual. ✉ *Rue du Centenaire, Gustavia* ☎ *0590/27–86–87.*

Le Yacht Club. Although ads call it a private club, dress right and you can probably get in to this hot spot anyway. Nothing much happens till midnight, when the terrific DJs get things going. Check the local papers for details of special parties. ✉ *Rue Jeanne d'Arc, Gustavia* ☎ *0690/49–23–33* ⊕ *www.caroleplaces.com.*

Supper Club The Strand. This suavely white-draped "boite" above Gustavia's Casa Nikki offers tapas and cocktails starting at 7. Dinner is served until about 11, when it turns into a Champagne Lounge with a fun party. Star DJs spin, and, at this writing, on Thursdays wine and champagne are buy one, get one free. ✉ *Gustavia Harbor, Gustavia* ☎ *0590/27–63–77* ⊕ *www.the-strand.fr.*

ST-JEAN

★ **Le Nikki Beach.** This place rocks on weekends during lunch, when the scantily clad young and beautiful lounge on the white canvas banquettes. At night there are beach BBQs, theme parties, fashion shows, and other creative events. The hip and the gorgeous flock here Sunday afternoons for a great beach party. ⊠ *St-Jean* ☎ *0590/27–64–64* ⊕ *www. nikkibeach.com.*

SHOPPING

★ **Fodor's**Choice St. Barth is a duty-free port, and with its sophisticated crowd of visitors, shopping in the island's 200-plus boutiques is a definite delight, especially for beachwear, accessories, jewelry, and casual wear. It would be no overstatement to say that shopping for fashionable clothing, jewels, and designer accessories is better in St. Barth than anywhere else in the Caribbean. New shops open all the time, so there's always something new to discover. Stores close for lunch from noon to 3, and many on Wednesday afternoon as well, but they are open until 7 in the evening. A popular afternoon pastime is strolling about the two major shopping areas in Gustavia and St-Jean.

In Gustavia, boutiques line the three major shopping streets. Quai de la République, which is right on the harbor, rivals New York's Madison Avenue or Paris's avenue Montaigne for high-end designer retail, including shops for **Louis Vuitton, Bulgari, Cartier, Chopard,** and **Hermès.** These shops often carry items that are not available in the United States. The elegant Carré d'Or plaza is great fun to explore. Shops are also clustered in **La Savane Commercial Center** (across from the airport), **La Villa Créole** (in St-Jean), and **Espace Neptune** (on the road to Lorient). It's worth working your way from one end to the other at these shopping complexes—just to see or, perhaps, be seen. Boutiques in all three areas carry the latest in French and Italian sportswear and some haute couture. Bargains may be tough to come by, but you might be able to snag that *Birkin* that has a long waiting-list stateside, and in any case, you'll have a lot of fun hunting around.

Shopping for up-to-the-minute fashions is as much a part of a visit to St. Barth as going to the beach. Shops change all the time, both in ownership and in the lines that are carried. Current listings are just a general guide. The best advice is simply to go for a long stroll in the late afternoon and check out all the shops on the way.

If you are looking for locally made art and handicrafts, call the tourist office, which can provide information, and arrange visits to the studios of some of the island artists, including Christian Bretoneiche, Robert Danet, Nathalie Daniel, Patricia Guyot, Rose Lemen, Aline de Lurin, and Marion Vinot. A few good gallery/craft boutiques are also scattered around Gustavia, and the larger hotels.

ANSE DE TOINY

HANDICRAFTS

Chez Pompi. Chez Pompi is little more than a cottage whose first room is a gallery for the naive paintings of Pompi (also known as Louis Ledée). ⊠ *Rte. de Toiny, Petit Cul de Sac* ☎ *0590/29–76–90.*

Couleurs Provence. This store stocks beautiful, handcrafted, French-made items like jacquard table linens in brilliant colors; decorative tableware, including trays in which dried flowers and herbs are suspended; and the island home fragrance line by L'Occitane. ⊠ *Route de Saline, St-Jean* ☎ *0590/52–48–51.*

GRAND CUL DE SAC

LIQUOR AND TOBACCO

La Cave de Saint-Barths. For more than 30 years, this cellar has maintained its excellent collection of French vintages and small-production rums in temperature-controlled cellars. ⊠ *Marigot* ☎ *0590/27–63–21.*

GUSTAVIA

BOOKS

Clic Bookstore and Gallery. This bookstore is an island outpost of the SoHo NYC and Hamptons concept gallery bookstore devoted to books on photography and monthly exhibits of fine modern photography. It's the brainchild of Calypso founder Christine Celle. ⊠ *Rue de la République, Gustavia* ☎ *590/29–70–17* ⊕ *www.clicgallery.com.*

Shops on Rue de la France, Gustavier

CLOTHING

Black Swan. Black Swan has an unparalleled selection of bathing suits for men, women, and children. The wide range of styles and sizes is appreciated. They also have souveneir-appropriate island logo-wear and whatever beach equipment you might require. ⊠ *Le Carré d'Or, Gustavia* ☎ *590/52–48–30.*

Boutique Lacoste. This store has a huge selection of the once-again-chic alligator-logo wear, as well as a shop next door with a complete selection of the Petit Bateau line of T-shirts popular with teens. ⊠ *Rue du Bord de Mer, Gustavia* ☎ *0590/27–66–90.*

Café Coton. Café Coton is a great shop for men, especially for long-sleeve linen shirts in a rainbow of colors and Egyptian cotton dress shirts. ⊠ *Rue du Bord du Mer, Gustavia* ☎ *0590/52–48–42.*

Calypso. Calypso carries sophisticated, sexy resort wear and accessories by Balenciaga, Chloe, and D Squared, among others. ⊠ *Le Carré d'Or, Gustavia* ☎ *0590/27–69–74* ⊕ *www.saint-barths.com/calypso/.*

Filles Des Iles. Shop here for high-quality, flattering attire by designers like Shamane, Scooter, and Dyrberg Kern, and sophisticated swimwear by Princess Tam Tam, which even women "of a certain" age can wear. The shop also stocks delicious artisanal fragrances and chic accessories. ⊠ *8, Villa Creole, St-Jean* ☎ *590/29–04–08.*

Hermès. The Hermès store in St. Barth is an independently owned franchise, and prices are slightly below those in the States. ⊠ *Rue de la République, Gustavia* ☎ *0590/27–66–15.*

Kokon. Kokon offers a nicely edited mix of designs for on-island or off, including the ho'em, Lotty B. Mustique, and Day Birger lines, and cute shoes to go with them by Heidi Klum for Birkenstock. ⊠ *Rue Fahlberg, Gustavia* ☎ *0590/29–74–48.*

Linde Gallery. Linde sells vintage sunglasses, accessories, vintage ready-to-wear from the 1970s and '80s, as well as books, CDs, and DVDs. ⊠ *Les Hauts de Carré d'Or, Gustavia* ☎ *590/29–73–86* ⊕ *www.lindegallery.com.*

Linen. Linen has tailored linen shirts for men in a rainbow of soft colors, and their soft slip-on driving mocs in classic styles are a St. Barth must. ⊠ *Rue du Général de Gaulle, Gustavia* ☎ *0590/27–54–26.*

Lolita Jaca. Don't miss this store for trendy, tailored sportswear. ⊠ *Le Carré d'Or, Gustavia* ☎ *0590/27–59–98* ⊕ *www.lolitajaca.com.*

Longchamp. Fans of the popular travel bags, handbags, and leather goods will find a good selection at about 20% off stateside prices. ⊠ *Rue Général de Gaulle, Gustavia* ☎ *0590/51–96–50.*

Pati de Saint Barth. This is the largest of the three shops that stock the chic, locally made T-shirts, totes, and beach wraps that have practically become the logo of St. Barth. The newest styles have hand-done graffiti-style lettering. The shop also has some handicrafts and other giftable items. ⊠ *Rue du Bord de Mer, Gustavia* ☎ *0590/29–78–04* ⊕ *www.madeinstbarth.com.*

Poupette St. Barth. All the brilliant color-crinkle silk and chiffon batik and embroidered peasant skirts and tops are designed by the owner. There also are great belts and beaded bracelets. ⊠ *Rue de la République, Gustavia* ☎ *0590/27–55–78* ⊕ *www.poupettestbarth.com.*

Saint-Barth Stock Exchange. On the far side of Gustavia Harbor is the island's consignment and discount shop. ⊠ *La Pointe-Gustavia, Gustavia* ☎ *0590/27–68–12.*

Stéphane & Bernard. This store stocks a well-edited, large selection of superstar French fashion designers, including Rykiel, Missoni, Valentino, Versaci, Ungaro, Christian Lacroix, and Eres beachwear. ⊠ *Rue de la République, Gustavia* ☎ *0590/27–65–69* ⊕ *www.stephaneandbernard.com.*

St. Tropez KIWI. Look to this popular boutique with two branches (one in Gustavia and one in St-Jean) for resort wear. ⊠ *Gustavia* ☎ *0590/27–57–08.*

Vanita Rosa. This store showcases beautiful lace and linen sundresses and peasant tops, with accessories galore. ⊠ *Rue du Roi Oscar II, Gustavia* ☎ *0590/52–43–25* ⊕ *www. vanitarosa.com.*

Victoire. Classic, well-made sportswear in luxurious fabrics and great colors, with a French twist on preppy, will please shoppers eager for finds that will play as well in Nantucket or Greenwich as they do on St. Barth. ⊠ *Rue du Général de Gaulle, Gustavia* ☎ *590/29–84–60* ⊕ *www. victoire-paris.com.*

FOODSTUFFS

A.M.C. This supermarket is a bit older than Marché U in St-Jean but able to supply nearly anything you might need for housekeeping in a villa or for a picnic. ⊠ *Quai de la République, Gustavia.*

HANDICRAFTS

Fabienne Miot. Look for unusual and artistic jewelry, featuring rare stones and natural pearls at this shop. ⊠ *Rue de la République, Gustavia* ☎ *0590/27–73–13.*

Kalinas Perles. Beautiful freshwater pearls are knotted onto the classic St. Barth–style leather thongs by artist Jeremy Albaledejo, who also has a great eye for other artisans' works showcased in a gallery-like setting. ⊠ *Rue du Bord de Mer, Gustavia* ☎ *690/65–93–00.*

Le P'tit Collectionneur. Encouraged by his family and friends, André Berry opened his private musuem, "le P'tit Collectionneur," in early 2007 to showcase his lifelong passion for collecting fascinating objects such as 18th-century English pipes and the first phonograph to come to the island. He will happily show you his treasures. ⊠ *La Pointe, Gustavia* 🖾 *€2* ⊙ *Mon.–Sat., 10–noon and 4–6 pm.*

JEWELRY

Bijoux de la Mer. This store carries beautiful and artistic jewelry made of South Sea pearls in wonderful hues strung in clusters on leather to wrap around the neck or arms. ⊠ *Rue de la Républic, Gustavia* ☎ *590/52–37–68* ⊕ *www. bijouxdelamerstbarth.com.*

Carat. Carat has Chaumet and a large selection of Breitling watches, plus rarities by Richard Mille, Breguet. ⊠ *Quai de la République, Gustavia* ☎ *590/27–67–22 No phone* ⊕ *www.caratsaintbarth.com/.*

Cartier. For fine jewelry, visit this branch of the famous jeweler. ⊠ *Quai de la République, Gustavia.*

Diamond Genesis. A good selection of watches, including Patek Phillippe and Chanel, can be found at this store. Pendants and charms in the shape of the island are a popular purchase. ⊠ *Rue Général-de-Gaulle, Gustavia* ⊕ *www. diamondgenesis.com.*

Donna del Sol. Next door to Cartier, designer Donna del Sol carries beautiful handmade gold chains, Tahitian pearl pieces, and baubles in multicolor diamonds of her own designs. Have something special in mind? She'll work with clients to design and produce custom items. ⊠ *Quai de la République, Gustavia* ⊕ *www.donnadelsol.com.*

Sindbad. This tiny shop, an island favorite since 1977, curates funky, unique couture fashion jewelry by Gaz Bijou of St Tropez, crystal collars for your pampered pooch, and other reasonably priced, up-to-the-minute styles. Current favorites are the South Sea pearls strung on leather thongs or colorful silky cords. ⊠ *Carré d'Or, Gustavia* ☎ *0590/27–52–29* ⊕ *www.sindbad-st-barth.com.*

LIQUOR AND TOBACCO

La Cave du Port Franc. This store has a good selection of wine, especially from France. ⊠ *Rue de la République, Gustavia* ☎ *0590/27-65-27* ⊕ *www.lacaveduportfranc.com.*

Le Comptoir du Cigare. This tobacco shop run by Jannick and Patrick Gerthofer, is a top purveyor of cigars. The walk-in humidor has an extraordinary selection, with encyclopedic stocks of Cohiba and Montecristo (even the rare Monte No. 4 Reserva), Vegas Robaina, and Romeo y Julieta. Smoke Cubans while you are on the island, and take home the Davidoffs. Refills can be shipped stateside. Be sure to try on the genuine Panama hats. ⊠ *6 Rue du*

Up to 40 yachts can moor in Gustavia's harbor

Général de Gaule, Gustavia ☎*0590/27–50–62* ⊕*www.comptoirducigare.com.*

Couleurs des Iles 120% Lin. This shop has many rare varieties of smokeables and good souvenir T-shirts, too. Head to the back for the stash of rare Puro Vintage. ⊠ *Rue Général de Gaulle, Gustavia* ☎*0590/27–79–60.*

M'Bolo. Be sure to sample the varieties of infused rums, including lemongrass, ginger, and the island favorite, vanilla. Bring home some in the beautiful hand-blown bottles. Chefs will like the selection of Laguiole knives, and the local spices, too. ⊠ *Rue duGénéral de Gaulle, Gustavia* ☎*0590/27–90–54.*

LORIENT

COSMETICS
Ligne de St. Barth. Don't miss the superb skin-care products made on-site from local tropical plants by this St. Barth company. ⊠ *Rte. de Saline, Lorient* ☎*0590/27–82–63* ⊕*www.lignestbarth.com.*

FOODSTUFFS
JoJo Supermarché. JoJo is the well-stocked counterpart to Gustavia's large supermarket and gets daily deliveries of bread and fresh produce. JoJoBurger, next door, is the local surfers' favorite spot for a (very good) quick burger. ⊠ *Lorient.*

ST-JEAN

CLOTHING

Black Swan. Black Swan has an unparalleled selection of bathing suits. The wide range of styles and sizes is appreciated. ⊠ *La Villa Créole, St-Jean* ⊕ *www.blackswanstbarth.com*.

Iléna. This boutique has incredible beachwear and lingerie by Chantal Thomas, Sarda, and others, including Swarovski crystal–encrusted bikinis for the young and gorgeous. ⊠ *Villa Créole, St-Jean* ☎ *0590/29–84–05*.

Lili Belle. Check out Lili Belle for a nice selection of wearable and current styles. ⊠ *Pelican Plage, St-Jean* ☎ *0590/87–46–14*.

Morgan. Morgan has a line of popular casual wear in the trendy vein. ⊠ *La Villa Créole, St-Jean* ☎ *0590/27–71–00*.

St. Tropez KIWI. Look to this popular boutique with two branches (one in Gustavia and one in St-Jean) for resort wear. ⊠ *3 Villas Créole, St-Jean* ☎ *0590/27–57–08*.

SUD SUD.ETC.Plage. This store stocks everything for the beach: inflatables, mats, bags, and beachy shell jewelry, as well as bikinis and gauzy cover-ups. ⊠ *Galerie du Commerce, St-Jean* ☎ *0590/27–90–56*.

FOODSTUFFS

Marche U. This fully stocked supermarket across from the airport has a wide selection of French cheeses, pâtés, cured meats, produce, fresh bread, wine, and liquor. There is also a good selection of prepared foods and organic grocery items. ⊠ *St-Jean* ☎ *0590/27–68–16*.

Maya's to Go. This is the place to go for prepared picnics, meals, salads, rotisserie chickens, and more from the kitchens of the popular restaurant in Gustavia. ⊠ *Galleries du Commerce, St-Jean* ☎ *0590/29–83–70* ⊕ *www.mayastogo. com* ⊗ *Closed Mon.*

SPORTS AND ACTIVITIES

BOATING AND SAILING

St. Barth is a popular yachting and sailing center, thanks to its location midway between Antigua and St. Thomas. Gustavia's harbor, 13 to 16 feet deep, has mooring and docking facilities for 40 yachts. There are also good anchorages available at Public, Corossol, and Colombier. You can charter sailing and motorboats in Gustavia Harbor for as

Snorkeling at Anse à Colombier

little as a half day. Stop at the tourist office in Gustavia, or ask at your hotel for an up-to-the minute list of recommended charter companies.

Jicky Marine Service. Jicky Marine Service offers full-day outings, either on a variety of motorboats, or 42- or 46-foot catamaran, to the uninhabited Île Fourchue for swimming, snorkeling, cocktails, and lunch. The cost starts at about $100 per person; an unskippered motor rental runs about $260 a day. ⊠ *Ferry dock, Gustavia* ☎ *0590/27–70–34* ⊕ *www.jickymarine.com.*

🕲 **Yellow Submarine.** Yellow Submarine takes you "six feet under" (the surface of the sea) for a close-up view of St. Barth's coral reefs through large glass portholes. It costs €40 for adults, €25 for children under 12. Trips depart daily, from the Ferry Dock in Gustavia with departures at 11 am and 2 pm, with night excursions Wednesday and Friday at 5:45 pm but more often depending on demand, so call first. ⊠ *Ferry Dock, Gustavia* ☎ *0590/52–40–51* ⊕ *www.yellow-submarine.fr.*

DIVING AND SNORKELING

Several dive shops arrange scuba excursions to local sites. Depending on weather conditions, you may dive at **Pain de Sucre, Coco Island,** or toward nearby **Saba.** There's also an underwater shipwreck to explore, plus sharks, rays, sea tortoises, coral, and the usual varieties of colorful fish. The waters on the island's leeward side are the calmest. For the uncertified who still want to see what the island's waters hold, there's an accessible shallow reef right off the beach at Anse de Cayes that you can explore if you have your own mask and fins, and a hike down the hill to the beach at Corossol brings you to a very popular snorkeling spot for locals.

Réserve Marine de St-Barth. Most of the waters surrounding St. Barth are protected in the island's Réserve Marine de St-Barth, which also provides information at its office in Gustavia. The diving here isn't nearly as rich as in the more dive-centered destinations like Saba and St. Eustatius, but the options aren't bad either, and none of the smaller islands offer the ambience of St. Barth. ⊠ *Gustavia* ☎ *0590/27–88–18.*

☾ **Plongée Caraïbe.** Plongée Caraïbe is recommended for its up-to-the-minute equipment and dive boat. They also run two-hour group snorkeling trips on the *Blue Cat Catamaran*; a half-day is €40. ☎☎ *0590/27–55–94* ⊕ *www.plongeecaraibes.com.*

Splash. In Gustavia, Splash offers PADI and CMAS (Confederation Mondiale des Activites Subaquatiques—World Underwater Federation) courses in diver training at all levels. All the instructors speak French and English. Although their boat normally leaves daily at 9 am, 11:30 am, 2 pm, and in the evening for a night dive, they will adjust their times to suit your preferences. ⊠ *Gustavia* ☎ *590/54–75–98* ⊕ *www.divestbarth.com.*

West Indies Dive. Marine Service operates the only five-star, PADI-certified diving center on the island, called West Indies Dive. Scuba trips, packages, resort dives, night dives, and certifications start at $90, including gear. ☎ *0590/27–70–34.*

FISHING

Most fishing is done in the waters north of Lorient, Flamands, and Corossol. Popular catches are tuna, marlin, wahoo, and barracuda. There's an annual St. Barth Open Fishing Tournament, organized by Océan Must, in mid-July.

Jicky Marine Service. Jicky Marine Service arranges ocean-fishing excursions. ⊠ *Gustavia* ☎ *0590/27–70–34* ⊕ *www.jickymarine.com.*

Océan Must Marina. Océan Must Marina arranges deep-sea fishing expeditions as well as bare boat and staffed boat charters. ⊠ *La Pointe, Gustavia* ☎ *0590/27–62–25* ⊕ *www. oceanmust.com.*

GUIDED TOURS

You can arrange island tours by minibus or car at hotel desks or through any of the island's taxi operators in Gustavia or at the airport. The tourist office runs a variety of tours with varying itineraries that run about €46 for a half day for up to eight people. You can also download up-to-the-minute walking and driving tour itineraries from the Tourist Board's website.

Mat Nautic. Mat Nautic can help you arrange to tour the island by water on a Jet Ski or WaveRunner. ⊠ *Quai du Yacht Club, rue Jeanne d'Arc, Gustavia* ☎ *0690/49–54–72.*

St-Barth Tours & Travel. St-Barth Tours & Travel will customize a tour of the island. They can also book ferry trips. ⊠ *Rue Saint Thomas, Gustavia* ☎ *0590/52–41–38.*

Anguilla

WORD OF MOUTH

"[W]e just prefer Anguilla because of the beaches, the people, and the food. Much more of an island vibe."

—MaryD

By Elise
Meyer

PEACE, PAMPERING, GREAT FOOD, and a wonderful local music scene are among the star attractions on Anguilla (pronounced ang-*gwill*-a). Beach lovers may become giddy when they first spot the island from the air; its blindingly white sand and lustrous blue-and-aquamarine waters are intoxicating. And if you like sophisticated cuisine served in casually elegant open-air settings, this may be your culinary Shangri-la.

The island's name, a reflection of its shape, is most likely a derivative of *anguille,* which is French for "eel." (French explorer Pierre Laudonnaire is credited with having given the island this name when he sailed past it in 1556.) In 1631 the Dutch built a fort here, but so far no one has been able to locate its site. English settlers from St. Kitts colonized the island in 1650, with plans to cultivate tobacco and, later, cotton and then sugar. But the thin soil and scarce water doomed these enterprises to fail. Except for a brief period of independence, when it broke from its association with St. Kitts and Nevis in the 1960s, Anguilla has remained a British colony ever since.

From the early 1800s various island federations were formed and disbanded, with Anguilla all the while simmering over its subordinate status and enforced union with St. Kitts. Anguillians twice petitioned for direct rule from Britain and twice were ignored. In 1967, when St. Kitts, Nevis, and Anguilla became an associated state, the mouse roared; citizens kicked out St. Kitts's policemen, held a self-rule referendum, and for two years conducted their own affairs. To what *Time* magazine called "a cascade of laughter around the world," a British "peacekeeping force" of 100 paratroopers from the Elite Red Devil unit parachuted onto the island, squelching Anguilla's designs for autonomy but helping a team of royal engineers stationed there to improve the port and build roads and schools. Today Anguilla elects a House of Assembly and its own leader to handle internal affairs, and a British governor is responsible for public service, the police, the judiciary, and external affairs.

The territory of Anguilla includes a few islets (or cays, pronounced "keys"), such as Scrub Island, Dog Island, Prickly Pear Cay, Sandy Island, and Sombrero Island. The 16,000 or so residents are predominantly of African descent, but there are also many of Irish background, whose ancestors came over from St. Kitts in the 1600s. Histori-

LOGISTICS

Getting to Anguilla:
There are no nonstop flights to Anguilla (AXA) from the United States, so you will almost always have to fly through San Juan, St. Maarten, or some other Caribbean island. You'll ordinarily be making the hop on a smaller plane. You can also take a ferry from St. Maarten.

Hassle Factor: Medium.

On the Ground: Some hotels provide transfers from the airport or ferry pier, especially the more expensive ones. For everyone else, if you don't rent a car, the taxi ride from the airport to your hotel will be less than $25 even to the West End (and considerably less if you're going to Sandy Ground).

Getting Around the Island: It's possible to base yourself in Sandy Ground, Rendezvous Bay, Meads Bay, or Shoal Bay without a car, but restaurants and resorts are quite spread out, so for the sake of convenience you may wish to rent a car for a few days or for your entire stay. If you do, prepare to drive on the left. Taxis are fairly expensive on Anguilla, another reason to consider renting a car.

cally, because the limestone land was unfit for agriculture, attempts at enslavement never lasted long; consequently, Anguilla doesn't bear the scars of slavery found on so many other Caribbean islands. Instead, Anguillians became experts at making a living from the sea and are known for their boatbuilding and fishing skills. Tourism is the stable economy's growth industry, but the government carefully regulates expansion to protect the island's natural resources and beauty. New hotels are small, select, and casino-free; Anguilla emphasizes its high-quality service, serene surroundings, and friendly people.

PLANNING

WHEN TO GO

As in much of the Caribbean, high season runs from mid-December through mid-April, and some resorts in Anguilla still close from August through mid-December, though many remain open year-round. Many resorts require long minimum stays until after New Year's Day.

ACCOMMODATIONS

Anguilla is known for its luxurious resorts and villas, but there are also a few places that mere mortals can afford (and some that are downright bargains).

HOTEL AND RESTAURANT PRICES

Prices in the restaurant reviews are the average cost of a main course at dinner or, if dinner is not served, at lunch; taxes and service charges are generally included. Prices in the hotel reviews are the lowest cost of a standard double room in high season, excluding taxes, service charges, and meal plans (except at all-inclusives). Prices for rentals are the lowest per-night cost for a one-bedroom unit in high season.

EXPLORING ANGUILLA

Exploring on Anguilla is mostly about checking out the spectacular beaches and resorts. The island has only a few roads, but they have been improving significantly in recent years, and the lack of adequate signage is being addressed. Locals are happy to provide directions, but using the readily available tourist map is the best idea. Visit the Anguilla Tourist Board, centrally located on Coronation Avenue in The Valley.

The Anguilla Heritage Trail is a free, self-guided tour of 10 important historical sights that can be explored independently in any order. Wallblake House, in The Valley, is the main information center for the trail, or you can just look for the large boulders with descriptive plaques.

WHAT TO SEE

Bethel Methodist Church. Not far from Sandy Ground, this charming little church is an excellent example of skillful island stonework. It also has some colorful stained-glass windows. ⊠ *South Hill* ☎ *No phone.*

Heritage Museum Collection. Don't miss this remarkable opportunity to learn about Anguilla. Old photographs and local records and artifacts trace the island's history over four millennia, from the days of the Arawaks. The tiny museum (complete with gift shop) is painstakingly curated by Colville Petty. High points include the historical documents of the Anguilla Revolution and the albums of photographs chronicling island life, from devastating hurricanes to a visit from Queen Elizabeth in 1964. You can see examples of ancient pottery shards and stone tools

Cacti growing on one of Anguilla's scrub-covered coral flats

along with fascinating photographs of the island in the early 20th century—many depicting the heaping and exporting of salt and the christening of schooners—and a complete set of beautiful postage stamps issued by Anguilla since 1967. ✉ *East End at Pond Ground* ☎ *264/235–7440* 💳 *$5* ☻ *Mon.–Sat. 10–5.*

★ **Island Harbour.** Anguillians have been fishing for centuries in the brightly painted, simple, handcrafted fishing boats that line the shore of the harbor. It's hard to believe, but skillful pilots take these little boats out to sea as far as 50 or 60 miles (80 or 100 km). Late afternoon is the best time to see the day's catch.■TIP→ Hail the free boat to Gorgeous Scilly Cay, a classic little restaurant offering sublime lobster and Eudoxie Wallace's knockout rum punches on Wednesday and Sunday. ✉ *Island Harbor Rd.* ⊕ *www.scillycayanguilla.com.*

Old Factory. For many years the cotton grown on Anguilla and exported to England was ginned in this beautiful historic building, now home of the Anguilla Tourist Office. Some of the original ginning machinery is intact and on display. ✉ *The Valley* ☎ *264/497–2759* ⊕ *www.old-factory-anguilla.ai* 💳 *Free* ☻ *Weekdays 10–noon and 1–4.*

Old Prison. The ruins of this historic jail on Anguilla's highest point—213 feet above sea level—offer outstanding views. ✉ *Valley Rd. at Crocus Hill.*

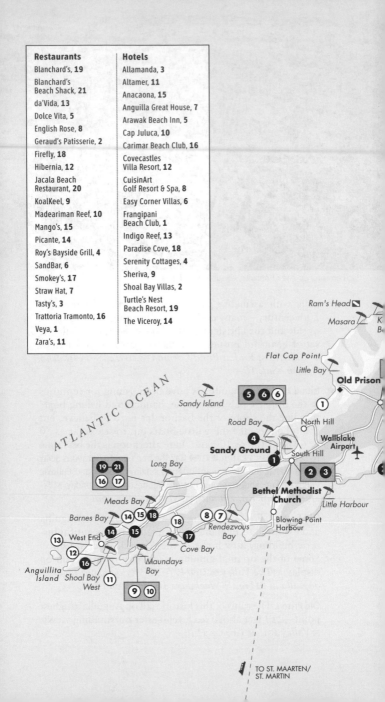

Restaurants

Blanchard's, **19**
Blanchard's
Beach Shack, **21**
da'Vida, **13**
Dolce Vita, **5**
English Rose, **8**
Geraud's Patisserie, **2**
Firefly, **18**
Hibernia, **12**
Jacala Beach
Restaurant, **20**
KoalKeel, **9**
Madeariman Reef, **10**
Mango's, **15**
Picante, **14**
Roy's Bayside Grill, **4**
SandBar, **6**
Smokey's, **17**
Straw Hat, **7**
Tasty's, **3**
Trattoria Tramonto, **16**
Veya, **1**
Zara's, **11**

Hotels

Allamanda, **3**
Altamer, **11**
Anacaona, **15**
Anguilla Great House, **7**
Arawak Beach Inn, **5**
Cap Juluca, **10**
Carimar Beach Club, **16**
Covecastles
Villa Resort, **12**
CuisinArt
Golf Resort & Spa, **8**
Easy Corner Villas, **6**
Frangipani
Beach Club, **1**
Indigo Reef, **13**
Paradise Cove, **18**
Serenity Cottages, **4**
Sheriva, **9**
Shoal Bay Villas, **2**
Turtle's Nest
Beach Resort, **19**
The Viceroy, **14**

ATLANTIC OCEAN

Sandy Island

Ram's Head

Masara

Flat Cap Point
Little Bay
Old Prison

Road Bay
North Hill

Sandy Ground
Wallblake
Airport
South Hill

Long Bay

Bethel Methodist
Church

Little Harbour

Meads Bay

Barnes Bay

West End
Rendezvous
Bay
Blowing Point
Harbour

Cove Bay

Anguillita
Island

Shoal Bay
West

Maundays
Bay

TO ST. MAARTEN/
ST. MARTIN

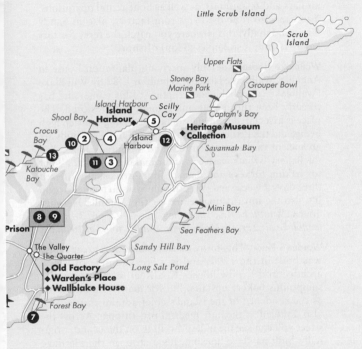

Anguilla

Little Scrub Island

Scrub Island

Upper Flats

Stoney Bay Marine Park

Grouper Bowl

Island Harbour

Island Harbour

Shoal Bay

Crocus Bay

Katouche Bay

Island Harbour

Scilly Cay

(5)

12

Heritage Museum Collection

Captain's Bay

Savannah Bay

13 10 (2) (4)

11 (3)

8 9

Prison

The Valley
The Quarter

◆ **Old Factory**
◆ **Warden's Place**
◆ **Wallblake House**

Mimi Bay

Sea Feathers Bay

Sandy Hill Bay

Long Salt Pond

Forest Bay

7

our

KEY

⌐	*Beaches*
◥	*Dive Sites*
●	*Restaurants*
①	*Hotels*
⛴	*Ferry lines*

```
0                    2 mi
0          2 km
```

WORD OF MOUTH. "Anguilla has the best beaches I have ever seen in the Caribbean. The sand is so soft and white and the colors of the water are more vibrant than any other Caribbean island I have visited. If you want to visit a very laid back, uncrowded island with amazing beaches . . ." —lauren27

Sandy Ground. Almost everyone who comes to Anguilla stops by this central beach, home to several popular open-air bars and restaurants, as well as boat-rental operations. You can also tour the Pyrat rum factory, also in Sandy Ground. Finally, this is where you catch the ferry for tiny Sandy Island, just 2 miles (3 km) offshore.

Wallblake House. The only surviving plantation house in Anguilla, Wallblake House was built in 1787 by Will Blake (Wallblake is probably a corruption of his name) and has recently been thoroughly and thoughtfully restored. The place is associated with many a tale involving murder, high living, and the French invasion in 1796. On the grounds are an ancient vaulted stone cistern and an outbuilding called the Bakery (which wasn't used for making bread at all but for baking turkeys and hams). Tours are usually offered three days a week, and you can only visit on a guided tour. It's also the information center for the Anguilla Heritage Tour. ⊠ *Wallblake Rd., The Valley* ☎ *264/497–6613* ⊕ *www.wallblake.ai* ⊜ *Free* ⊘ *Mon., Wed., and Fri. tours at 10 and 2.*

Warden's Place. This former sugar-plantation great house was built in the 1790s and is a fine example of island architecture. It now houses KoalKeel restaurant and a sumptuous bakery upstairs. But for many years it served as the residence of the island's chief administrator, who also doubled as the only medical practitioner. Across the street you can see the oldest dwelling on the island, originally built as slave housing. It's a stop on the Heritage Trail. ■ **TIP→** Go in the morning from 8 to 10 for breakfast, then tour the historic building. ⊠ *Coronation Ave., The Old Valley* ☎ *264/497–2930* ⊕ *www.koalkeel.com.*

BEACHES

NORTHEAST COAST

Captain's Bay. On the north coast just before the eastern tip of the island, this quarter-mile stretch of perfect white sand is bounded on the left by a rocky shoreline where Atlantic waves crash. If you make the tough, four-wheel-drive-only trip along the dirt road that leads to the northeastern end of the island toward Junk's Hole, you'll be rewarded with peaceful isolation. The surf here slaps the sands with a vengeance, and the undertow is strong—so wading is the safest water sport.

Island Harbour. These mostly calm waters are surrounded by a slender beach. For centuries Anguillians have ventured from these sands in colorful handmade fishing boats. It's not much of a beach for swimming or lounging, but there a several restaurants (Hibernia, Arawak Café, Côtée Mer, and Smitty's), and this is the departure point for the three-minute boat ride to Scilly Cay, where a thatched beach bar serves seafood. Just hail the restaurant's free boat and plan to spend most of the day (the all-inclusive lunch starts at $40 and is worth the price—Wednesday, Friday, and Sunday only).

NORTHWEST COAST

Barnes Bay. Between Meads Bay and West End Bay, this little cove is a good spot for windsurfing and snorkeling, but at this writing the beach still hasn't recovered from Hurricane Omar in 2008. Public access is on the road to Mango's restaurant and Caribella resort.

Little Bay. Little Bay is on the north coast between Crocus Bay and Shoal Bay, not far from The Valley. Sheer cliffs lined with agave and creeping vines rise behind a small gray-sand beach, usually accessible only by water (it's a favored spot for snorkeling and night dives). The easiest way to get here is a five-minute boat ride from Crocus Bay (about $10 round-trip). The young and agile can clamber down the cliffs by rope to explore the caves and surrounding reef; this is the only way to access the beach from the road and is not recommended to the inexperienced climber. Do not leave personal items in cars parked here, because theft can be a problem.

Road Bay (*Sandy Ground*). The big pier here is where the cargo ships dock, but so do some pretty sweet yachts, sailboats, and fishing boats. The brown-sugar sand is home to terrific restaurants that hop from day through dawn, including Veya, Roy's Bayside Grille, Ripples, Barrel Stay, the Pumphouse, and Elvis's quintessential beach bar. There are all kinds of boat charters available here. The snorkeling isn't very good, but the sunset vistas are glorious, especially with a rum punch in your hand.

Shoal Bay, considered by many to be the most beautiful beach on Anguilla

Sandy Island. A popular day trip for Anguilla visitors, tiny Sandy Island shelters a pretty lagoon, nestled in coral reefs about 2 miles (3 km) from Road Bay. Most of the operators in Sandy Ground can bring you here.

★ **Fodor's Choice Shoal Bay.** Shoal Bay. Anchored by sea grape and coconut trees, the 2-mile (3-km) powdered-sugar strand at Shoal Bay (not to be confused with Shoal Bay West at the other end of the island) is universally considered one of the world's prettiest beaches. You can park free at any of the restaurants, including Elodia's, Uncle Ernie's, or Gwen's Reggae Grill, most of which either rent or provide chairs and umbrellas for patrons for about $20 a day per person. There is plenty of room to stretch out in relative privacy, or you can bar-hop, take a ride on Junior's Glass Bottom Boat, or arrange a wreck dive at PADI-certified Shoal Bay Scuba near Kú, where ZaZaa, the island's chic-est boutique will satisfy fans of St. Barth shopping. The relatively broad beach has shallow water that is usually gentle, making this a great family beach; a coral reef not far from the shore is a wonderful snorkeling spot. Sunsets over the water are spectacular. You can even enjoy a beachside massage at Malakh, a little spa near Madeariman's.

SOUTHEAST COAST

Sandy Hill. You can park anywhere along the dirt road to Sea Feathers Bay to visit this popular fishing center. What's good for the fishermen is also good for snorkelers. But the beach here is not much of a lounging spot. The sand is too narrow and rocky for that. However, it's a great place to buy lobsters and fish fresh out of the water in the afternoon.

SOUTHWEST COAST

★ **Fodor's Choice Cove Bay.** Follow the signs to Smokey's at the end of Cove Road, and you will find water that is brilliantly blue and sand that is as soft as sifted flour. It's just as spectacular as its neighbors Rendezvous Bay and Maundays Bay. You can walk here from Cap Juluca for a change of pace, or you can arrange a horseback ride along the beach. Weekend barbecues with terrific local bands at Smokey's are an Anguillian must.

★ **Fodor's Choice Maundays Bay.** The dazzling, mile-long platinum-white beach is especially great for swimming and long beach walks. It's no wonder that Cap Juluca, one of Anguilla's premier resorts, chose this as its location. Public parking is straight ahead at the end of the road near Cap Juluca's Pimms restaurant. You can have lunch or dinner at Cap Juluca (just be prepared for the cost). Depending on the season you can book a massage in one of the beachside tents.

Rendezvous Bay. Follow the signs to Anguilla Great House for public parking at this broad swath of pearl-white sand that is some 1½ miles (2½ km) long. The beach is lapped by calm, bluer-than-blue water and a postcard-worthy view of St. Martin. The expansive crescent is home to three resorts; stop in for a drink or a meal at one of the hotels, or rent a chair and umbrella at one of the kiosks. Don't miss the daylong party at the tree-house Dune Preserve, where Bankie Banx, Anguilla's most famous musician, presides.

Shoal Bay West. This glittering bay bordered by mangroves and sea grapes is a lovely place to spend the day. The mile-long beach is home to the dazzling Covecastles and Altamer villas. The tranquillity is sublime, with coral reefs for snorkeling not too far from shore. Punctuate your day with a meal at beachside Trattoria Tramonto. Reach the beach by taking the main road to the West End and bearing left at the fork, then continuing to the end. Note that similarly named Shoal Bay is a separate beach on a different part of the island.

WHERE TO EAT

Despite its small size, Anguilla has around 70 restaurants ranging from stylish temples of haute cuisine to classic, barefoot beachfront grills, roadside barbecue stands, food carts, and casual cafés. Many have breeze-swept terraces, where you can dine under the stars. Call ahead—in winter to make a reservation and in late summer and fall to confirm whether the place you've chosen is open. Anguillian restaurant meals are leisurely events, and service is often at a relaxed pace, so settle in and enjoy. Most restaurant owners are actively and conspicuously present, especially at dinner. It's a special treat to take the time to get to know them a bit when they stop by your table to make sure you are enjoying your meal.

What to Wear: During the day, casual clothes are widely accepted: shorts will be fine, but don't wear bathing suits and cover-ups unless you're at a beach bar. In the evening, shorts are okay at the extremely casual eateries. Elsewhere, women wear sundresses or nice casual slacks; men will be fine in short-sleeve shirts and casual pants. Some hotel restaurants are slightly more formal, but that just means long pants for men.

★ **Fodor's**Choice ✕ **Blanchard's.** *American.* This absolutely delight-
$$$$ ful restaurant, a mecca for foodies, is considered one of
the best in the Caribbean. Proprietors Bob and Melinda
Blanchard moved to Anguilla from Vermont in 1994 to fulfill their culinary dreams. A festive atmosphere pervades the
handsome, airy white room, which is accented with floor-
to-ceiling teal-blue shutters to let in the breezes, and colorful
artwork by the Blanchards' son Jesse on the walls. A master-
ful combination of creative cuisine, an upscale atmosphere,
attentive service, and an excellent wine cellar (including a
selection of aged spirits) pleases the star-studded crowd. The
nuanced contemporary menu is ever changing but always
delightful; house classics like corn chowder, lobster and
shrimp cakes, and a Caribbean sampler are crowd-pleasers,
and vegetarians will find ample choices. For dessert, you'll
remember concoctions like the key lime "pie-in-a-glass" or
the justly famous "cracked coconut" long after your suntan
has faded. A recent addition is a three-course prix-fixe menu
that includes many of the signature dishes and is a bargain at
$45. ⇨ *Blanchard's Beach Shack, on the beach next to the res-
taurant.* Ⓢ *Average main: $49* ✉ *Meads Bay* ☎ 264/497–6100
⊕ *www.blanchardsrestaurant.com* ♠ *Reservations essential*
⊘ *Closed Sun. Closed Mon. May–mid-Dec. No lunch.*

$ ✕ **'Blanchards Beach Shack.** *Modern American.* You'll find the
☺ perfect antidote to high restaurant prices right on the sands
★ of Meads Bay Beach. Opened in late 2011 by, and located
right beside, 'Blanchards, this chartreuse-and-turquoise
cottage serves yummy lunches and dinners of lobster rolls,
all-natural burgers, tacos, and terrific salads and sandwiches—you can dine at nearby picnic tables. Frozen drinks
like mango coladas and icy mojitos please grown-ups, while
kids dig into the fresh-made frozen yogurt concoctions.
Organic produce, compostable paper goods, and happy
smiles are always on offer. Lots of choices for kids and
vegetarians, too. ■TIP➔ Diners are welcome to hang around on the
beach. Ⓢ *Average main: $20* ✉ *Meads Bay* ☎ 264/498–6100.

$$$ ✕ **da'Vida.** *Caribbean.* Sometimes you really can have it all.
☺ Right on exquisite Crocus Bay, this beautifully designed
resort-cum-restaurant-cum-club is a place where you could
spend the whole day dining, drinking, and lounging under
umbrellas on the comfortable chairs. New in 2012 is a
beachside spa. Snorkeling equipment and kayaks are avail-
able for rent, and there's even a boutique. You can picnic at
the Beach Grill (burgers, hot dogs, wraps, salads) or head
inside the main building for contemporary choices such as
dumplings, soups, pastas, and pizzas. Lunch starts at 11,

4

and you can get tapas and sunset drinks from about 3. At dinner, the stylish wood interior (built by craftsmen from St. Vincent) is accented by candlelight. On the menu are such dishes as tasty seared snapper with gingered kale, coconut-crusted scallops, and Angus steaks. Go for the music on weekend nights. Owners David and Vida Lloyd, brother and sister, who also operate Lloyd's Guest House, grew up right here, and they have taken pains to get it all just right. $ *Average main: $35* ✉ *Crocus Bay* ☎ *264/498–5433* 🌐 *www.davidaanguilla.com* ⏲ *Closed Mon.*

$$$$ ★ ✕ **Dolce Vita Italian Beach Restaurant & Bar.** *Italian.* Long-time visitors remember proprietors Abbi and Christopher from previous stints at Caprice and Luna Rosa. They now run their own restaurant, preparing serious Italian cuisine and providing warm and attentive service in a romantic beachside pavillion in Sandy Ground. Fresh-made pasta stars in classic lasagna, fettuccini bolognese, pappardelle with duck sauce, and a meatless eggplant parmigiana. A carniverous quartet can pre-order suckling pig, or sample first-quality chops and steaks. Italian wine fans will discover new favorites from the cellar. What's for dessert? Limoncello Cheese Cake! $ *Average main: $32* ✉ *Sandy Ground* ☎ *264/497–8668* 🌐 *www.dolcevitasandyground.com* ✍ *Reservations essential* ⏲ *Closed Sun. No lunch Sat.*

$ ✕ **English Rose.** *Caribbean.* Lunchtime finds this neighborhood hangout packed with locals: cops flirting with sassy waitresses, entrepreneurs brokering deals with politicos, schoolgirls in lime-green outfits doing their homework. The decor is not much to speak of, but this is a great place to eavesdrop or people-watch while enjoying island-tinged specialties like beer-battered shrimp, jerk-chicken Caesar salad, snapper creole, and buffalo wings. There is karaoke on Friday. $ *Average main: $12* ✉ *Carter Rey Blvd., The Valley* ☎ *264/497–5353.*

$$$ ☺ ★ ✕ **Firefly Restaurant.** *Caribbean.* Set on a breezy poolside patio, Firefly—the restaurant at Anacaona Boutique Hotel—serves huge portions of tasty Caribbean fare by an Anguillian chef appropriately named "Fresh." The pumpkin-coconut soup is a winner, as are preparations of local snapper, mahimahi, and crayfish. Breakfast and Lunch are served also. ■ **TIP→** For great value, and terrific fun, book a table at the Thursday night buffet, with a lively performance by the folkloric theater company Mayoumba, or the Monday night three-course prix-fixe dinner with musical entertainment by the Happy Hits. $ *Average main: $26* ✉ *Meads Bay* ☎ *264/497–6827* 🌐 *anacaonahotel.com.*

Asian-inspired cuisine at Hibernia restaurant

$ ✕ **Geraud's Patisserie.** *French.* A stunning array of absolutely delicious French pastries and breads—and universal favorites like cookies, brownies, and muffins—are produced by Le Cordon Bleu dynamo Geraud Lavest in this tiny, well-located shop. Come in the early morning for cappuccino and croissants, and pick up fixings for a wonderful lunch later (or choose from among the list of tempting daily lunch specials). The little shop carries a small selection of interesting condiments, teas, and gourmet goodies. During the high season (December through May), there's a terrific Sunday brunch. Geraud also does a lively off-site catering business, from intimate villa and yacht dinners to weddings. [$] *Average main: $13* ✉ *South Hill Plaza* ☎ *264/497–5559* 🌐 *www.anguillacakesandcatering.com* ⏰ *Closed Mon. No dinner.*

★ $$$$ **Fodor's Choice** ✕ **Hibernia.** *Eclectic.* Some of the island's most creative dishes are served in this wood-beam cottage restaurant–art gallery overlooking the water at the far eastern end of Anguilla. Unorthodox yet delectable culinary pairings—inspired by chef-owners Raoul Rodriguez and Mary Pat's annual travels to the Far East (most recently Japan)—constantly bring new tastes and energy to the tables. The restaurant uses local organic products whenever possible. Long-line fish is served with a gratin of local pumpkin, shiitake mushrooms, and an essence of bitter oranges grown beside the front gate. Every visit here is an opportunity to share in Mary Pat and Raoul's passion for life, expressed through the vibrant combination of setting, art, food, unique tableware, beautiful gardens, and thoughtful hospitality. ■TIP→ Mary Pat stocks the tiny art gallery with amazing, and surprisingly reasonable, finds from her roaming around the globe. Ⓢ *Average main: $41* ⊠ *Island Harbour* ☎ *264/497–4290* ⊕ *www.hiberniarestaurant.com* ⊙ *Closed mid-Aug.–mid-Oct. Call for seasonal hrs.*

WORD OF MOUTH. "Take a cab to Shoal Bay East—lots of choices to eat (Mandeariman's, Ku, Gwen's around the point) and an absolutely stunning beach." —MaryD.

$$$ ✕ **Jacala Beach Restaurant.** *French.* Right on beautiful Meads
★ Bay, this restaurant opened to raves in 2010. Alain the chef and Jacques the maître d' (from Malliouhana) have joined forces, and the happy result is carefully prepared and nicely presented French food served with care in a lovely open-air restaurant, accompanied by good wines and a lot of personal attention. A delicious starter terrine of feta and grilled vegetables is infused with pesto. For an entrée, you must try hand-chopped steak tartare, or seared and marinated sushi-grade tuna on a bed of delightful mashed plantain. Lighter lunchtime options include a tart cucumber-yogurt soup garnished with piquant tomato sorbet. After lunch you can digest on the beach in one of the "Fatboy" loungers. In any case, save room for the chocolate *pot de crème*. Ⓢ *Average main: $25* ⊠ *Meads Bay* ☎ *264/498–5888* ⊙ *Closed Mon.–Tues. and Aug.–Sept.*

★ **Fodor's**Choice ✕ **KoalKeel.** *Caribbean.* Dinner at KoalKeel is
$$$ a unique culinary and historic treat not to be missed on Anguilla. Originally part of a sugar and cotton plantation, the restaurant, with its beautiful dining veranda, is owned and lovingly overseen by Lisa Gumbs, a descendant of the slaves once housed here. A tour of the history-rich buildings is a must. A 200-year-old rock oven is used in the bakery upstairs, and with a day's notice you can enjoy a slow-roasted whole chicken from that oven. New, young chef Nick Dellinger concentrates on island produce and local fish. Try Island Pigeon-Pea soup, or spiny lobster salad with mango and grilled avocado. Be sure to save room for the incredible desserts. Wine lovers, take note of the exceptional 15,000-bottle wine cellar, in an underground cistern. Anguilla's savvy early risers show up here for the fresh French bread, croissants, and *pain au chocolat,* which are sold out by 9 am. The no-cell-phone rule means quiet conversations. ■TIP→ At this writing there is a shuttle service between West End hotels and the restaurant, so you don't have to

worry about drinking and driving. ⑤ *Average main: $33* ✉ *Coronation Ave., The Valley* ☎ *264/497-2930* ⊕ *www.koalkeel.com* ⚘ *Reservations essential* ⊘ *Closed Mon.*

$$ ✕**Madeariman Reef Bar and Restaurant.** *Brasserie.* This casual, feet-in-the-sand bistro right on busy, beautiful Shoal Bay is open for breakfast, lunch, and dinner; the soups, salads, and simple grills here are served in generous portions with a bit of French flair, and the pizza is cooked in a stone oven. Come for lunch and stay to lounge on the beach chaises ($20 for two includes umbrella) or barhop between here and Uncle Ernie's barbecue next door. At night it feels like St. Barth. ⑤ *Average main: $14* ✉ *Shoal Bay East* ☎ *264/497-5750.*

$$$$ ✕**Mango's.** *Seafood.* One meal at Mango's and you'll understand why it's a perennial favorite of repeat visitors to Anguilla. Sparkling-fresh fish specialties have starring roles on the menu here. Light and healthful choices include spicy grilled whole snapper, and Cruzan Rum barbecued chicken. Save room for dessert—the warm apple tart and the coconut cheesecake are worth the splurge. Come at lunch for sandwiches and burgers. There's an extensive wine list, and the Cuban cigar humidor is a luxurious touch. ⑤ *Average main: $37* ✉ *Barnes Bay* ☎ *264/497-6479* ⊕ *www.mangosseasidegrill.com* ⚘ *Reservations essential* ⊘ *Closed Tues.*

$$ ✕**Picante.** *Mexican.* This casual, bright-red roadside Carib-
ⓒ bean *taquería,* opened by a young California couple, serves huge, tasty burritos with a choice of fillings, fresh warm tortilla chips with first-rate guacamole, seafood enchiladas, and tequila-lime chicken grilled under a brick. Passion-fruit margaritas are a must, and the creamy Mexican chocolate pudding makes a great choice for dessert. Seating is at picnic tables; the friendly proprietors cheerfully supply pillows on request. Reservations are recommended. ⑤ *Average main: $21* ✉ *West End Rd., West End* ☎ *264/498-1616* ⊕ *www.picante-restaurant-anguilla.com* ⊘ *Closed Tues. and Sept. and Oct. No lunch.*

$$$ ✕**Roy's Bayside Grille.** *Caribbean.* Some of the best grilled
★ lobster on the island is served here, along with burgers, great fish-and-chips, and good home-style cooking. On Friday there's a happy hour with a special menu. On Sunday you can get roast beef and Yorkshire pudding, and there's free Wi-Fi. ⑤ *Average main: $25* ✉ *Road Bay, Sandy Ground* ☎ *264/497-2470* ⊕ *www.roysbaysidegrill.com* ⊘ *No lunch Mon.*

$ ★ 🍴 **SandBar.** *Tapas.* Tasty, sharable small plates, great cocktails, a friendly vibe, and gorgeous sunsets add up to an Anguilla "must" on the beach at Sandy Ground. Cool music combines with gentle prices, a hammock on the beach, and potent, inventive drinks—at Whisky's Rum Bar you can sample a flight of rums or mixed cocktails like the sea cooler, a mix of rum, cucumber juice, lime, mint, and sugar syrup. Inventive tapas are freshly made to order, with choices for any palate. The spicy fries are a favorite, as are the ginger beef wontons, salt-fish beignets with lemon-chive aioli, and a refreshing dish of watermelon, feta, and olives. Check them out on Facebook for specials. [$] *Average main: $9* ✉ *Sandy Ground* ☎ *264/498–0171* ⏲ *Closed Sun. No lunch.*

$$ 👶 ★ 🍴 **Smokey's.** *Barbecue.* This quintessential Anguillian beach barbecue, part of the Gumbs family mini-empire of authentic and delicious eateries, is on pretty Cove Bay. On the beach, lounges with umbrellas welcome guests. Hot wings, honey-coated smoked ribs, curry goat, smoked chicken salad, and grilled lobsters are paired with local staple side dishes such as spiced-mayonnaise coleslaw, hand-cut sweet-potato strings, and crunchy onion rings. If your idea of the perfect summer lunch is a roadside lobster roll, be sure to try the version here, served on a home-baked roll with a hearty kick of hot sauce. The dinner menu includes lobster fritters, grilled tuna with lemon-caper butter, and rum chicken. On Saturday afternoon a popular local band enlivens the casual, laid-back atmosphere, and on Sunday the restaurant is party central for locals and visitors alike. [$] *Average main: $25* ✉ *Cove Rd., Cove Bay* ☎ *264/497–6582* 🌐 *www.smokeysatthecove.com.*

★ $$$ 👶 **Fodor's Choice** 🍴 **Straw Hat.** *Eclectic.* Since this Anguilla favorite moved to the beautiful sands of Meads Bay (at the Frangipani) its many fans now enjoy breakfast, lunch, and dinner on the tropical beachfront patio. Charming owners Peter and Anne Parles, the sophisticated and original food, and friendly service are the main reasons the restaurant has been in business since the late 1990s. The menu features appealing small plates like lobster spring rolls and clever "chips 'n fish," which diners can share or mix and match for the perfect meal. The curried goat here sets the bar for the island. And "fish of the day" truly means fish caught that day. A terrific redesign in 2011 put big flat-screens with satellite TV in the bar—a fine place to catch the game or make some new friends. [$] *Average main: $39* ✉ *Frangipani*

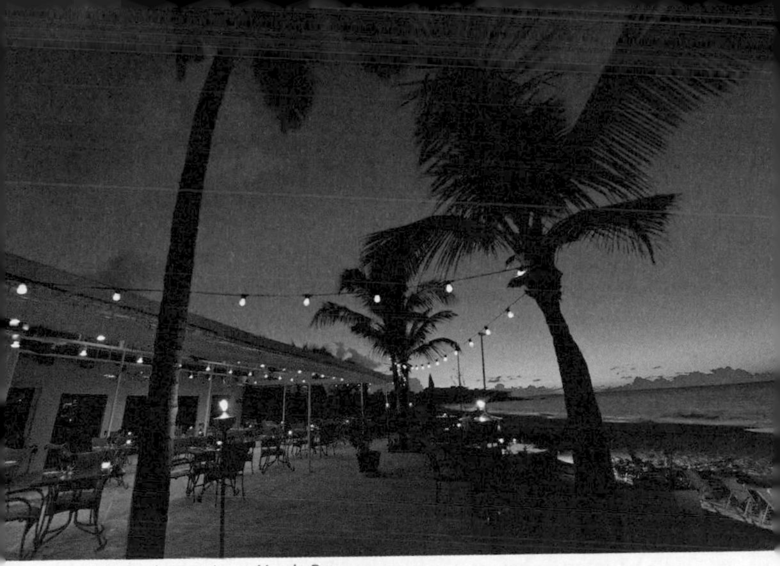

Straw Hat's outdoor patio on Meads Bay

Beach Club, Meads Bay ☎ *264/497-8300* 🌐 *www.strawhat.com* ✍ *Reservations essential* ⏲ *Closed Sept. and Oct.*

$$$ 🍴 **Tasty's.** *Caribbean.* Once your eyes adjust to the quirky kiwi, lilac, and coral color scheme, you'll find that breakfast, lunch, or dinner at Tasty's is, well, very tasty. It's open all day long, so if you come off a midafternoon plane starving, head directly here—it's right near the airport. Chef-owner Dale Carty trained at Malliouhana, and his careful, confident preparation bears the mark of French culinary training, but the menu is classic Caribbean. It's worth leaving the beach at lunch for the lobster salad here. A velvety pumpkin soup garnished with roasted coconut shards is superb, as are the seared jerk tuna and the garlic-infused marinated conch salad. Yummy desserts end meals on a high note. This is one of the few restaurants that do not allow smoking, so take your Cubans elsewhere for an after-dinner puff. The popular Sunday brunch buffet features island specialties like salt-fish cakes. [$] *Average main: $26* ✉ *Main Rd., South Hill Village, South Hill* ☎ *264/497–2737* 🌐 *www.tastysrestaurant.com/* ✍ *Reservations essential.*

$$$ 🍴 **Trattoria Tramonto and Oasis Beach Bar.** *Italian.* The island's only beachfront Italian restaurant features a dual (or dueling) serenade of Andrea Bocelli on the sound system and gently lapping waves a few feet away. Chef Valter Belli artfully adapts recipes from his home in Emilia-Romagna. Try the delicate lobster ravioli in truffle-cream sauce. For dessert, don't miss the tiramisu. Though you might wander in

here for lunch after a swim, when casual dress is accepted, you'll still be treated to the same impressive menu. You can also choose from a luscious selection of champagne fruit drinks, a small but fairly priced Italian wine list, and homemade grappa. ⓢ *Average main: $28* ⊠ *Shoal Bay West* ☎ *264/497–8819* ⊕ *www.trattoriatramonto.com* ⚑ *Reservations essential* ⊘ *Closed Mon. and Aug.–Oct.*

★ **Fodor's**Choice ✕**Veya.** *Eclectic.* On the suavely minimalist,
$$$$ draped, four-sided veranda, the stylishly appointed tables glow with flickering candlelight (in white-matte, sea urchin–shape votive holders made of porcelain). A lively lounge where chic patrons mingle and sip mojitos to the purr of soft jazz anchors the room. Inventive, sophisticated, and downright delicious, Carrie Bogar's "Cuisine of the Sun" features thoughtful but ingenious preparations of first-rate provisions. Ample portions are sharable works of art—sample Moroccan-spiced shrimp "cigars" with roast tomato–apricot chutney or Vietnamese-spiced calamari. Jerk-spiced tuna is served with a rum-coffee glaze on a juicy slab of grilled pineapple with curls of plantain crisps, and crayfish in beurre blanc is beyond divine. Dessert is a must. Sublime warm chocolate cake with chili-roasted banana ice cream and caramelized bananas steals the show. Great music in the lounge invites after-dinner lingering. Downstairs is a café that serves breakfast and light lunches such as salads and panini, as well as delicious bakery goodies. It opens at 6:30 am for early risers. ⓢ *Average main: $37* ⊠ *Sandy Ground* ☎ *264/498–8392* ⊕ *www.veya-axa.com* ⚑ *Reservations essential* ⊘ *Closed Sun., Aug., and weekends June–Oct.*

WORD OF MOUTH. "The best meal we had in Anguilla was Veya, near Sandy Ground. (We also had great dinners at Deon's Overlook, The Barrel Stay, and Zara's.)" —Callaloo

$$$ ✕**Zara's.** *Eclectic.* Chef Shamash Brooks presides at this cozy restaurant with beamed ceilings, terra-cotta floors, and colorful artwork. His kitchen turns out tasty fare that combines Caribbean and Italian flavors with panache (Rasta Pasta is a specialty). Standouts include a velvety pumpkin soup with coconut milk, crunchy calamari, lemon pasta scented with garlic, herbed rack of lamb served with a roasted applesauce, and spicy fish fillet steamed in banana leaf. ⓢ *Average main: $25* ⊠ *Allamanda Beach Club, Upper Shoal Bay* ☎ *264/497–3229* ⊘ *No lunch.*

WHERE TO STAY

Tourism on Anguilla is a fairly recent phenomenon—most development didn't begin until the early 1980s, so most hotels and resorts are of relatively recent vintage. The lack of native topography and, indeed, vegetation, and the blindingly white expanses of beach have inspired building designs of some interest; architecture buffs might have fun trying to name some of the most surprising examples. Inspiration largely comes from the Mediterranean: the Greek Islands, Morocco, and Spain, with some Miami-style art deco thrown into the mixture.

Anguilla accommodations basically fall into two categories: grand resorts and luxury resort-villas, or low-key, simple, locally owned inns and small beachfront complexes. The former can be surprisingly expensive, the latter surprisingly reasonable. In the middle are some condo-type options, with full kitchens and multiple bedrooms, which are great for families or for longer stays. Private villa rentals are becoming more common and are increasing in number and quality every season as development on the island accelerates.

A good phone chat or email exchange with the management of any property is a good idea, as units within the same complex can vary greatly in layout, accessibility, distance to the beach, and view. When calling to reserve a room, ask about special discount packages, especially in spring and summer. Most hotels include continental breakfast in the price, and many have meal-plan options. But keep in mind that Anguilla is home to dozens of excellent restaurants before you lock yourself into an expensive meal plan that you may not be able to change. All hotels charge a 10% tax, a $1 per room/per day tourism marketing levy, and—in most cases—an additional 10% service charge. A few properties include these charges in the published rates, so check carefully when you are evaluating prices.

For expanded reviews, facilities, and current deals, visit Fodors.com.

PRIVATE VILLAS AND CONDOS

The tourist office publishes an annual *Anguilla Travel Planner* with informative listings of available vacation apartment rentals.

DID YOU KNOW?

With almost two miles of powdery white sand, Rendezvous Bay has only three resorts, including the luxurious CuisinArt Resort & Spa.

Anguilla Luxury Collection. Anguilla Luxury Collection is operated by Sue and Robin Ricketts, longtime Anguilla real estate experts, who manage a collection of first-rate villas. They also manage a range of attractive properties in the Anguilla Affordable Collection linked through the same website. ☎ *264/497–6049* 🌐 *www.anguillaluxurycollection.com.*

Ani Villas. Two stunning cliffside villas for up to 24 guests, offer breathtaking views and total luxury to families or groups looking for total pampering. Included in the rental rate comes private boat transfers from St. Martin, rental car, a full service team: concierge, butler, chef, housekeepers, breakfasts, dinner chef service, and all beverages. Tennis pros, spa services, trainers and guides are all available on demand. There is room for 100 guests for a party or a wedding; and a dramatic and romantic promontory for the ceremony. A tennis court, bikes, fitness room, pool, cliffside hot-tubs, and playrooms mean that except for beach going, you never have to leave. Check for promotions that include unlimited golf at the Cuisinart Golf Course. ☎ *264/497–7888* 🌐 *www.anivillas.com.*

myCaribbean. myCaribbean is the largest local private villa-rental company. Gayle Gurvey and her staff manage and rent more than 100 local villas, and have been in business since 2000. ☎ *877/392–0828* 🌐 *www.mycaribbean.com.*

RECOMMENDED HOTELS AND RESORTS

$ 🏨 **Allamanda Beach Club.** *Rental.* Youthful, active couples from around the globe happily fill this casual, three-story, white-stucco building hidden in a palm grove just off the beach, opting for location and price over luxury. **Pros:** front row for all Shoal Bay's action; young crowd; good restaurant. **Cons:** location requires a car; rooms are clean, but not at all fancy. [$] *Rooms from: $170* ✉ *The Valley* ☎ *264/497–5217* 🌐 *www.allamanda.ai* 🛏 *20 units* 🍴 *No meals.*

$$$$ 🏨 **Altamer.** *Rental.* Architect Myron Goldfinger's geometric symphony of floor-to-ceiling windows, cantilevered walls, and curvaceous floating staircases is fit for any king (or CEO)—as is the price tag that goes along with it. **Pros:** plenty of space; lots of electronic diversions; great for big groups. **Cons:** a bit out of the way; interiors are starting to show some wear and tear. [$] *Rooms from: $6050* ✉ *Shoal Bay West, The Valley* ☎ *264/498–4000* 🌐 *www.altamer.com* 🛏 *3 5-bedroom villas* 🍴 *Multiple meal plans.*

$$$ 🏨 **Anacaona.** *Hotel.* Veteran Anguilla hoteliers Sue and Robin Ricketts run this low-key resort (its name is pronounced "an-nah-cah-*oh*-na") overlooking Meads Bay, having created an affordable yet chic hideaway imbued with the culture and traditions of the island. **Pros:** friendly clientele, sensitive to local culture; modern, clean, and good value; nice high-tech amenities. **Cons:** bit of a walk to beach; smallish rooms. [$] *Rooms from: $250* ✉ *Meads Bay* ☎ *264/497–6827, 877/647–4736* 🌐 *www.anacaonahotel.com* 🛏 *27 rooms* 🍴 *Multiple meal plans.*

$$ 🏨 **Anguilla Great House Beach Resort.** *Hotel.* These traditional West Indian—style bungalows strung along one of Anguilla's longest beaches are old-school Caribbean, and the gentle prices and interconnected rooms appeal to families and groups of friends traveling together. **Pros:** real, old-school Caribbean; right on the gorgeous beach, young crowd; gentle prices. **Cons:** rooms are very simple, and bathrooms are the bare basics. [$] *Rooms from: $210* ✉ *Rendezvous Bay* ☎ *264/497–6061, 800/583–9247* 🌐 *www.anguillagreathouse.com* 🛏 *31 rooms* 🍴 *No meals.*

$$ 🏨 **Arawak Beach Inn.** *B&B/Inn.* These hexagonal two-story villas are a good choice for a funky, budget-friendly, low-key guesthouse experience. **Pros:** funky, casual crowd; friendly owners; gentle rates. **Cons:** not on the beach; isolated location makes a car a must. [$] *Rooms from: $165* ✉ *The Valley, Island Harbour* ☎ *264/497–4888, 877/427–2925 reservations* 🌐 *www.arawakbeach.com* 🛏 *17 rooms* 🍴 *Multiple meal plans.*

$$$$ 🏨 **Cap Juluca.** *Resort.* Sybaritic and serene, this 179-acre 👪 resort wraps around breathtaking Maundays Bay. **Pros:** lots of space to stretch out on miles of talcum-soft sand; warm service; romantic atmosphere; all on-site water sports are included, even waterskiing. **Cons:** bathrooms need updating. [$] *Rooms from: $995* ✉ *Maundays Bay* ☎ *264/497–6779, 888/858–5822 in U.S.* 🌐 *www.capjuluca.com* 🛏 *72 rooms, 7 patio suites, 6 pool villas* 🍴 *Multiple meal plans.*

$$$$ 🏨 **Carimar Beach Club.** *Rental.* This horseshoe of bougainvillea-draped Mediterranean-style buildings on beautiful Meads Bay has the look of a Sun Belt condo. **Pros:** tennis courts; easy walk to restaurants and spa; great beach location; laundry facilities. **Cons:** no pool or restaurant; only bedrooms have a/c. [$] *Rooms from: $425* ✉ *Meads Bay* ☎ *264/497–6881, 866/270–3764* 🌐 *www.carimar.com* 🛏 *24 apartments* 🕓 *Closed Sept.–Oct. 15* 🍴 *No meals.*

CuisinArt Resort & Spa

The Viceroy

$$$$ ☷ **Covecastles Villa Resort.** *Rental.* Though this secluded Myron Goldfinger–designed enclave resembles a series of giant concrete baby carriages from the outside, the airy curves and angles of the skylighted interiors are comfortable, if a little dated, with the sort of oversize wicker furniture and raw-silk accessories that defined resort-chic in the late 1980s. **Pros:** secluded, large, private villas; private beach with reef for snorkeling; great service. **Cons:** beach is small and rocky; located at the far end of the island; redecoration is a bit overdue. ⓢ *Rooms from: $895* ✉ *Shoal Bay West* ☎ *264/497–6801, 800/223–1108* ⊕ *www.covecastles. com* ⇨ *16 apartments* ⓘⓞⓘ *No meals.*

★ **Fodor's**Choice ☷ **CuisinArt Golf Resort and Spa.** *Resort.* This
$$$$ family-friendly beachfront resort's design—gleaming
☼ white-stucco buildings, blue domes and trim, glass-block walls—blends art deco with a Greek Islands feel. **Pros:** family-friendly; great spa and sports; gorgeous beach and gardens. **Cons:** food service can be slow; pool area is noisy. ⓢ *Rooms from: $800* ✉ *Rendezvous Bay* ☎ *264/498–2000, 800/943–3210* ⊕ *www.cuisinartresort.com* ⇨ *93 rooms, 2 penthouses, 6 villas* ⊙ *Closed Sept. and Oct.* ⓘⓞⓘ *Multiple meal plans.*

$ ☷ **Easy Corner Villas.** *Rental.* The price is right at these modest villas on a bluff overlooking Road Bay. They're a five-minute walk (up a steep hill) from the beach and have spectacular views of Salt Pond and the ocean beyond. **Pros:** good value; large units; central location. **Cons:** not all units have views; maid service is extra; not upscale on an upscale island. ⓢ *Rooms from: $125 South Hill* ☎ *264/497–6433, 264/497–6541, 800/633–7411 reservations only* ⇨ *12 villas* ⓘⓞⓘ *No meals.*

$$$ ☷ **Frangipani Beach Club.** *Resort.* This flamingo-pink Mediterranean-style property perches on the beautiful champagne sands of Meads Bay. **Pros:** great beach; good location for restaurants and resort-hopping; first-rate on-site restaurant; helpful staff. **Cons:** some rooms have no view, so be sure to ask. ⓢ *Rooms from: $395* ✉ *Meads Bay* ☎ *264/497–6442, 877/593–8988* ⊕ *www.frangipaniresort.com* ⇨ *18 rooms, 7 suites* ⊙ *Closed Sept. and Oct.* ⓘⓞⓘ *No meals.*

$$ ☷ **Indigo Reef.** *Rental.* If you are looking for the antidote
☼ to the big resort developments on the island but still want
★ attractive, modern, private villa accommodations close to the restaurants, resorts, and beautiful beaches of West End, this intimate enclave of eight small villas (with one to four bedrooms) nestled at the tip of the island could be just the thing. **Pros:** cozy, fresh, and well designed; great for groups

traveling together; far from the madding crowd but still on the West End. **Cons:** the beach here is rocky and the water's rough; a/c only in bedrooms; must have car. [$] *Rooms from: $285* ✉ *Indigo Reef, West End* ☎ *264/497–6144* 🌐 *www.indigoreef.com* ⇨ *8 villas* 🍴 *No meals.*

$$$ 🏨 **Paradise Cove.** *Rental.* This simple complex of reasonably priced one- and two-bedroom apartments compensates for its location away from the beach with two whirlpools, a large pool, and tranquil tropical gardens where you can pluck fresh guavas for breakfast. **Pros:** reasonable rates; great pool; lovely gardens. **Cons:** a bit far from the beach; decor is bland. [$] *Rooms from: $320* ✉ *The Cove* ☎ *264/497–6959, 264/497–6603* 🌐 *www.paradise.ai* ⇨ *12 studio suites, 17 1- and 2-bedroom apartments* 🍴 *No meals.*

$$ 🏨 **Serenity Cottages.** *Rental.* Despite the name of this property, it comprises not cottages but rather large, fully equipped, and relatively affordable one- and two-bedroom apartments (and studios created from lockouts) in a small complex set in a lush garden at the farthest end of glorious Shoal Bay Beach. **Pros:** big apartments; quiet end of beach; snorkeling right outside the door; very reasonable rates for weeklong packages. **Cons:** no pool; more condo than hotel in terms of staff; location at the end of Shoal Bay pretty much requires a car and some extra time to drive to the West End. [$] *Rooms from: $325* ✉ *Shoal Bay East* ☎ *264/497–3328* 🌐 *www.serenity.ai* ⇨ *2 1-bedroom suites, 8 2-bedroom apartments* ⏲ *Closed Sept.* 🍴 *No meals.*

$$$$ 🏨 **Sheriva Villa Hotel.** *Rental.* This intimate, luxury-villa hotel comprises three cavernous private villas containing a total of 20 guest rooms and seven private swimming pools overlooking a broad swath of turquoise sea. **Pros:** incredible staff to fulfill every wish; all the comforts of home and more; good value for large family groups. **Cons:** not on the beach; you risk being spoiled for life by the staff's attentions. [$] *Rooms from: $1,500* ✉ *Maundays Bay Rd., West End* ☎ *264/498–9898* 🌐 *www.sheriva.com* ⇨ *20* 🍴 *Multiple meal plans.*

$$$ 🏨 **Shoal Bay Villas.** *Rental.* Some recent redecorating, and the addition of air-conditioning in the rooms, has spiffed up this old-style property well located right on Shoal Bay's incredible 2-mile beach. **Pros:** friendly; casual; full kitchens; beachfront. **Cons:** not fancy; at this writing, construction is under way for a new building. [$] *Rooms from: $370* ✉ *Shoal Bay* ☎ *264/497–2051* 🌐 *sbvillas.ai* ⇨ *12 units* 🍴 *No meals.*

4

$$$ 🏨 **Turtle's Nest Beach Resort.** *Rental.* This collection of studios and one- to three-bedroom oceanfront condos is right on Meads Bay beach, with some of the island's best restaurants a sandy stroll away. **Pros:** beachfront; huge apartments; well-kept grounds and pool. **Cons:** no elevator. [$] *Rooms from: $340* ✉ *Meads Bay* ☎ *264/462–6378* 🌐 *www.turtlesnestbeachresort.com* 🛏 *29 units* 🍴 *No meals.*

★ **Fodor'sChoice** 🏨 **The Viceroy.** *Resort.* On a promontory over 3,200 feet of the gorgeous pearly sand on Meads Bay, Kelly Wurstler's haute-hip showpiece will wow the chic international-sophisticate set, especially those lucky enough to stay in one of the spacious two- to five-bedroom villas, complete with private infinity pools and hot tubs, indoor-outdoor showers, electronics galore, and a gourmet professional kitchen stuffed with high-end equipment, not to mention a house manager to keep it all running smoothly. **Pros:** state-of-the-art luxury; cutting-edge contemporary design; flexible, spacious rooms. **Cons:** international rather than Caribbean in feel; very large resort; kind of a see-and-be-seen scene. [$] *Rooms from: $795* ✉ *Barnes Bay, West End* ☎ *264/497–7000, 866/270–7798 in U.S.* 🌐 *www.viceroyhotelsandresorts.com* 🛏 *163 suites, 3 villas* ⏲ *Closed Sept.* 🍴 *Breakfast.*

$$$$

NIGHTLIFE

In late February or early March, reggae star and impresario Bankie Banx stages Moonsplash, a three-day music festival that showcases local and imported talent around the nights of the full moon. At the end of July is the International Arts Festival, which hosts artists from around the world. BET (Black Entertainment Television) sponsors the Tranquility Jazz Festival in November, attracting major musicians such as Michel Camilo, James Moody, Bobby Watson, and Dee Dee Bridgewater.

Most hotels and many restaurants offer live entertainment in high season and on weekends, ranging from pianists and jazz combos to traditional steel and calypso bands. Check the local tourist magazines and newspaper for listings. Friday and Saturday, Sandy Ground is the hot spot; Wednesday and Sunday the action shifts to Shoal Bay East.

The nightlife scene here runs late into the night—the action doesn't really start until after 11 pm. If you do not rent a car, be aware that taxis are not readily available at night. If you plan to take a taxi back to your hotel or villa at the end of the night, be sure to make arrangements in advance with the driver who brings you or with your hotel concierge.

Dune Preserve. The funky Dune Preserve is the driftwood-fabricated home of Bankie Banx, Anguilla's famous reggae star. He performs here weekends and during the full moon. There's a dance floor and a beach bar, and sometimes you can find a sunset beach barbecue in progress. In high season there's a $15 cover charge. ⊠ *Rendezvous Bay* ☎ *264/497–6219* ⊕ *www.bankiebanx.net.*

★ **Fodor's**Choice **Elvis' Beach Bar.** This is the perfect locale (it's actually a boat) to hear great music and sip the best rum punch on earth. The bar is open every day but Tuesday, and there's live music on Wednesday through Sunday nights during the high season—as well as food until 1 am. Check to see if there's a full-moon LunaSea party. You won't be disappointed. ⊠ *Sandy Ground* ☎ *264/772–0637* ⊕ *www.elvisbeachbar.net.*

★ **Johnno's Beach Stop.** Things are lively at Johnno's, where there is live music and alfresco dancing every night and on Sunday afternoon, when just about everybody drops by. This is *the* classic Caribbean beach bar, attracting a funky eclectic mix, from locals to movie stars. It's open Tuesday–Sunday from 11 to 9. ⊠ *Sandy Ground* ☎ *264/497–2728.*

★ **Pumphouse.** At the Pumphouse, in the old rock-salt factory, you can find live music most nights—plus surprisingly good pub grub, and a mini-museum of artifacts and equipment from 19th-century salt factories. There's calypso-soca on Thursday; it's open from noon until 3 am daily, except Sunday. ⊠ *Sandy Ground* ☎ *264/497–5154* ⊕ *www.pumphouse-anguilla.com.*

SHOPPING

Anguilla is by no means a shopping destination. In fact, if your suitcase is lost, you will be hard-pressed to secure even the basics on-island. If you're a hard-core shopping enthusiast, a day trip to nearby St. Martin will satisfy. Well-heeled visitors sometimes organize boat or plane charters through their hotel concierge for daylong shopping excursions to St. Barth, and Anguilla Air Services started a reasonably priced daily round-trip to St. Barth in 2012. The island's tourist publication, *What We Do in Anguilla,* has shopping tips and is available free at the airport and in shops. Pyrat rums—golden elixirs blending up to nine aged and flavored spirits—are a local specialty available at the Anguilla Rums distillery and several local shops. For upscale designer sportswear, check out the small boutiques in hotels (some are branches of larger stores in Marigot on St. Martin). Outstanding local artists sell their work in galleries, which often arrange studio tours (you can also check with the Anguilla Tourist Office).

Anguilla Arts and Crafts Center. This gallery carries island crafts, including textiles and ceramics. Of particular interest are unique ceramics by Otavia Fleming, lovely spotted-glaze items with adorable lizards climbing on them. Look for special exhibits and performances—ranging from puppetry to folk dance—sponsored by the Anguilla National Creative Arts Alliance. ⊠ *Brooks Building, The Valley* ☎ *264/497–2200.*

Cheddie's Carving Studios. Cheddie's showcases Cheddie Richardson's fanciful wood carvings and coral and stone sculptures. ⊠ *West End Rd., The Cove* ☎ *264/497–6027* ⊕ *www.cheddieonline.com.*

Devonish Art Gallery. This gallery purveys the wood, stone, and clay creations of Courtney Devonish, an internationally known potter and sculptor, plus creations by his wife, Carolle, a bead artist. Also available are works by other Caribbean artists and regional antique maps. ⊠ *West End Rd., George Hill* ☎ *264/497–2949.*

★ **Hibernia Restaurant and Gallery.** Hibernia has striking pieces culled from the owners' travels, from contemporary Eastern European artworks to traditional Indo-Chinese crafts. ⊠ *Island Harbour* ☎ *264/497–4290.*

★ **Savannah Gallery.** Here you'll find works by local Anguillian artists as well as other Caribbean and Central American art, including oil paintings by Marge Morani. You'll also find works by artists of the renowned Haitian St. Soleil school, as well as Guatemalan textiles, Mexican pottery, and brightly painted metalwork. ⊠ *Coronation St., Lower Valley* ☎ *264/497–2263* ⊕ *www.savannahgallery.com.*

★ **The Galleria at World Art and Antiques.** The peripatetic proprietors of World Arts, Nik and Christy Douglas, display a veritable United Nations of antiquities: exquisite Indonesian ikat hangings to Thai teak furnishings, Aboriginal didgeridoos to Dogon tribal masks, Yuan Dynasty jade pottery to Uzbeki rugs. There is also handcrafted jewelry and handbags. ⊠ *Cove Rd., West End* ☎ *264/497–5950, 264/497–2767.*

CLOTHING

Boutique Blu. This store at CuisinArt carries custom designs by the renowned jewelers Alberto e Lina, as well as Helen Kaminski accessories and more brand-name merchandise. ✉ *CuisinArt Resort and Spa, Rendezvous Bay* ☎ *264/498–2000.*

Irie Life. This boutique sells vividly hued beach and resort wear and flip-flops. ✉ *South Hill* ☎ *264/497–6526.*

ZaZaa. Sue Ricketts, the first lady of Anguilla marketing, owns ZaZaa boutiques in South Hill on the Main Road, and at Anacaona Resort, on Meads Bay. Buy Anguillian crafts as well as wonderful ethnic jewelry and beachwear from around the globe, such as sexy Brazilian bikinis and chic St. Barth goodies. There are beach sundries and souvenirs as well. ✉ *Lower South Hill, West End Rd, South Hill* ☎ *264/235–8878* ⊕ *www.anguillaluxurycollection.com.*

SPORTS AND ACTIVITIES

Anguilla's expanding sports options are enhanced by its beautiful first golf course, designed by Greg Norman to accentuate the natural terrain and maximize the stunning ocean views over Rendezvous Bay. Players say the par-72, Troon-managed course is reminiscent of Pebble Beach. Personal experience says bring a lot of golf balls! The Anguilla Tennis Academy, designed by noted architect Myron Goldfinger, operates in the Blowing Point area. The 1,000-seat stadium, equipped with pro shop and seven lighted courts, was created to attract major international matches and to provide a first-class playing option for tourists and locals.

BOATING AND SAILING

Anguilla is the perfect place to try all kinds of water sports. The major resorts offer complimentary Windsurfers, paddleboats, and water skis to their guests.

Sandy Island Enterprises. If your hotel lacks facilities, you can get in gear at Sandy Island Enterprises, which rents Sunfish and Windsurfers and arranges fishing charters. ✉ *Sandy Ground* ☎ *264/476–6534* ⊕ *www.mysandyisland.com.*

A Day at the Boat Races

If you want a different kind of trip to Anguilla, try for a visit during Carnival, which starts on the first Monday in August and continues for about 10 days. Colorful parades, beauty pageants, music, delicious food, arts-and-crafts shows, fireworks, and nonstop partying are just the beginning. The music starts at sunrise jam sessions—as early as 4 am—and continues well into the night. The high point? The boat races. They are the national passion and the official national sport of Anguilla.

Anguillians from around the world return home to race old-fashioned, made-on-the-island wooden boats that have been in use on the island since the early 1800s. Similar to some of today's fastest sailboats, these are 15 to 28 feet in length and sport only a mainsail and jib on a single 25-foot mast. The sailboats have no deck, so heavy bags of sand, boulders, and sometimes even people are used as ballast. As the boats reach the finish line, the ballast—including some of the sailors—gets thrown into the water in a furious effort to win the race. Spectators line the beaches and follow the boats on foot, by car, and from even more boats. You'll have almost as much fun watching the fans as the races.

DIVING

Sunken wrecks; a long barrier reef; terrain encompassing walls, canyons, and hulking boulders; varied marine life, including greenback turtles and nurse sharks; and exceptionally clear water—all of these make for excellent diving. Prickly Pear Cay is a favorite spot. **Stoney Bay Marine Park,** off the northeast end of Anguilla, showcases the late-18th-century *El Buen Consejo,* a 960-ton Spanish galleon that sank here in 1772. Other good dive sites include **Grouper Bowl,** with exceptional hard-coral formations; **Ram's Head,** with caves, chutes, and tunnels; and **Upper Flats,** where you are sure to see stingrays.

Anguillian Divers. This is a full-service dive operator with a PADI five-star training center. The five-dive packages are a good deal, and they offer open-water certifications, too. ✉ *Meads Bay* ☎ *264/497–4750* ⊕ *www.anguilliandiver.com.*

Shoal Bay Scuba and Watersports. Single-tank dives start at $50 and two-tank dives at $90 at this shop in beautiful Shoal Bay. They run up to five different dives daily.

DID YOU KNOW?

Fishermen in Anguilla often fish for albacore tuna, wahoo, barracuda, and kingfish in local waters.

Daily snorkeling trips at 1 pm are $25 per person. ⊠ *Shoal Bay East Beach, Shoal Bay* ☏ *264/497–4371* ⊕ *www. shoalbayscuba.com.*

GOLF

CuisinArt Golf Club. This 7,200-yard, $50 million wonder designed by superstar Greg Norman has 13 of its 18 holes directly on the water. The course features sweeping sea vistas and an ecologically responsible watering system of ponds and lagoons that snake through the grounds. Players thrill to the spectacular vistas of St. Maarten and blue sea at the tee box of the 390-yard starting hole. Pro Ryan Bowey runs teaching clinics and programs to suit every player, and experienced golfers love the state-of-the-art equipment. The greens fee for 18 holes during peak times is $225 (less if you are a CuisinArt guest). There is a gorgeous Italian restaurant for lunch. ■TIP→ Appropriate dress is required, including long shorts or slacks and a collared shirt. ⊠ *Long Bay* ☏ *264/498–5602* ⊕ *www.cuisinartresort.com.*

GUIDED TOURS

A round-the-island tour by taxi takes about 2½ hours and costs $55 for one or two people, $5 for each additional passenger.

Anguilla Tourist Office. Contact the Anguilla Tourist Office to arrange the tour by Sir Emile Gumbs, the island's former chief minister, of the Sandy Ground area. This tour, which highlights historic and ecological sites, is on Tuesday at 10 am. The $20 fee benefits the Anguilla Archaeological Historical Society. Gumbs also organizes bird-watching expeditions that show you everything from frigate birds to turtledoves. ⊠ *Coronation Ave., The Valley* ☏ *264/497–2759, 800/553–4939* ⊕ *ivisitanguilla.com.*

Bennie's Travel & Tours. This is one of the island's more reliable tour operators. ⊠ *Blowing Point* ☏ *264/497–2788.*

Malliouhana Travel and Tours. Malliouhana Travel and Tours will create personalized package tours of the island. ⊠ *Albert Lake Dr., The Quarter* ☏ *264/497–2431* ⊕ *www. malliouhanatravel.com/.*

Little Bay, on Anguilla's northwest shore

HORSEBACK RIDING

Seaside Stables. Seaside Stables, located in Cove Bay, offers rides and instruction, if a sunset gallop (or slow clomp) has always been your fantasy. Private rides at any time of the day are about $85, group rides in the morning or afternoon are $70; or try a full-moon ride for $90; prior riding experience is not required. Choose from English, Western, or Australian saddles. ⊠ *Paradise Dr., Cove Bay* ☎ *264/497–3667* ⊕ *www.seaside-stables-anguilla.com.*

SEA EXCURSIONS

A number of boating options are available for airport transfers, day trips to offshore cays or neighboring islands, night trips to St. Martin, or just whipping through the waves en route to a picnic spot.

Chocolat. This 35-foot catamaran is available for private charter or scheduled excursions to nearby cays. Captain Rollins is a knowledgeable, affable guide. Rates for day sails with lunch (prepared by the captain's wife, Jacquie, of Ripples Restaurant) are about $80 per person. ⊠ *Sandy Ground* ☎ *264/497–3394.*

Funtime Charters. This charter and shuttle service operates five powerboats ranging in size from 32 to 38 feet. They will arrange private boat transport to the airport ($65 per person), day trips to St. Barth, or other boat excursions. ⊠ *The Cove* ☎ *264/497–6511, 866/334–0047* ⊕ *www. funtime-charters.com.*

☾ **Junior's Glass Bottom Boat.** For an underwater peek without getting wet, catch a ride ($20 per person) on Junior's Glass Bottom Boat. Snorkeling trips and instruction are available, too. Just show up at Shoal Bay Beach and look for the boat or ask for Junior at the Dive Shop. ⊠ *Sandy Ground* ☎ *264/497–4456* ⊕ *www.junior.ai.*

No Fear Sea Tours. In addition to private airport transportation, day snorkeling trips, sunset cruises, and fishing trips on three 32-foot speedboats and a 19-foot ski boat, this charter service offers water-sports rentals (tubing, skiing, knee-boarding). ⊠ *The Cove* ☎ *264/235–6354* ⊕ *www. nofearseatours.com.*

Sandy Island Enterprises. Picnic, swimming, and diving excursions to Prickly Pear Cay, Sandy Island, and Scilly Cay are available through Sandy Island Enterprises. Fans of TV's *The Bachelor* might recall the Valentine's Day picnic date in 2011. You, too, can enjoy rum punch and lobster here. The Sandy Island sea shuttle leaves from the small pier in Sandy Ground daily November–July, and by reservation August–October. ⊠ *The Valley* ☎ *264/476–6534* ⊕ *mysandyisland.com.*

Travel Smart
St. Maarten/
St. Martin, St. Barth
& Anguilla

GETTING HERE AND AROUND

St. Maarten/St. Martin, St. Barthé-lemy, and Anguilla are part of a cluster of islands in the Lesser Antilles that are fairly close together. In fact, the islands are linked by both frequent ferries and small-plane flights. St. Maarten/St. Martin, which has the only international airport among the three, is the international flight hub. Most travelers, regardless of which island they plan to visit, land in St. Maarten/St. Martin and make their way to their final destination.

▌ AIR TRAVEL

ANGUILLA

There are no nonstop flights to Anguilla from the United States. TransAnguilla Airways offers daily flights from Antigua, St. Thomas, and St. Kitts. Windward Islands Airways flies several times a day from St. Maarten. Anguilla Air Services is a reliable charter operation. LIAT comes in from Antigua, Nevis, St. Kitts, St. Thomas, and Tortola. Cape Air has two daily flights from San Juan (three on peak travel days).

Airport Clayton J. Lloyd Airport ☎ 264/497–3510.

Local Airline Contacts
Anguilla Air Services ☎ 264/498–5922, 264/235–7122 ⊕ www.anguillaairservices.com. **Cape Air** ☎ 866/227–3247, 508/771–6944 ⊕ www.capeair.net. **LIAT** ☎ 264/497–5002 ⊕ www.liatairline.com. **TransAn-guilla Airways** ☎ 264/497–8690 ⊕ www.transanguilla.com. **Windward Islands Airways** ☎ 264/497–2748 ⊕ www.fly-winair.com.

ST. BARTHÉLEMY

There are no direct flights to St. Barth. Most North Americans fly first into St. Maarten's Queen Juliana International Airport (⇨ Chapter 2, St. Maarten/St. Martin for more information), from which the island is 10 minutes by air. Winair has regularly scheduled flights from St. Maarten. Tradewind Aviation has regularly scheduled service from San Juan and also does charters. Anguilla Air Services and St. Barth Commuter have scheduled flights and also do charters. You must reconfirm your return interisland flight, even during off-peak seasons, or you may very well lose your reservations. Be certain to leave ample time between your scheduled flight and your connection in St. Maarten—three hours is the minimum recommended (and be aware that luggage frequently doesn't make the trip; your hotel or villa-rental company may be able to send someone to retrieve it). It's a good idea to pack a change of clothes, required medicines, and a bathing suit in your carry-on—or better yet, pack very light and don't check baggage at all.

In business since 2002, Tradewind Aviation, a charter airline, provides convenient scheduled service to St. Barth from San Juan in modern, air-conditioned, turbine-powered aircraft flown by two pilots. Connecting through San Juan affords St. Barth visitors the most nonstop commercial flight options from the U.S. mainland and a convenient, domestic transfer point that is more convenient than St. Maarten.

Airports Aéroport de St-Jean ☎ *0590/27-63-56.*

Local Airline Contacts Anguilla Air Services ☎ *264/498-5922* ⊕ *www.anguillaairservices.com.* **St. Barth Commuter** ☎ *0590/27-54-54* ⊕ *www.stbarthcommuter.com.* **Tradewind Aviation** ☎ *800/376-7922, 203/267-3305* *in Connecticut* ⊕ *www.tradewinda-viation.com.* **Winair** ☎ *0590/27-61-01, 866/466-0410* ⊕ *www.fly-winair.com.*

ST. MAARTEN/ST. MARTIN
There are nonstop flights from Atlanta (Delta, seasonal), Charlotte (US Airways), Miami (American), New York–JFK (American, JetBlue), New York–Newark (United), Philadelphia (US Airways), and Boston (JetBlue). There are also some nonstop charter flights (including GWV/Apple Vacations from Boston). You can also connect in San Juan, primarily on American. Many smaller Caribbean-based airlines, including Air Caraïbes, Caribbean Airlines, Dutch Antilles Express, Insel, LIAT, and Winair (Windward Islands Airways), offer service from other islands in the Caribbean.

Airports Aéroport de L'Espérance. Aéroport de L'Espérance, on the French side, is small and handles only island-hoppers. ⊠ *SFG*

Route l'Espérance, Grand Case ☎ *590/27-11-00* ⊕ *www.aeroport-saintmartin.com.* **Princess Juliana International Airport.** Princess Juliana International Airport on the Dutch side handles all the large jets. ☎ *721/546-7542* ⊕ *www.pjiae.com.*

Airline Contacts Air Caraïbes ☎ *590/590-87-10-36* ⊕ *www. aircaraibes-usa.com.* **American Airlines** ☎ *599/545-2040, 800/433-7300.* **Caribbean Airlines** ☎ *721/546-7610.* **Delta Airlines** ☎ *721/546-7615.* **Dutch Antilles Express** ☎ *721/546-7640.* **Insel Air** ☎ *721/546-7690.* **JetBlue** ☎ *721/546-7664, 721/546-7663.* **LIAT** ☎ *721/546-7677.* **St. Barths Commuter** ☎ *721/546-7698.* **United Airlines** ☎ *721/546-7671.* **US Airways** ☎ *721/546-7683.* **Winair** ☎ *721/546-7690.* **Windward Express Airways** ☎ *721/545-2001.*

▮ BOAT AND FERRY TRAVEL

ANGUILLA
Ferries run frequently between Anguilla and St. Martin. Boats leave from Blowing Point on Anguilla approximately every half hour from 7:30 am to 6:15 pm and from Marigot, St. Martin, every 45 minutes from 8 am to 7 pm. You pay a $20 departure tax before boarding ($5 for day-trippers—but be sure to make this clear at the window where you pay), in addition to the $15 one-way fare. On very windy days the 20-minute trip can be bouncy. Remember that the drive between the Marigot ferry terminal and the airport can take up to 45 minutes with traffic. Private transfers by speedboat are

sometimes offered from a dock right at the airport, at a cost of about $75 per person (arranged through your Anguilla hotel). Private ferry companies run six or more round-trips a day, coinciding with major flights, from Blowing Point direct to the airport in St. Maarten. On the St. Maarten side they will bring you right to the terminal in a van, or you can just walk across the parking lot. These trips are $35 one-way or $60 round-trip (cash only). Shauna Ferries also can arrange charters.

Contacts Anguilla Ferries ☎ 264/235-6205 ⊕ www. anguillaferry.com. **Link Ferries** ☎ 264/497-2231 ⊕ www.link.ai. **Shauna Ferries** ☎ 264/476-6534.

ST. BARTHÉLEMY

St Barth can be reached by sea via ferry service or charter boat. There are three companies that provide passenger ferry service between St. Maartin and St. Barth, so check each provider's timetable to determine the most convenient departure. All service is to and from Quai de la République in Gustavia. Voyager offers round-trips for about $100 per person from either Marigot or Oyster Pond. Great Bay Express has several round-trips a day from Bobby's Marina in St. Maarten for €55 if reserved in advance, or €60 for same-day departures. *Babou One*, a new, stabilized, air-conditioned boat run by West Indies Ferry Express with service between Marigot and Gustavia, takes only 70 minutes. There are three convenient departures daily, at a cost of about €50 for adults, €35 for children under

12 (each way). Master Ski Pilou offers private boat charters, but they are very expensive.

Boat and Ferry Contacts
Great Bay Express Ferry. This express service provides quick ferry transportation between Phillipsburg and Gustavia two or three times daily. You can now book online. ☎ 690/71-83-01 ⊕ www. sbhferry.com. **Master Ski Pilou.** Master Ski Pilou provides private boat transfers to St. Barth from St. Maarten. ☎ 0590/27-91-79 ⊕ www. masterskipilou.com. **Voyager.** Voyager has several daily departures to Gustavia from Marigot or Oyster Pond in St. Martin ☎ 0590/87-10-68 ⊕ www.voy12.com. **West Indies Ferry Express** ☎ 590/590-29-63-70 ⊕ www.westindiesferry.com.

ST. MAARTEN/ST. MARTIN

You can take ferries to St. Barth (45–80 minutes, €67–€93 [you can pay in dollars] from the Dutch or French side); to Anguilla (20 minutes, $25 from the French side); and to Saba (one to two hours, $90–$100 from the Dutch side). *Babou One*, a new, stabilized, air-conditioned boat run by West Indies Ferry Express, offers service between Marigot and Gustavia in 70 minutes, timed to connect with international flights to and from St. Maarten's Princess Juliana Airport.

Contacts Dawn II. Service to Saba ✉ Philipsburg, St. Maarten ☎ 599/ 416-2299 ⊕ www.sabactransport. com. **Edge I** and **Edge II**. Daytrips to Saba, St. Barth. ✉ Pelican Marina, Simpson Bay, St. Maarten ☎ 599/544-2640, 599/544-2631 ⊕ www.stmaarten-activities.com.

Link Ferries. Service to Anguilla. ⊠ *Marigot, St. Martin* ☎ *264/497–2231 in Anguilla, 264/497–3290 in Anguilla* ⊕ *www.link.ai.* **Shauna.** Service to Anguilla ⊠ *Simpson Bay, St. Maarten* ☎ *264/772–2031 in Anguilla.* **Voyager II.** Service to St. Barth from Marigot. ⊠ *Marigot, St. Martin* ☎ *590/87–10–68* ⊕ *www.voy12.com.* **West Indies Ferry Express.** Service to St. Barth. ⊠ *Marigot* ☎ *590/590–29–63–70* ⊕ *www.westindiesferry.com.*

▌ CAR TRAVEL

ANGUILLA

Although most of the rental cars on-island have the driver's side on the left as in North America, Anguillian roads are like those in the United Kingdom—driving is on the left side of the road. The roads can be rough, so be cautious, and observe the 30 mph (48 kph) speed limit. Roundabouts are probably the biggest obstacle for most. As you approach, give way to the vehicle on your right; once you're in the rotary, you have the right of way.

Car Rentals: A temporary Anguilla driver's license is required to rent a car—you can get into real trouble if you're caught driving without one. You get it for $20 (good for three months) at any of the car-rental agencies at the time you pick up your car; you'll also need your valid driver's license from home. Rental rates start at about $45 to $55 per day, plus insurance.

Car-Rental Contacts Apex/Avis ⊠ *Airport Rd.* ☎ *264/497–2642* ⊕ *www.avisanguilla.com.* **Bryans Car Rental** ⊠ *Blowing*

Point ☎ *264/497–6407.* **Triple K Car Rental/Hertz** ⊠ *Airport Rd.* ☎ *264/497–2934.*

ST. BARTHÉLEMY

Roads are sometimes unmarked, so get a map and look for signs pointing to a destination. These will be nailed to posts at all crossroads. Roads are narrow and sometimes very steep, but recent work has improved roads all over the island; even so, check the brakes and gears of your rental car before you drive away. ▪ TIP→ Take a careful inventory of existing dents and scrapes on your rental vehicle with pictures on your smartphone or digital camera. Maximum speed on the island is 30 mph (50 kph). Driving is on the right, as in the United States and Europe. Parking is an additional challenge. There are two gas stations on the island, one near the airport and one in Lorient. They aren't open after 5 pm or on Sunday, but the station near the airport has pumps that accept automated payment by chip-and-pin credit card (such as those used throughout Europe), although at this writing most U.S. credit cards don't have the chip required for credit payments. Considering the short distances, a full tank of gas should last you most of a week.

Car Rentals. You must have a valid driver's license and be 25 or older to rent, and in high season there may be a three-day minimum. During peak periods, such as Christmas week and February, be sure to arrange for your car rental ahead of time. When you make your hotel reservations, ask if the hotel has its own cars available to rent;

some hotels provide 24-hour emergency road service—something most rental companies don't offer. A tiny but powerful Smart car is a blast to buzz around in, and also a lot easier to park than larger cars. Expect to pay at least $55 per day. A Mini-Cooper convertible makes the most of sunny drives.

Car-Rental Contacts
Avis ☎ 0590/27-71-43 ⊕ www.avis-stbarth.com. **Budget** ☎ 0590/27-66-30. **Cool Rental** ☎ 590/27-52-58. **Europcar** ☎ 0590/27-73-33 ⊕ www.st-barths. com/europcar/index.html. **Gumbs** ☎ 0590/27-75-32. **Gust Smart of St-Barth** ☎ 0590/27-95-06. **Hertz** ☎ 0590/27-71-14. **Turbe** ☎ 0590/27-71-42 ⊕ www.saint-barths.com/turbecarrental/.

ST. MAARTEN/ST. MARTIN

It's easy to get around the island by car. Most roads are paved and in good condition. However, they can be crowded, especially when the cruise ships are in port; you might experience traffic jams around Marigot and Philipsburg. Be alert for potholes and speed bumps, as well as the island tradition of stopping in the middle of the road to chat with a friend or yield to someone entering traffic. Few roads are identified by name or number, but most have signs indicating the destination. Driving is on the right. There are gas stations in Simpson Bay near the airport.

Car Rentals: You can book a car at Juliana International Airport, where all major rental companies have booths. They provide a shuttle to the rental-car lot. Rates are among the best in the Caribbean, as little as $20–$35 per day. You can rent a car on the French side, but this rarely makes sense for Americans because of the unfavorable exchange rates.

Car-Rental Contacts
Avis ☎ 721/545-2847, 590-0690/634-947 on the French side. **Budget** ☎ 721/545-4030, 721/55-40-30. **Dollar/Thrifty Car Rental** ☎ 721/545-2393. **Empress Rent-a-Car** ☎ 721/545-2062. **Golfe Car Rental** ☎ 0590/51-94-81 on the French side ⊕ www.golfecarrental. com. **Hertz** ☎ 721/545-4541. **Unity** ☎ 721/520-5767 ⊕ www. unitycarrental.com.

▌ MOPED, SCOOTER, AND BIKE TRAVEL

ST. BARTH

Several companies rent motorbikes, scooters, mopeds, and mountain bikes. Motorbikes go for about $30 per day and require a $100 deposit. Helmets are required. Scooter and motorbike rental places are mostly along rue de France in Gustavia and around the airport in St-Jean.

Contacts Barthloc Rental ✉ Rue de France, Gustavia ☎ 0590/27-52-81 ⊕ www.barthloc.com. **Chez Béranger** ✉ Rue de France, Gustavia ☎ 0590/27-89-00. **Ets Denis Dufau** ✉ St-Jean ☎ 0590/27-70-59.

ST. MAARTEN/ST. MARTIN

Though traffic can be heavy, speeds are generally slow, so a moped can be a good way to get around. Scooters rent for as low as €25 per day and motorbikes for €37 a day at Eugene Moto, on the French side. The Harley-Davidson dealer, on the Dutch side, rents hogs for $150 a day or $900 per week.

Contacts Eugene Moto ✉ *Sandy Ground Rd., Sandy Ground, St. Martin* ☎ *590/87-13-97.* **Harley-Davidson** ✉ *71 Union Rd., Cole Bay, St. Maarten* ☎ *721/544-2704* ⊕ *www.h-dstmartin.com.*

▌ TAXI TRAVEL

ANGUILLA

Taxis are fairly expensive, so if you plan to explore the island's many beaches and restaurants, it may be more cost-effective to rent a car. Taxi rates are regulated by the government, and there are fixed fares from point to point, which are listed in brochures the drivers should have handy and are also published in the local guide *What We Do in Anguilla.* It's $24 from the airport or $22 from Blowing Point Ferry to West End hotels. Posted rates are for one or two people; each additional passenger adds $5 to the total, and there is a $1 charge for each piece of luggage beyond the allotted two. You can also hire a taxi for the hourly rate of $28. Surcharges of $4–$10 apply to trips after 6 pm. You'll always find taxis at the Blowing Point Ferry landing and at the airport. You'll need to call them to pick you up from hotels and restaurants, and arrange ahead with the driver who took you if you need a taxi late at night from one of the nightclubs or bars.

Taxi Contacts Airport Taxi Stand ☎ *264/235-3828.* **Blowing Point Ferry Taxi Stand** ☎ *264/497-6089.*

ST. BARTHÉLEMY

Taxis are expensive and not particularly easy to arrange, especially in the evening. There's a taxi station at the airport and another in Gustavia; from elsewhere you must contact a dispatcher in Gustavia or St-Jean. Fares are regulated by the Collectivity, and drivers accept both dollars and euros. If you go out to dinner by taxi, let the restaurant know if you will need a taxi at the end of the meal, and they will call one for you.

Contacts Gustavia taxi dispatcher ☎ *0590/27-66-31.* **St-Jean taxi dispatcher** ☎ *0590/27-75-81.*

ST. MAARTEN/ST. MARTIN

There is a government-sponsored taxi dispatcher at the airport and at the harbor. Fares are for one or two people. Add $5 for each additional person, $1 to $2 per bag, $1 for a box. It costs about $18 from the airport to Philipsburg or Marigot, and about $30 to Dawn Beach. After 10 pm fares go up 25%, and after midnight 50%. Licensed drivers can be identified by the "taxi" license plate on the Dutch side and the window sticker on the French. You can hail cabs on the street or call the taxi dispatch to have one sent for you. Fixed fares apply from Juliana International Airport and the Marigot ferry to the various hotels. The Dutch St. Maarten Taxi Association can be reached day or night at its hotline number.

Taxi Contacts Airport Taxi Dispatch ☎ *721/545-4317.* **Dutch St. Maarten Taxi Association** ☎ *721/543-7815, 9247 24 Hour Hotline.*

ESSENTIALS

■ ACCOMMODATIONS

St. Maarten/St. Martin has the widest array of accommodations of any of the three islands, with a range of large resort hotels, small resorts, time-shares, condos, private villas, and small B&Bs scattered across the island. Most of the larger resorts are concentrated in Dutch St. Maarten. Visitors find a wide range of choices in many different price ranges.

Anguilla has several large luxury resorts, a few smaller resorts and guesthouses, and a rather large mix of private condos and villas. Lodging on Anguilla is generally fairly expensive, but there are a few more modestly priced choices.

The vast majority of accommodations on St. Barth are in private villas in a wide variety of levels of luxury and price; villas are often priced in U.S. dollars. The island's small luxury hotels are exceedingly expensive, made more so for Americans because prices are in euros. A few modest and moderately priced hotels do exist on the island, but there's nothing on St. Barth that could be described as cheap, though there are now a few simple guest houses and inns that offer acceptable accommodations for what in St. Barth is a bargain price (under €100 per night in some cases).

■ COMMUNICATIONS

INTERNET

ANGUILLA

In Anguilla, Internet access is common at hotels, but Internet cafés are not. Many hotels offer only Wi-Fi access, so you may need to bring your own laptop or tablet computer to stay connected.

ST. BARTHÉLEMY

Most hotels and restaurants on the island now offer free Wi-Fi for customers, and there is also a free hot spot at the port area.

Contacts Centre Alizes.
Centre Alizes offers Internet service, fax and secretarial services.
✉ *Rue de la République, Gustavia*
☎ *0590/29-89-89.*

ST. MAARTEN/ST. MARTIN

Many hotels offer Internet service—some complimentary and some for a fee. There are free Wi-Fi hotspots (look for signs) all over the island, including on the Phillipsburg boardwalk, if you have your own laptop or tablet computer.

PHONES

ANGUILLA

Most hotels will arrange with a local provider for a cell phone to use during your stay (or you can rent one). A prepaid, local cell gives you the best rates. Some U.S. GSM phones will work in Anguilla, some not. To call Anguilla from the United States, dial 1 plus the area code 264, then the local seven-digit number. To call the United States and Canada, dial 1, the area code, and the seven-digit number.

ST. BARTHÉLEMY

Many hotels will provide or rent you a cell phone to use during your stay. Some U.S. cell companies work in St. Barth. The country code for St. Barth is 590. Thus, to call St. Barth from the United States, dial 011 + 590 + 590 and the local six-digit number. Some cell phones use the prefix 690. For calls on St. Barth, you must dial 0590 plus the six-digit local number.

ST. MAARTEN/ST. MARTIN

Calling from one side of the island to another is an international call. To phone from the Dutch side to the French, you first must dial 00–590–590 for local numbers, or 00–590–690 for cell phones, then the number. To call from the French side to the Dutch, dial 00–721, then the local number. To call a local number on the French side, dial 0590 plus the six-digit number. On the Dutch side, just dial the seven-digit number with no prefix. Any of the local carriers—and most hotel concierges—can arrange for a prepaid rental phone for your use while you are on the island for about $5 a weekday plus a per-minute charge.

▮ EATING OUT

St. Maarten/St. Martin, Anguilla, and St. Barth are known for their fine restaurants. For more information on local cuisine and dining possibilities, see the individual island chapters. ⇨ *For information*

on food-related health issues, see Health below.

PAYING

Credit cards are widely accepted on all three islands. For more information, see the individual island chapters.

▮ ELECTRICITY

Generally, Dutch St. Maarten and Anguilla operate on 110 volts AC (60-cycle) and have outlets that accept flat-prong plugs—the same as in North America. You will need neither an adaptor nor a transformer in these islands.

French St. Martin and St. Barth operate on 220 volts AC (60-cycle), with round-prong plugs, as in Europe; you need an adapter and sometimes a converter for North American appliances. The French outlets have a safety mechanism—equal pressure must be applied to both prongs of the plug to connect to the socket. Most hotels have hair dryers, so you should not need to bring one (but ask your hotel to be sure), and some hotels have shaver outlets in the bathroom that accept North American electrical plugs.

∎ EMERGENCIES

ANGUILLA

As in the United States, dial 911 in any emergency.

ST. BARTHÉLEMY

Emergency Services Air Ambulance ☏ 545-4744. Ambulance and Fire ☏ 0590/18. Hospital Emergency ☏ 590/51-19-00. Police ☏ 17, 0590/27-66-66.

ST. MAARTEN/ST. MARTIN

Emergency Services Dutch-side emergencies ☏ 911, 721/542-2222. French-side emergencies ☏ 17, 590/52-25-52.

∎ HEALTH

An increase in dengue fever has been reported across the Caribbean since early 2007. While Puerto Rico, Martinique, and Guadeloupe have been the islands most heavily affected, instances have been reported in other parts of the Caribbean as well, including St. Barth. Since there are no effective vaccines to prevent dengue fever, visitors to the region should protect themselves with mosquito repellent (particularly repellant containing DEET, which has been deemed the most effective) and keep arms and legs covered at sunset, when mosquitoes are particularly active.

There are no particular problems regarding food and water safety in St. Maarten/St. Martin, Anguilla, or St. Barth. If you have an especially sensitive stomach, you may

wish to drink only bottled water; also be sure that food has been thoroughly cooked and is served to you fresh and hot. Peel fruit. If you have problems, mild cases of traveler's diarrhea may respond to Pepto-Bismol. Generally, Imodium (known generically as loperamide) just makes things worse, but it may be necessary if you have persistent problems. Be sure to drink plenty of fluids; if you can't keep fluids down, seek medical help immediately.

MEDICAL INSURANCE AND ASSISTANCE

Consider buying trip insurance with medical-only coverage. Neither Medicare nor some private insurers cover medical expenses anywhere outside the United States. Medical-only policies typically reimburse you for medical care (excluding that related to pre-existing conditions) and hospitalization abroad, as well as medical evacuation.

Another option is to sign up with a medical-evacuation assistance company. A membership in one of these companies provides doctor referrals, emergency evacuation or repatriation, 24-hour hotlines for medical consultation, and other assistance. International SOS Assistance Emergency and AirMed International provide evacuation services and medical referrals. MedjetAssist offers medical evacuation.

Medical Assistance Companies AirMed International ☏ 800/356-2161 ⊕ www.airmed.com. **International SOS** ☏ 215/942-

8000 ⊕ www.internationalsos.com.
MedjetAssist ☎ 800/527–7478
⊕ www.medjetassist.com.

Medical-Only Insurers
International Medical Group
☎ 800/628–4664 ⊕ www.imglobal.
com. **Wallach & Company**
☎ 800/237–6615, 540/687–3166
⊕ www.wallach.com.

▪ HOURS OF OPERATION

ANGUILLA
Banks are open Monday through
Thursday from 8 to 3 and Friday 8
to 5. Most shops are open from 10
to 5 on weekdays only. Most commercial establishments are closed
weekends, although some small
groceries open for a few hours on
Sunday afternoon, but call first,
or adopt the island way of doing
things: if it's not open when you
stop by, try again.

ST. BARTHÉLEMY
Banks are generally open weekdays from 8 to noon and 2 to 3:30,
but most have 24-hour ATMs. The
main post office on rue Jeanne
d'Arc in Gustavia is open Monday, Tuesday, Thursday, and Friday from 8 to 3, on Wednesday
and Saturday until noon. The
branch in Lorient is open weekdays from 7 am to 11 am and Saturday from 8 am to 10 am. The
post office in St-Jean is open on
Monday and Tuesday from 8 to 2
and on Wednesday through Saturday from 8 to noon. Stores are
generally open weekdays from
8:30 to noon and 2 to 5, Saturday
from 8:30 to noon. Some of the
shops across from the airport and
in St-Jean stay open on Saturday

afternoon and until 7 pm on weekdays. A few around St-Jean even
stay open on Sunday afternoon
during the busy season. Although
some shops are closed on Wednesday afternoon, most are open from
8:30 to noon and 3 to 6.

ST. MAARTEN/ST. MARTIN
Banks on the Dutch side are open
weekdays 8:30 to 4:30, Saturday
9 to noon. French banks are open
weekdays 7:45 to 12:30 and 2:30
to 4; they're usually closed on
Wednesday and Saturday afternoons and afternoons preceding
public holidays. Dutch-side post
offices are open weekdays 7:30 to
5. On the French side, post offices
are open weekdays 7:30 to 4:45
and Saturday 7:30 to 11:30. Shops
on the Dutch side are generally
open Monday through Saturday
9 to 6; on the French side, Monday through Saturday from 9 to
12:30 and 3 to 7. In Grand Case
and around the Sonesta Maho
Beach, the shops generally stay
open until 11 pm to cater to the
dinner crowd. Increasingly, shops
on both sides remain open during
lunch. Some of the larger shops
are open on Sunday and holidays
when cruise ships are in port.

▪ MAIL

ANGUILLA
Airmail postcards and letters cost
EC$1.50 (for the first ½ ounce) to
the United States. The only post
office is in The Valley; it's open
weekdays 8 to 3:30. There's a
FedEx office near the airport. It's
open weekdays 8 to 5 and Saturday 9 to 1.

ST. BARTHÉLEMY

Mail is slow and can take up to three weeks to arrive. The main post office is in Gustavia, but smaller post offices are in St-Jean and Lorient. DHL, FedEx, and UPS all provide service to the island.

ST. MAARTEN/ST. MARTIN

Letters from the Dutch side to North America and Europe cost ANG2.85; postcards to all destinations are ANG1.65. From the French side, letters up to 20 grams and postcards are €1 to North America. Postal codes are used only on the French side.

▌ MONEY

Prices throughout this guide are given for adults. Substantially reduced fees are almost always available for children, students, and senior citizens. Refrences to credit cards are made only in those cases where they are not accepted.

ANGUILLA

Legal tender is the Eastern Caribbean (EC) dollar, but U.S. dollars are widely accepted. ATMs dispense both U.S. and EC dollars. All prices quoted in this chapter are in U.S. dollars.

ST. BARTHÉLEMY

Legal tender is the euro, but U.S. dollars are widely accepted. ATMs are common and dispense only euros.

ST. MAARTEN/ST. MARTIN

Legal tender on the Dutch side is the Netherlands Antilles florin, but almost everyone accepts dollars. On the French side, the currency is the euro, but most establishments accept dollars. ATMs dispense dollars or euros, depending on where you are.

▌ PASSPORTS

A valid passport and a return or ongoing ticket is required for travel to Anguilla, St. Barthélemy, and St. Maarten/St. Martin. There are no border controls whatsoever between the Dutch and French sides of St. Maarten/St. Martin.

▌ SAFETY

ANGUILLA

Anguilla is a quiet, relatively safe island, but crime has been on the rise, and there's no sense in tempting fate by leaving your valuables unattended in your hotel room, on the beach, or in your car. Avoid remote beaches, and lock your car, hotel room, and villa. Most hotel rooms are equipped with a safe for stashing your valuables.

ST. BARTHÉLEMY

There's relatively little crime on St. Barth. Visitors can travel anywhere on the island with confidence. Most hotel rooms have safes for your valuables. As anywhere, don't tempt loss by leaving cameras, laptops, or jewelry out in plain sight in your hotel room or villa or in your car. Don't walk barefoot at night. There are venomous centipedes that can inflict a remarkably painful sting.

ST. MAARTEN/ST. MARTIN

Petty crime can be a problem on both sides of the island (though less so on the French side than on the Dutch side), and robberies (including armed robberies) have been on the upswing. Always lock your valuables and travel documents in your room safe or your hotel's front-desk safe. Don't ever leave anything in the car, even in the glove compartment. When driving, keep your seatbelt on and the car doors locked. Never leave anything unattended at the beach. Despite the romantic imagery of the Caribbean, it's not good policy to take long walks along the beach at night. You should be on guard even during the day. Don't flash cash or jewelry, carry your handbag securely and zipped, and park in the busier areas of parking lots in towns and at beaches. Other suggestions include carrying only your driver's license and a photocopy of your passport with you for identification, leaving the original in your hotel safe. In general, use the same caution here as you would use at home.

▋ TAXES AND SERVICE CHARGES

ANGUILLA

The departure tax is $20 for adults and $10 for children, payable in cash, at the airport at Blowing Point Ferry Terminal. If you are staying in Anguilla but day-tripping to St. Martin, be sure to mention it, and the rate will be only $5. A 10% accommodations tax is added to hotel bills along with a $1-per-night marketing tax, plus whatever service charge the hotel adds.

ST. BARTHÉLEMY

The island charges a $5 departure tax when your next stop is another French island, $10 to anywhere else payable in cash only

(dollars or euros). Some hotels add a 10% service charge. Sometimes it is included in the room rate, so check. There is a 5% room tax on hotels and villa rentals.

ST. MAARTEN/ST. MARTIN

Departure tax from Juliana Airport is $10 to destinations within the Netherlands Antilles and $30 to all other destinations. It is usually included in your air ticket. It will cost you €3 (usually included in the ticket price) to depart by plane from Aéroport de L'Espérance and $5 (the rate can change) by ferry to Anguilla from Marigot's pier. Hotels on the Dutch side add a 15% service charge to the bill as well as a 5% government tax. Hotels on the French side add 10%–15% and generally 5% tax.

▋ TIME

St. Maarten, Anguilla, and St. Barth are in the Atlantic Standard Time zone, which is one hour later than Eastern Standard and four hours earlier than GMT. Caribbean islands don't observe daylight saving time, so during the period when it's in effect, Atlantic Standard and Eastern Standard are the same.

▋ TIPPING

ANGUILLA

Despite any service charge, it's usually expected that you will tip more—$5 per day for housekeeping, $20 for a helpful concierge, and $10 per day to beach attendants. Many restaurants include a service charge of 10% to 15% on the bill; if there's no surcharge, tip about 15%. Taxi drivers should receive 10% of the fare.

ST. BARTHÉLEMY

Restaurants include a 15% service charge in their published prices, but it's common French practice to leave 5% to 10% more in cash, even if you have paid by credit card. Most taxi drivers don't expect a tip.

ST. MAARTEN/ST. MARTIN

Service charges may be added to hotel and restaurant bills on the Dutch side (otherwise tip 15%–18%). On the French side, a service charge is customary; on top of the included service it is customary to leave an extra 5%–10% *in cash* for the server. Taxi drivers, porters, and maids depend on tips. Give 10% to 15% to cabbies, $1 per bag for porters, and $2 to $5 per night per guest for chambermaids.

▮ TRIP INSURANCE

Comprehensive trip insurance is valuable if you're booking a very expensive or complicated trip (particularly to an isolated region) or if you're booking far in advance. Comprehensive policies typically cover trip cancellation and interruption, letting you cancel or cut your trip short due to illness or, in some cases, acts of terrorism in your destination. Such policies might also cover evacuation and medical care. (For trips abroad you should have at least medical-only coverage. *See Medical Insurance and Assistance under Health.*) Some policies also cover you for trip delays due to bad weather or

mechanical problems, as well as for lost or delayed luggage.

Another type of coverage to consider is financial default—that is, when your trip is disrupted because a tour operator, airline, or cruise line goes out of business. Generally, you must buy this when you book your trip or shortly thereafter; also, it's available only if your operator doesn't appear on a list of excluded companies.

Always read the fine print of your policy to make sure that you're covered for the risks that most concern you. Compare several policies to be sure you're getting the best price and range of coverage available.

Insurance Comparison Sites Insure My Trip.com ☎ *800/487–4722* ⊕ *www.insuremytrip.com.* **SquareMouth.com** ☎ *800/240–0369* ⊕ *www.squaremouth.com.*

Comprehensive Travel Insurers Allianz Travel Insurance ☎ *800/284–8300* ⊕ *www.allianztravelinsurance.com.* **Chartis Travel Guard** ☎ *800/826–4919* ⊕ *www.travelguard.com.* **CSA Travel Protection** ☎ *800/711–1197* ⊕ *www.csatravelprotection.com.* **HTH Worldwide** ☎ *610/254–8700* ⊕ *www.hthworldwide.com.* **Travel Insured International** ☎ *800/243–3174* ⊕ *www.travelinsured.com.* **Travelex Insurance** ☎ *800/228–9792* ⊕ *www.travelex-insurance.com.*

■ VISITOR INFORMATION

ANGUILLA

Contacts Anguilla Tourist Office ✉ *Coronation Ave., The Valley* ☎ *264/497–2759, 800/553–4939 from U.S.* ⊕ *www.anguilla-vacation.com.*

ST. BARTHÉLEMY

Contact Office du Tourisme ✉ *Quai Général-de-Gaulle* ☎ *0590/27–87–27* ⊕ *www.saintbarth-tourisme.com.*

ST. MAARTEN/ST. MARTIN

Contacts Dutch-side Tourist Information Bureau ✉ *Vineyard Park Bldg., 33 W. G. Buncamper Rd., Philipsburg, St. Maarten* ☎ *721/542–2337* ⊕ *www.vacationstmaarten.com.* **French-side Office de Tourisme** ✉ *Rte. de Sandy Ground, near Marina de la Port-Royale, Marigot, St. Martin* ☎ *590/87–57–21* ⊕ *www.st-martin.org.*

■ WEDDINGS

ANGUILLA

Anguilla's beaches and sybaritic resorts, such as Cap Juluca and Malliouhana, provide ideal settings for destination weddings and honeymoons. Several resorts will help plan everything in advance. Some people are discouraged by a fairly lengthy residency period to get an inexpensive marriage license: if one partner lives on Anguilla at least 15 days before the wedding date, the license costs $40; otherwise, you must pay a fee of $284 for a wedding stamp. Allow two working days to process applications, which can be obtained weekdays from 8:30 to 4 at the Judicial Department. Both parties must present proof of identity (valid passport, birth certificate, or driver's license with photo), as well as an original decree of divorce where applicable and death certificate if widowed. Blood tests are not required. There are additional requirements if you wish to marry in the Catholic Church.

ST. BARTHÉLEMY

Because of the long legal residency requirement, it's not really feasible to get married on St. Barth unless you're a French citizen.

ST. MAARTEN/ST. MARTIN

Getting married on the French side really isn't feasible because of stringent residency requirements, identical to those in St. Barth. Marriages in Dutch St. Maarten follow the same rules as on the other Netherlands Antilles islands. Couples must be at least 18 years old and submit their documents at least 14 days prior to the wedding date. The application requires notarized original documents to be submitted to the registrar, including birth certificates, passports (for non-Dutch persons), divorce decrees from previous marriages, death certificates of deceased spouses, and passports for six witnesses (they can be locals—the Tourist Board maintains a list of contacts) if the ceremony is to take place outside of the Marriage Hall. The documents must be submitted in Dutch or English—or else they must be translated into Dutch. The cost for this process is $285.90.

Information Chief Registrar ✉ *Census Office, Souliga Rd., Philipsburg* ☎ *599/542-4267.*

INDEX

PHOTO CREDITS

NOTES

NOTES

FODOR'S IN FOCUS ST. MAARTEN/ST. MARTIN, ST. BARTH & ANGUILLA

Editor: Douglas Stallings, *series editor*

Editorial Contributor: Elise Meyer

Production Editor: Carrie Parker

Maps & Illustrations: David Lindroth, *cartographer*; Rebecca Baer, *map editor*; William Wu, *information graphics*

Design: Fabrizio La Rocca, *creative director*; Tina Malaney, Chie Ushio, Jessica Ramirez, *designers*; Melanie Marin, *senior picture editor*

Cover Photo: (Anguilla) Chris Caldicott/Axiom Photographic Agency/Getty Images

Production Manager: Angela L. McLean

COPYRIGHT

3rd Edition

ISBN 978-0-89141-966-2
ISSN 1942-7344

SPECIAL SALES

This book is available for special discounts for bulk purchases for sales promotions or premiums. Special editions, including personalized covers, excerpts of existing books, and corporate imprints, can be created in large quantities for special needs. For more information, write to Special Markets/Premium Sales, 1745 Broadway, MD 3-1, New York, NY 10019, or e-mail specialmarkets@randomhouse.com.

AN IMPORTANT TIP & AN INVITATION

Although all prices, opening times, and other details in this book are based on information supplied to us at press time, changes occur all the time in the travel world, and Fodor's cannot accept responsibility for facts that become outdated or for inadvertent errors or omissions. **So always confirm information when it matters**, especially if you're making a detour to visit a specific place. Your experiences—positive and negative—matter to us. If we have missed or misstated something, **please write to us**. Share your opinion instantly through our online feedback center at fodors.com/contact-us.

PRINTED IN CHINA
10 9 8 7 6 5 4 3 2 1

ABOUT OUR WRITER

Elise Meyer's friends insist that her middle name is "Let's Go." With an academic background in art history, she opened a gallery in SoHo in the 1970s, which was a great excuse to travel frequently to Europe. A life-long resident of New England, she believes that her regular trips to the Caribbean have always been a wintertime necessity despite a passion for skiing. For 20 years, St. Barth and Anguilla have been frequent destinations, when she is not pursuing (and chronicling) interests in gardening, food, golf, the arts, and things that are funny. Now that the two kids are off on their own adventures, she's been enjoying longer and more exotic trips with a husband who shares her wanderlust, as well as a firm resolve never to check in luggage, and she's taken on St. Maarten/St. Martin as well. She's a long-time contributor to *Fodor's Caribbean*.